The Writer and the
Overseas Childhood

The Writer and the Overseas Childhood

The Third Culture Literature of Kingsolver, McEwan and Others

ANTJE M. RAUWERDA

McFarland & Company, Inc., Publishers
Jefferson, North Carolina, and London

LIBRARY OF CONGRESS CATALOGUING-IN-PUBLICATION DATA

Rauwerda, Antje M.
 The writer and the overseas childhood : the third culture literature of Kingsolver, McEwan and others / Antje M. Rauwerda.
    p.   cm.
 Includes bibliographical references and index.

 ISBN 978-0-7864-4900-2
 softcover : acid free paper ∞

 1. Expatriate authors. 2. Exiles' writing — History and criticism. I. Title.
 PN495.R38 2012
 809'.8920691 — dc23   2012020556

BRITISH LIBRARY CATALOGUING DATA ARE AVAILABLE

© 2012 Antje M. Rauwerda. All rights reserved

No part of this book may be reproduced or transmitted in any form or by any means, electronic or mechanical, including photocopying or recording, or by any information storage and retrieval system, without permission in writing from the publisher.

Front cover images © 2012 Shutterstock

Manufactured in the United States of America

*McFarland & Company, Inc., Publishers
 Box 611, Jefferson, North Carolina 28640
 www.mcfarlandpub.com*

For my family

Table of Contents

Acknowledgments — viii
Preface — 1
Introduction: When Writers Grow Up Expat — 7

One — Third Culture Reading — 27
Two — Adult Situations and Secret Perversions in the Writings of Former Military Brats — 62
Three — When Your Parents Work for God: The Fiction Writing of Former Missionary Kids — 116

Conclusion: Barbara Kingsolver's The Poisonwood Bible *as Third Culture Literature* — 157
Chapter Notes — 179
Works Cited — 182
Index — 189

Acknowledgments

One evening at an American Thanksgiving party in London, England, the wife of one of my husband's friends told me about a book she had read called *Third Culture Kids*. It turns out that one random conversation (in a suitably trans–Atlantic setting) would redefine both my academic career and my personal history. In Googling the book, I also found Families in Global Transition (FIGT). In attending the 2007 FIGT convention, I discovered exactly how apt the terminology "third culture" was for describing the literature I wanted so badly to define, and how well it defined *me*. I owe a debt to David Pollock and Ruth Van Reken's work. I could, in fact, likely have communicated with Van Reken while writing this book, but opted not to try: I wasn't sure I could do the work I needed to do without feeling overshadowed by such a prominent thinker in the field.

The early stages of researching this book were surprisingly emotional. First, and most unexpectedly, on a personal level, for the 2007 FIGT convention gave me essential vocabulary, but it also, for reasons I took a long time to figure out, felt like grieving for a shared culture I didn't know I'd lost. I would go to sessions and find myself fighting back tears halfway through them. Having spent more than thirty years convinced that my experiences were fairly unique, it was disconcerting to talk to other FIGT attendees with lives completely different from mine and find we shared experiences of dislocation: I was flummoxed to feel allied to both an archly religious Filipino missionary and an American officer in full naval uniform. Second, I was surprised, as I began compiling a corpus of literature to analyze, by how graphically alarming the writings of third culture individuals tended to be. I had thought, when initially imagining this book, that I would spill my words in defining a new area within international writing, one characterized by neo-colonial privilege. However, it almost immediately became clear that I was going to have to reckon, at length, with images of abused children. I joke now that my next project will have to be on rainbows and kittens, for the prevalence of sexually exploited, sick and dead children in my reading material over these last years has been staggering.

When I was writing this, there were no other studies of literature produced by third culture individuals. Though this book has nothing to do with my dissertation (which was on whiteness in postcolonial literature), I owe my willingness to embark on literary analyses predicated on theoretical and analytical approaches developed in other disciplines to my dissertation supervisors: Asha Varadharajan and Tracy Ware. The two of them scared me silly by forcing me to tackle whiteness studies, but the experience of taking on that great unknown made me much more comfortable, a decade later, in taking on third culture studies and applying them to big names like Ian McEwan, Ann-Marie MacDonald and (big on readers, though not necessarily prominent in academia) William Paul Young. Sneja Gunew also deserves credit for being inspiringly terrifying: from my undergraduate studies with her to a more recent lunch after I delivered a conference paper based on early phases of this work, she has consistently pushed me to think more stringently, carefully and encompassingly, particularly in theoretical matters (and perhaps most particularly in terms of my efforts to understand Homi Bhabha's work).

As a Canadian passport holder working in the United States, I found getting grants almost impossible: there are so few one is actually eligible for as a resident non-citizen of the United States, and a non-resident citizen of Canada. My employer, Goucher College, has been generous in providing summer research funding for this project (twice), as well as conference funding to get me to FIGT and the conference at which I was able to talk to Sneja. I feel triumphant that I've managed to pull off writing this without any extra leave from teaching, especially as I have done it with two children under the age of five. I owe my children (Clara and Winton) thanks for tolerating my absences, my apologies, and a depth of love deeper than fathoms can measure. I'd like them to know, in future years, that I gave up almost all adult social interaction, as well as yoga classes, in order to juggle just two commitments (work and kids) and thereby try to do both justice. Thank you (and also apologies) to the friends of mine who have been willing to wait these years out (Ella Ophir and Alice Petersen particularly).

It has been an unexpected pleasure to make a *new* friend in the process of writing this: Juniper Ellis. We have been meeting regularly for over a year to offer feedback on each other's work. From this professional relationship I have benefited immensely: having June as a reader meant I completed work on time, and worked knowing that I had an intelligent, insightful, and gentle reader on the other end. Over the months, I got to know June better so that I now happily anticipate our meetings as a chance to squeeze in a bit of restorative adult interaction in the midst of work. So much do I enjoy our meetings, I might have to write something else as soon as this is done. I eagerly anticipate seeing June's work in print. Watch for her novel (working title *Antidote*). It's worth noting that June's current academic work is on humor, and her current novel is itself humorous; the influence seeps over into my own writing, in which, despite the gravity of the images I discuss, I have tried to introduce a bit of levity.

I have been lucky to have Goucher colleagues read parts of this work as well. Dan Marcus organizes a writing group that has helped me with several pieces, including a chapter of this book. The group includes Mark Ingram, Rebecca Free, Florence Martin, Jamie Mullaney and John Turner. In the book's very earliest stages, Shira Tarrant was also a member (we still miss you here in Baltimore, Shira). Arnie Sanders and Penny Cordish read sections of this in the closing stages of my preparation of the manuscript. I was also fortunate enough to have the opportunity to develop a seminar for Goucher's senior English majors that dealt in part with third culture literature: I consider the students in that class an up-and-coming group of third culture specialists.

And, of course, Mitchell Jones. There's a lot that should be said by way of thanks. You have been immensely forgiving, and denied the evidence that writing on a tight schedule was making me crazy. Thank you for not harping on about how much of my hair was falling out and for providing coffee ice cream after my stomach made it clear that actual coffee was off the menu. Perhaps most of all, thank you for *not* wanting to read this in draft form. I value your opinion such that critique from you would have paralyzed me.

Preface

This book arose from my search for appropriate terminology for international authors writing in English who are not really "from" the former colonies and are also neither immigrants nor exiles. For decades, the question lurking behind my research has been "What about the writers with backgrounds like mine?" I have Canadian parents who were themselves originally Dutch and German (my father, representing the Dutch side, was actually born and raised in Indonesia). I have a Canadian passport and an American green card. In my formative years (0–18) I lived in Calgary, North Wales, Calgary again, Singapore, North Wales again, Dallas (just for school holidays), England and Vancouver. In one especially eventful year, I had four home addresses and two boarding school ones. Sociologists and psychologists would call me a *third culture kid*.

Beyond my personal interest in the research on individuals with a dislocated culture like mine lies my professional interest in literature written by individuals who share this experience of displacement. If postcolonial literature is influenced by the legacy of colonialism, by resistance movements, and by the re-assertion of a national culture post independence, what characterizes *third culture literature*? Its progenitors are de-territorialized, global, displaced and dislocated, but also privileged and associated with bloodlines that are often (though not always) traceable to the West rather than the East. This book is intended to suggest how "growing up expat" creates a distinct international culture, and that literature produced out of such a culture is a coherent field of its own.

Many children raised by business people (my father was in oil), diplomats, missionaries and the military grow up in conditions very similar to those of my childhood. There is a sizeable number of us who have been "raised expat." "Just Landed" (a website for expatriates worldwide) states that "in 2010, more than 200 million people will be living abroad" ("Expatriates Worldwide"). The number is large, and larger still when you consider that in any given year a portion of that 200 million will repatriate, and a number of new expatriates will go abroad for the first time, so that the number of people *actually* abroad at any time is quite smaller than the number of people *who have lived overseas* at one point or another. Some people raised abroad grow up to be writers. I tend to think that the number of writers emerging from this demographic is unusually high, storytelling being an art we practice every time someone asks, "So, where're you from?" but statistical proclivities toward careers in writing are not part of the study that follows. Growing up overseas, or in contexts in which moving frequently is the norm, is a life experience shared by many authors who do not fit under the label "postcolonial" but also are not really "from" the countries in which they reside, or even the countries in which they have citizenships. This book is intended to provide a vocabulary for "writers who grew up expat." It imports the description of these individuals as "third culture" from the social sciences, and applies it to literature for the first time.

When I recount my own upbringing, people tend to be jealous. I have traveled so much, seen so many other cultures and had so many opportunities. I have also lived well (perhaps better at age ten, as a privileged expatriate in Singapore, than I will ever again). I frequently encounter the assumption that international/intercultural experiences are categorically, overwhelmingly, good for children. In some respects this is true. However, the leaving and losing of places and people is never easy, nor is losing the conviction that a particular place in the world is "home." (I myself now feel mostly unaffiliated with any place, and pretty much equally foreign no matter where I go.) The assumption that living overseas does children "a world of good" omits a great deal. One of the objectives of this book is to show how third culture fiction highlights, elaborates on and responds to what is *not* so positive about growing up in perpetual transition.

When I left Singapore, I was fourteen and had spent seven years on the small island republic. It was like finally being recognized as an outsider and expelled from a place that was much loved, but emphatically not mine to call home. While there, I had attended Tanglin Preparatory School and the United World College (both British), not local schools. I had friends at the Dutch Club and the Saddle Club. I left behind Singapore's heat, humidity and excellent papaya; I also left behind life as an expatriate, and the peculiar, privileged culture associated with life as that kind of outsider. My family moved from Singapore to Rhos-on-Sea in North Wales, where I attended a small Catholic school. I felt like I had moved into an Enid Blyton novel, so foreign and fantastic were the uniforms, priests and chapel services. My new classmates called me a "Yank" despite the fact that I had a British accent (thanks to my Singapore schooling), and a Canadian passport. I lost touch with my Singapore friends almost immediately, the new place was so overwhelming. Then my parents went to Dallas (maybe calling me "Yank" had been prophetic?), my brother (older by a substantial margin) went to Montreal, and I stayed on to finish my "A" levels at a school in Shropshire, supposedly far better than its Welsh counterpart. I lost contact with my brother almost entirely after this point. At school in Shropshire, I had a room next to a girl whose family played tennis with members of the royal family. Canadian/Singaporean/Texan/*Welsh*, and saddled with a name both unpronounceable and unspellable to Anglophones, I did not make the teen social cut and was quickly wildly unpopular. I also fell out of touch with my recently-made Welsh friends. Once my "A" level exams were over, I returned to Canada to start at the University of British Columbia in Vancouver (at which no one cared about my good "A" level marks): I was "home" in a city in which I had never lived, among peers who didn't get my largely British sense of humor, hadn't watched *Top of the Pops*, didn't care about the Falklands War, didn't know the words to "Majulah Singapura," hadn't ever sat through swarming insects on *larong* night, didn't know anything about Lee Kuan Yew and had eaten neither a Flake 99 nor ikan bilis. I looked like everyone else, but I did not fit in. I promptly lost contact with Britain almost entirely. Since returning to North America, I have been to Singapore once (11 days that reaffirmed how much of an expat I had been as a child, not a Singaporean) and Britain once (but only to London, a city I spent scant time in as a teen).

One can draw key third culture kids' characteristics out of my experiences: dislocation, feeling perpetually like an outsider, difficulties with national-cultural identity development, being an invisible immigrant once repatriated to my "home" nation, and having my past add up to a succession of losses of places and people. I had a very privileged childhood, but it was not *all* good. In his work on the effects of growing up in the military, psychiatrist Sidney Werkman suggests,

> Let us not forget that the lifestyle shares many advantages with that of the fortunate man in a cartoon, pictured lounging beside his swimming pool in the shadow of his mansion who tells us: "It's not all peaches and cream, but it's mostly peaches and cream." My position is that what is not "peaches and cream" can lead to subtle personality difficulties in children raised in military households. These may not be measurable by standard checklists, but they often lead to clinical disturbances [985].

Werkman's observation about military children applies to me, and to many other children brought up as expatriates: it is indeed a "peaches and cream" life, but it also produces certain distinct problems. Perhaps these are not always "clinical," but they are often significant and influential throughout an individual's life. Because the lifestyle is so privileged, who would think that expatriate children (and the adults they grow up to be) have so much to mourn? If, like the children of most diplomats, military personnel or business people, they move every few years, then the total losses happen repeatedly. Everything is left behind, again and again. I knew this from my own experience, but was shocked when I began my research at how much of the work on children raised as expatriates focuses on unresolved grief and problems with identity. I was more shocked when I began analyzing the works of third culture authors, for the proliferation of images of devastating loss appeared consistently and ubiquitously, suggesting a significant literary rebuttal of the assumption that a life on the move is categorically a good life.

Though there are many third culture authors, it is sometimes challenging to find them. One cannot currently type "third culture literature" into a search engine and come up with a tidy list. In looking, I ran up against the mores of publishing and book reviewing, in which the tendency is to identify authors by nation, and in which there is little accommodation possible for authors whose origin is unclear, or whose "nationality" includes a lengthy series of countries. My best strategies have been fairly random. Standing in bookstores reading the biographical blurbs on book covers found me a few useful names. Perhaps because loss and devastation feature so prominently in the works of third culture authors, a surprising number have shown up as Oprah's Book Club choices. Also surprising is how many Man Booker Prize winners have third culture (expatriate) upbringings.

The Man Booker is a prominent and well-reputed prize. It was depressing to see how many third culture authors make the list for it, or even *win* it, and then fail to make a crossover to academia as subjects of literary criticism or as texts on course reading lists. It seems likely that the texts and authors do not enter academic study because there is no classification for them. They are not really part of a single nation's literary tradition, and they are not international in ways the academy understands. They don't fit in a British, Canadian, or American literature course, for instance, but they don't fit in a postcolonial course either. They do fit as third culture literature. Academia *needs* a third culture rubric, for the only ways it currently recognizes international writers writing in English are: (1) in terms of their marginality and (somatic) alterity; or (2) in terms of their status as immigrants.

Third culture literature is not a category defined by race, and, indeed, race is somewhat beside the point in the chapters that follow. It tends, however, to be written by individuals who were dislocated in privileged circumstances; these authors are seldom on the disadvantaged side of a socio-cultural or economic scale. It is unpopular to study the "over-dog," and while this isn't an argument against studying postcolonial literature, it is imperative that readers, critics and publishers notice and examine the large number of international writers who do not fit any analytical profile or publishing definition currently in use.

Third culture literature defines an area that is currently unstudied, but has existed for decades, and will persist. Bringing the increasingly numerous social science studies of third culture to bear on the literature reveals how clearly defined this field actually is, and how distinctive. My analysis of third culture literature contributes significantly to what the social sciences know by explicating how the shared cultural details of this field emerge in literary themes and images. The urgency of this work is multiple: academia needs to recognize the existence of this body of literature and its distinguishing features; the social sciences need to see how this literary research complements their preexisting studies; publishers and reviewers need a functional category for these authors and their works; and authors themselves need the recognition that will prevent their works from disappearing into obscurity for want of a label. Third culture individuals who are readers will be able to take much from this book; academics, publishers and reviewers who read for a living but have never heard of "third culture" may, hopefully, be able to take even more.

Introduction: When Writers Grow Up Expat

In 2003, I sat in a café in Halifax, Canada, and scribbled a fervent letter, a love letter of sorts, on a napkin. It was addressed to Yann Martel, whose *Life of Pi* I had just read, but it grew especially out of my discovery that Martel was a diplomat's son and, though Canadian by passport, had been raised all over the world. Essentially, my absorbent little *billet doux* argued that because we had such similar backgrounds (myself also Canadian and raised around the world), we should know each other — in fact, we kind of *already did* (so convinced was I that his internationalized experience and mine meant we would understand things about each other that no other Canadian possibly could). Embarrassing, ardent, and I never sent it. It was not until 2007 that I encountered Ruth Van Reken, author of *Letters Never Sent* (her title uncannily reiterating the heartfelt feeling of shared experience that characterized my own un-sent letter to Martel), and one of the key proponents of research into the lives of "third culture kids," a term that was new to me at the time, and is still new to the field of English literary studies, but aptly describes Martel and authors like him: raised outside their passport nation (one culture), in a series of host countries (second cultures), as an expatriate (third culture).

It is perhaps surprising, once one begins looking for them, how many authors *are* like Martel in having been raised as expatriates (or even "intranational" expatriates, who have moved so many times within their home nation under the auspices of organizations like the military that their experience is of living as an expatriate on "home" soil). Some, like Sarah Bird (American Air Force bases, including Japan, France, Spain and the Yucatán) or Richard Lewis (USA/Indonesia), are comparative unknowns. Others are well reputed in the context of a national literature, with the result that the displacement which so informs their texts is omitted from critical considerations of them. For instance, Barbara Kingsolver, whose work has been used to define American approaches to water policy, indigeneity and food[1] (but who is also significantly influenced by a childhood sojourn in the Congo); Ann-Marie MacDonald, who is referred to as a Canadian author despite her geographically dislocated background (she was raised on Canadian Air Force bases, including one in West Germany); or Ian McEwan, who is generally taken to be a defining figure in contemporary British literature but grew up in part on British Army installations in Libya and Singapore. Some publish in mass-market genres that tend to be categorized by the material at hand (thriller, romance, etc.), not the author's national identity: consider William Paul Young (Canadian, with missionary parents who raised him in Indonesia) and his extraordinarily successful novel *The Shack*. One might be surprised that such different, so-called American writers as Pat Conroy (various American military bases) and Joseph O'Neill (Irish/Turkish descent, raised in Mozambique, Turkey, Iran and the Netherlands) share a cultural background of displacement, and yet they do.

I have included in the examples above only six of the seventeen authors I touch on in this book, and there are many more one could consider — for instance, Clark Blaise (USA, Canada, with more than two dozen moves during his developmental years), DBC Pierre (Australia, Spain, Mexico, England, West Indies), Helen Dewitt (USA, South America, United Kingdom, Germany) or James Scudamore (Japan, Brazil, United Kingdom). And there is a dizzying array of fantasy writers who are third culture kids, none of whom I treat here; they range in prominence from J.R.R. Tolkien (South Africa, United Kingdom) to Philip Pullman (many international British Air Force bases, then Australia), with some lesser-knowns like Jeff Vandermeer (USA and Fiji) and Fiona McIntosh (United Kingdom, Ghana, Australia) in between.

In this introductory chapter, I define the cultural experience authors such as these have in common. I also argue that literature emerging from this specific cultural context shares preoccupations with diasporic, (third world) cosmopolitan, and postcolonial literatures, but is *significantly different* from these because of the privileged expatriate perspective of its authors. The writings of Martel and others like him can be fruitfully treated as a subset of international writing that I call *third culture literature*. "Third culture" is a term I am adapting from other contexts.[2] "Third culture literature" is a term not previously used in literary scholarship.

Sociologist Ruth Hill Useem refers to "third culture" individuals as, among others like them, the children of diplomats, missionaries, the military, and international business people. These individuals are raised outside their parents' home country and tend to have frequently relocated from one nation to another. Useem's term indicates that people raised outside their home country as expatriates have a passport home, which is their first culture. This is typically somewhat foreign to them, as they do not live or have not lived much in it. They also have a relationship with a second culture (or series of them): their host country or countries. In their host countries, they are always aware that they are foreign and form a third, stronger connection with other expatriates: a *third culture*. Unlike many diasporic populations, third culture individuals do not foster an attachment to a home nation and then go abroad (they do not go "away" from a single "home"). Instead, they foster attachments to interstitial, international communities in the various countries in which they reside (Stephens and Reken 1).

For Pollock and Van Reken, living in many diverse locations *while a child* is crucial: "Unlike adults with similar experiences ... for [third culture kids] the moving back and forth from one culture to another happens before they have completed the developmental task of forming a sense of their own personal or cultural identity" (39). Children do not yet have a strong national/cultural identity: their idea of themselves, and of "home," is plastic. A third culture kid, mobile as she grows up, develops national/cultural identities contingent on context. A Spanish passport holder living in Canada might, when asked by a Canadian, say she is from Spain. Asked by a Spaniard, she would have to qualify what's missing in or different about her Spanishness: "I was born in Spain, but I live in Canada." Asked by a Chinese person, that same child might say "Canada" or even "Do you want the short or long version of where I am from?" Perpetually aware of being "new," or of lacking a full complement of the experiences others in any place share, "home" is an inaccessible notion for third culture individuals. Even when grown into adulthood, third culture kids remain profoundly shaped by the childhood transience that resulted in, and continues to result in, their feeling that they have no "home." An adult who goes abroad generally has a sense of the home that came before all their experiences of being away: they have a sense of who they were before they encountered other cultures. Even an immigrant, regardless of age, tends to have a sense of home, be it the place they started from or the new place in which they have arrived and into which they strive to grow roots. A third culture kid tends to be unrooted in both their past and present locations, even once grown up.

In addition to this crucial distinction between adults who travel (but have a "home" nation) and individuals raised away from their parents' home, it is important to note two aspects of this definition of third culture kids: the privilege of mobility (though peripheral to the cultures they are raised in, third culture kids are not restricted by their marginality) and interstitiality (raised among similarly out-of-place children, these individuals do not become hybrids of a home culture and a host culture, but rather acculturate themselves with other dislocated individuals).

I use "third culture literature" to describe fiction writings resulting from, and/or explicitly engaging with, a third culture context. Third culture is rooted in experiential similarity rather than geographical location. The terminology "third culture" is becoming more widespread in disciplines as diverse as education, linguistics and human resource development,[3] but in order to "locate" third culture authors, my study draws on seminal definitions of third culture from psychology and sociology as well as my own research into authors' biographies. I combine these resources to delineate a particular cultural context. I then go on to suggest what characterizes *literary work* produced out of such a cultural context. This introduction, and my book, thus deal with establishing what "third culture" is as well as with indicating what features are common to "third culture *literature*." It is worth noting that while author biography is important in establishing a shared culture, the readings of literary texts in this book do *not* suggest that third culture fictions are necessarily autobiographical. This introduction is also intended to position the idea of "third culture" as a category relative to others extant in the humanities, especially in philosophical and literary critical study, and so compares this idea to terms like "diasporic" and "cosmopolitan."

My work is to map a field that has no specific physical geography, describe a peripatetic culture with no shared location, and characterize a distinct and recognizable body of literature that has not yet been seen as a coherent corpus. My intervention is urgent, for many of the works I study in this book win accolades and then disappear from view for want of an appropriate national label (*Life of Pi*, as I suggest below, is a good example). Many others are repeatedly critiqued for not being international in a way that makes sense in any existing rubric for literary study (*The Poisonwood Bible*, for instance, is frequently critiqued for not *really* being a postcolonial novel). Third culture authors are unlikely to become less prevalent in our ever-globalizing world. It is becoming imperative that literary critics develop an appropriate vocabulary for discussing these writers; in fact, such a vocabulary is long overdue.

Why We Need "Third Culture Literature": The Reception of Yann Martel's *Life of Pi*

The reception of Martel's Man Booker Prize–winning *Life of Pi* in 2002 provides a useful example of the need for vocabulary describing international authors who are not tourists, immigrants, exiles, refugees, or third world cosmopolitans, but are instead what I refer to as third culture authors.

Martel's national identity was hotly debated in Canada. As Eva-Marie Kröller notes, Martel's nomination for the Man Booker Prize was "welcomed in Canada with great satisfaction" but, because Martel was born in Spain and raised in Costa Rica, France, Mexico and Alaska, it also launched a controversy about what determines the "Canadianness" of an author (1). "Yann Martel took home laurels for *Life of Pi*," writes Canadian journalist Sandra Martin in *The Globe and Mail*: "Our reaction? We tripped over ourselves to point out that none of the three alleged Canadians [nominated for the award] had actually been born here" (December 3, 2002). Canadian response to Martel's success, then, was initially to point out that Martel himself shouldn't really be classified as Canadian. There was, however, no obvious alternative vocabulary for Martin or others to use. Martin continues: "If people had bothered to check beyond 'place of birth' on the Spanish-born Mr. Martel's passport, they would have quickly discovered that his father, the Canadian diplomat and distinguished poet Emil Martel, can trace his lineage in Canada back to the early 17th century" (December 3, 2002). Martin's substitution of Emil's experience for Yann's indicates the elusiveness of Yann Martel's national identity, for though his father was Canadian *qua* Canadian, Yann was, as I note above, a Canadian passport holder born in Spain and raised elsewhere. Martin reclaims Martel's Canadianness on the basis of his passport and his father's life (both first culture), disregarding the second cultures to which Yann was exposed and the third culture of expatriatism that more fully represents "where he comes from."

The novel itself opens with a pseudo-biographical, fictional "Author's Note," which sets a stage as international as Martel's own life (the "author" travels to Canada, Portugal, India, Britain, Siberia, Bolivia and Japan). This fictionalized version of Martel is used to show how his works are received: "Reviewers [are] puzzled" (v). The novel proceeds to a fabulist plot involving a young boy (Pi Patel), curious about Islam, Christianity and Hinduism. The boy's family runs a zoo replete with specimens acquired from around the world; when it is closed, animals and family set sail, in the same ship, for other shores. The ship sinks and young Pi is set adrift in a lifeboat populated by a handful of unfriendly, hungry and fierce zoo animals. In later years, safe in Canada, Pi recounts his story to the novel's fictionalized "author." One can read many of Pi's experiences as analogous to those of a third culture kid. Pi may not explicitly *be* a third culture kid, but his losses, griefs and responses to dislocation are manifestly expressions of third culture experience.

In her study of loss and grief in third culture kids, Kathleen Gilbert observes that third culture individuals, "rather than thinking about the loss of home" thanks to many relocations, "related better to the concept of experiencing grief at the recognition that home was absent from their lives" (105). For third culture kids, there is no home; what one starts with is the absence of home itself. Pi's presiding characteristic is his homelessness. He is a castaway, literally "at sea," overwhelmed, in a rapidly changing and globalized, international, inter-species world, and "very few castaways have survived as long at sea as Mr. Patel" (354). The novel, in this regard, expresses two key third culture concerns: What if there *is* no home? What if one is always an outsider?

At the start of *Life of Pi*, Martel compares animal zoos and human homes: "Don't we say 'There's no place like home'? That's certainly what animals feel.... A house is a compressed territory where our basic needs can be met. A sound zoo enclosure is the equivalent for an animal" (19). He goes on to suggest that

> one might even argue that if an animal could choose with intelligence, it would opt for living in a zoo, since the major difference between a zoo and the wild is the absence of parasites and enemies and the abundance of food in the first and their respective abundance and scarcity in the second. Think about it yourself. Would you rather be put up in the Ritz with free room service and unlimited access to a doctor or be homeless without a soul to care for you? [20].

If the zoo is home, life without it is an unprotected wilderness. Pi, as a castaway, is in the unprotected wilderness without home. "In the literature [about zoos] can be found legions of examples of animals that could escape but did not, or did and returned," Pi muses wistfully (20). Who would *want* to be without a home, as Pi finds himself to be even when eventually married with a family and a comfortable house in the Toronto suburbs? Pi is a man who, in a secure Canadian adulthood, smiles for the camera at his graduation and wedding, "but his eyes tell another story" (95).

In *The Global Soul*, Pico Iyer (himself a third culture kid) on the one hand celebrates the plasticity of identity enjoyed by someone who is able to "claim or deny attachment" to what-, who-, and wherever they choose, and on the other recognizes the "nightmare of disorientation and disconnection" produced by being so loosed from national, cultural and even familial ties (21). "Liminality, in the form of being between identities, can be highly stressful," Kathleen Gilbert writes (105). In *Life of Pi*, Pi experiences the plasticity of his identity as purely nightmarish. It rapidly becomes clear that Pi must adapt himself to life with unpredictable threats (at first a hyena and a tiger, and later, after the tiger eats the hyena, only the tiger). Pi alters his habits because he has to in order to survive. He ceases to be a vegetarian and learns to kill fish, as well as turtles, and eat them raw. He trains the tiger using an emergency whistle. He becomes someone utterly unfamiliar to himself. Pi's transformations exaggerate the process by which third culture kids alter their identities (developing new languages or accents, habits, styles of dress, friendships, food preferences) in order to "survive" in new contexts.

Martel concludes his novel with a conversation that is at once ridiculous and consummately third culture. Pi, recuperating in Mexico, is questioned about his experiences by Japanese employees of the company that owned the sunken ship. We discover that the narrative of the animals as we have read it is the narrative that Pi tells the two Japanese men (and then later retells to the novel's faux "author"). The Japanese inquisitors think Pi is mocking them by telling a fiction (324). So Pi tells a different story to the men, a condensed one, that has him in the boat with his mother (for whom the orangutan has been a metaphor in the longer version), a Frenchman (the hyena) and a Taiwanese sailor (the zebra). Pi himself is the tiger in this version of the story. The shorter story is more plausible and yet in its factual credibility it fails to accurately provide the emotional impact of the massive losses Pi has experienced. It is, as Pi rails, "an immobile story ... a dry, yeastless factuality" (336). The short version loses the gist of displacement, dislocation and movement. In a sense, what Martel gives us is both the long and short versions of the perennially difficult-to-answer third culture question: "Where are you from?" The revised, short version Pi tells the men does not provide the vertiginous confusion, the "nightmare of disorientation and disconnection," that the animal story does. The hyena's killing of the orangutan in the fabulist version is actually far more poignant than the death of his mother at the hands of a rather depraved, hungry Frenchman. The animal's whimpers are "humanlike" and plausible (145), while his mother's dismembered head sinking is inhuman, incredible, and beyond a reader's emotional comprehension (344). Indeed, the loss of everything to dislocation and death, and the grief thereby occasioned, is far more striking in the long, metaphor-rich version of Pi's story. Mr. Okamoto, one of the men asking questions, concedes that "the story with the animals is the better story" (352).

The novel's conclusion also reminds us of the fictional "Author's Note" with which it began in evoking a range of nations (in this case Mexico, Japan, and France). The total number of places referred to in the text is thus large, resulting in a story that cannot be firmly located: its setting is not only Canada (though Pi tells his story while in Toronto), nor is it really India, nor Mexico, nor Japan. The story is adrift in international waters, without specific allegiances, as, perhaps, Martel is himself.

The national indeterminacy of both author and plot, while challenging for journalists, has likely made the book less relevant to literary critics working with contemporary fiction, as we are typically required to locate our specialties and publications in terms of geography. *Life of Pi* is hard to categorize as Canadian literature, and yet it is not postcolonial either: it falls between categories in terms of the regional specialities of university faculty and the courses we offer. In the academic writing that has been done on the novel, limiting the implications of *Life of Pi*'s scattered geography often results in reading the global patchwork Martel presents as characteristic of postmodernism rather than of displacement.[4] This emphasis on postmodernism reflects how hard it is — without a term like "third culture" — to deal with a story without national anchors attributable to either its plot or its author. More accurate than "diasporic," "(third world) cosmopolitan," "postcolonial" or even ersatz "colonial," "third culture" can provide a vocabulary for literary analysis that accounts for the internationalized, interstitial and ungrounded identities of a writer like Martel or his fictional characters.

Third Culture Literature and Existing Terminologies

In this section I invoke a range of existing terms, theories, and the nuances of their use by specific theorists, all by way of illustrating the hallmarks of what I take to be third culture literature. Thus this book proposes a designation that encompasses third culture literature's dislocation, loss despite privilege, disenfranchisement, and tacit awareness of neocolonial influence with guilt resulting from that awareness.

"Diasporic" does not quite describe writers like Martel. Powerfully evoking loss of homeland, and originating in descriptions of the Jewish diaspora, it has been used in subsequent centuries to suggest other kinds of mass (as well as individual) displacement, but in terms that appropriately, given the word's allusion to forced exile, evoke a single homeland lost to subsequent homes. However, Martel and other third culture writers generally do not have a homeland and, in addition, are not part of a forced exodus, refugees, immigrants from one single nation to another in which they seek out passports and citizenship, migrants sneaking across borders in the dark, or itinerant because they are literally homeless. As Pico Iyer[5] (born in England to Indian parents, raised between California and British boarding schools, and currently living in Japan) writes of himself, "A person like me can't really call himself an exile (who traditionally looked back to a home now lost), or an expatriate (who's generally posted abroad for a living); I'm not really a nomad (whose patterns are guided by seasons and tradition); and I've never been subject to the refugee's violent disruptions" (*The Global Soul* 23). Iyer answers the need for a new term for people like himself with the uncomfortably numinous "global soul," by which he means someone nationally unaffiliated (24), although his vocabulary unfortunately also suggests a transcendence redolent of identity snobbery ("I am more of an enlightened world citizen than you are"). "Global *nomad*" is in fact a term that is sometimes used as synonymous with "third culture kid," despite the fact that "nomad" implies the annually repeated routes of nomadic peoples. (See, for instance, Morten G. Ender's collection *Military Brats and Other Global Nomads*.) I have opted to use "third culture" instead, because, even though a reader might wrongly strain to find "third *world*" at its heart, "third culture" more precisely locates this culture as expatriate and transient.

At its core, Iyer's "global soul" has much in common with May Joseph's conception of "nomadic, conditional citizenship" experienced in "multiple national contexts" (2, 3). For Joseph, however, "contexts" are obdurately rooted in colonial history, which results in her reconsideration of a margin/periphery paradigm, as the later chapters of her *Nomadic Identities* (in which she focuses on topics like black Britishness) attest. Aihwa Ong's "flexible citizenship" initially sounds like it overlaps with Iyer and Joseph in its evocation of internationality and detachment from the passport nation (Ong writes about Asians with American passports) (56–57). However, her focus on detachment from the passport nation (America) *and* continued attachment to another place (an Asian country) (56) makes her argument fundamentally different from Joseph's (multiple attachments that ultimately give way to a home/away pairing) or Iyer's (no real attachment to any place).

Iyer writes of lacking "a sense of community" (24); he laments the disorienting (and ultimately isolating) effect of cultural adaptability ("[t]he Global Soul ... may grow so used to giving back a different self according to his environment [that] he loses sight of who he is when nobody's around") (25). Sociologists studying third culture corroborate this idea: Iyer's perceived isolation is fairly typical of third culture experience. Libby Stephens and Van Reken assert the need to "recognize and validate a [third culture kid's] identity and relationship with 'international culture'" (6). Many online organizations for third culture kids, missionary kids and military brats now attempt to foster a sense of community for individuals raised all over the world. Pollock and Van Reken suggest that recognizing a third culture community means individuals can affiliate themselves with it rather than trying to remain "eternal chameleons" (Pollock and Van Reken 271). Janet Bennett's keynote plenary at the 2007 Families in Global Transition convention in Houston, Texas, stressed that first-time convention participants would likely think they were alone in their experiences of displacement and would, to their surprise, discover they were in room full of people with similar experiences, not in terms of specific countries lived in, but in the results of frequent displacement (contextually flexible constructions of national/cultural identity and the absence of a grounding notion of home). Bennett invited conference participants to recognize that they were *not* indeed unique, but rather part of a shared third culture.

David Pollock defines a "third culture kid" as

> an individual who, having spent a significant part of the developmental years in a culture other than the parents' culture, develops a sense of relationship to all of the cultures, while not having full ownership in any. Elements from each culture are incorporated into the life experience, but the sense of belonging is in relationship to others of similar experience ["TCK Definition"].

Pollock coauthors a book with Van Reken, *Third Culture Kids: The Experience of Growing Up Among Worlds*, that explicates this definition in detail, emphasizing the evidence of a shared culture among individuals without specific geographical roots (20). They differentiate "third culture" from "third world," suggest that "significant part" as a time span can vary depending on an individual's age, and highlight the importance of the individual experiencing cultural dislocation between the ages of zero and eighteen (21, 27). A "sense of relationship to all of the cultures, while not having full ownership in any," produces, according to Pollock and Van Reken, "the sense of belonging 'everywhere and nowhere' at the same time" (30). Third culture kids are obviously exposed to widely divergent cultures, and yet there is a puzzling ease of understanding among fellow third culture kids that leads Pollock and Van Reken to ask, "What is it about growing up in multiple cultures and with high mobility that creates such instant recognition of each other's experiences and feelings?" (34). Their book proceeds to answer that question over its next three hundred pages, much as my book will proceed to suggest how literature answers the same question. The short version of the answer is that despite geographical disparities, third culture manifests the effects of this "similar experience."

Third culture, then, is international community based on like experiences and perspectives. In some respects this seems, conceptually, like the utopian, philosophical ideal of cosmopolitanism: third culture individuals are not attached to any one country and so can imagine values, morals, and responsibilities globally rather than parochially. This putatively ideal perspective is frequently invoked by sociologists and psychologists to tout the benefits of growing up in scattered locales. However, in practice the terms "cosmopolitan" and "third culture" do not overlap very much; the former often still, unexpectedly, invokes a binary home-and-away paradigm, while the latter involves multiple (dis)locations, necessarily occurring during the developmental years, for individuals who consequently have *no* sense of home. Ulf Hannerz insists, "Of course, cosmopolitans are usually somewhat footloose, on the move in the world. [But] among the several cultures with which they are engaged, at least one is presumably of the territorial kind" (240). This is not the case in third culture: for third culture individuals there is ultimately no "territorial" home culture on which their feet rest.

While "cosmopolitan" seems to imply a flexible internationalism, in literary analyses especially it is a concept frequently applied to contexts in which there is a periphery (often rural, and in the third world) and a center (generally a first world metropolis). Take the important and influential example of Timothy Brennan's "Cosmopolitans and Celebrities" (1989), which refers to "authors from the dominions who travel to London, Paris or New York"; "home" is "the dominions" and there is one possible "away" for each "cosmopolite"—"the center," be it "London, Paris, or New York" (6). Brennan also writes of cosmopolitanism as "janus-faced," the two faces foreclosing the possibility of multiple ones (7). His article sets the stage for the persistent general understanding that cosmopolitans are originally "from" the peripheral third world and tend to write about center-periphery (colonizer/colonized) conflicts. Essentially, Brennan's definition of cosmopolitan literature is postcolonial literature produced by a third world author who has relocated to a major first world city. Brennan asserts Salman Rushdie and Bharati Mukherjee's "authentic attachment to a Third World locale": they are different from unrooted writers like Martel. One part of their identity keeps a foot at home, regardless of how far the other travels, and, in addition, they are rooted in "the third world," which implies that any transition they make will be from a former colony to either a former colonial center or a new metropolitan one (like Manhattan) (2, 3). Brennan explicitly discusses Rushdie and Mukherjee in the context of "post-war immigrations to the metropolitan centres" (invoking an effect of postcoloniality demonstrated by substantial waves of immigration: the formerly colonized moves to the place associated with the power and privilege of the colonizer) (4).

I use the term "dislocation" in the chapters that follow, indicating the (many) moves that characterize third culture literature. These moves are non-hierarchical and multiple rather than in pairs. There is no privileged "home," nor is there a coveted metropolitan destination — all places tend to be equal, with the literatures of third culture authors placing an emphasis on characters who feel equally dislocated in all places. My use of "dislocation" thus differs from some existing uses, which perpetuate the periphery (home)/center (away) binary we see in Brennan. Writing about "the Politics of Dislocation" (1995) — and, like Brennan, binary in emphasis — Revathi Krishnaswamy observes that the "itinerant intellectual becomes an international figure" by "Journeying from the 'peripheries' to the metropolitan center" (125). "International" here entails a pair of places rather than a plethora: periphery and city. Likewise, Caren Kaplan's 1996 *Questions of Travel* opens as follows:

> In this book, I inquire into categories that are so often taken for granted, asking how and when notions of home and away, placement and displacement, dwelling and travel, location and dislocation, come to play a role in contemporary literary and cultural criticism in Europe and the United States [1].

Here Kaplan presents four pairs (all of which could be taken as shades of home/away) and an explicitly Western focus. In her discussion of "Rooted Cosmopolitanism" (2006), Domna Stanton shows the persistence of binaries when she stresses that "readers must negotiate the difference between 'over here' and 'over there'" (630). Even Kwame Anthony Appiah's *Cosmopolitanism* (also 2006), while discussing the philosophical possibilities of reconciling cultural relativism and universalism, repeatedly contrasts examples from Ghana with those from the United States — for instance, comparing/contrasting Ghana's Kumasi and the mores of life in Princeton, New Jersey (90ff).

Admittedly, there are diverse applications of the idea of cosmopolitanism, some of which involve more complex global patterns. One might consider Arjun Appadurai's well-known *-scapes*, his "five dimensions of cultural flows," used to allow more systematic analysis of the global *cultural* economy and its "overlapping, disjunctive order that cannot be understood anymore in terms of existing center-periphery models": ethnoscapes, mediascapes, technoscapes, financescapes and ideoscapes (32, 33). He considers the flow of culture through various kinds of economy, suggesting that the different avenues (or -scapes) through which culture travels allow one to get past the binaries explicit in center-periphery models. Nonetheless, his constructions of cultural economy and exchange do not quite get at the impetus of third culture, which is not so much flowing and changing but rather coalescing around an unexpected body of shared experience. Third culture individuals may move around the world, but their shared experience of dislocation is not indicative of different flowing economies so much as of similar experiences of being in the lifeboat riding the flow, to borrow an image from Martel.

Homi K. Bhabha works to complicate cosmopolitanism itself. In the preface to the 2004 Routledge Classics edition of *The Location of Culture*, he argues:

> There is, however, another cosmopolitanism of the Trinidadian variety, figuratively speaking, that emerges from the world of migrant boarding houses and the habitations of national and diasporic minorities. Julia Kristeva, in another context, calls it wounded cosmopolitanism. In my view it is better described as a vernacular cosmopolitanism which measures global progress from the minoritarian perspective [xvi].

Bhabha presents the possibility of a creolization of the cosmopolitan into the vernacular, so that it becomes several minorities internal to a nation. This is no longer a home/away paradigm. Bhabha here, as he so often does, elegantly conducts us toward a liminal position that accommodates diversity. What remains in his description, nonetheless, is the "minoritarian" perspective and the subaltern of disadvantaged "migrant boarding houses." The position of privileged internationalism (the inhabitant, perhaps, of a nice diplomatic residence, rather than a migrant's overcrowded "boarding house") is not under consideration. In addition, Bhabha's reference to Trinidad, even figuratively, reinscribes a long-growing (mis)understanding in contemporary Western literary and cultural criticism that the internationalisms of cosmopolitics are necessarily connected with racial alterities.

Third culture individuals tend to be privileged: we are not discussing the inhabitants of crowded boarding houses, but rather those of nice diplomatic residences, or decent military base apartments, or lavish (by local standards) mission houses. Annika Hylmö's analysis of children's literature dealing with expatriation includes a section on "Expatriate Living and the Reproduction of Social Privilege," and begins as follows: "The expatriate community draws on reified social privileges that its members actively participate in reproducing" (125). Children taken overseas are, it is generally (and rightly) assumed, fortunate enough to experience new things, new cultures, new places, new languages, and a certain level of expatriate luxury. It is common for moving to far-flung locales to be considered a categorically *good* experience for a child. However, the emphasis placed on the benefits of growing up abroad, or in multiple locations, tends to mean that genuine and significant losses are overlooked. Consider the typical diplomat's child (diplomats and business people are generally at the top of the heap among third culture individuals, enjoying the highest material levels of expatriate privilege): Her family might move every three or four years. Though they may move through a series of very nice houses, and enjoy access to swimming pools, tennis courts, exotic holidays and good food, what the child experiences every three or four years is, nonetheless, the loss of everything and everyone she knows: the house, her friends, her school, the family's pets, and even the nation and its culture. Moves happen often; the child knows she will soon lose track of friends left behind. The child also knows that every stint in a place is temporary: she does not and will not belong, even if she grows to love a place and/or its culture dearly.

The big surprise, in reading third culture *literature*, is the extent to which third culture losses are magnified. Contradicting as forcibly as possible the benefits assumed to come with growing up expatriate, one sees devastating losses occur again and again. Death proliferates in these texts (analogous to the seeming "death" of everything left behind when one moves). In addition, because the grief a child experiences is often overshadowed by the benefits her family insists she is enjoying, loss festers, unresolved. As Gilbert observes of third culture kids, "TCKs experiencing losses may be told to move on, to stop acting out.... Losses that are not successfully resolved in childhood have an increased likelihood of recurring in adulthood" (96). In third culture literature one sees a range of spectacular dysfunctions as unresolved losses are explored. In addition to death, images of pedophilia, underage sex, sick children and abandonment proliferate — they are not just here and there in the fiction, but *everywhere*.

In the social science analyses of third culture kids, sociologists consider the benefits of third culture individuals not being attached to any one place or nationality: a third culture individual might celebrate their expanded worldview, adaptability, lack of prejudice and cross-cultural skills (Pollock and Van Reken 78, 92, 97, 107–19; Stephens and Van Reken 1–2, 5). Alongside these benefits are documented problems: unresolved grief over losses of people and places, and difficulties in identity formation. Regarding identity, if, as Kathleen A. Finn Jordan writes, "home" and "roots" are "essential" to the process of identity formation, then the discontinuity that Barbara F. Schaetti notes as the key feature of a third culture individual's life must necessarily result in difficulty forging a stable, continuous identity (Jordan 212; Schaetti 109). Gilbert concludes of third culture kids that "a prominent aspect of their lives was the extent and pervasiveness of loss throughout their childhood and adolescence, as well as the echoes of grief resolution that have extended well into adulthood" (107). She adds that the "result of this unending processing of grief may be a person who feels rootless and alienated [living in] a perpetual state of liminality" (107). Jean-Marc Dewaele and Jan Pieter Oudenhoven test multilingual third culture kids who have repatriated to London. They expect to, and indeed do, find high levels of cultural empathy, open-mindedness, social initiative and flexibility (449, 453). However, they also find multilingual third culture kids to have "significantly" lower levels of emotional stability (453).

Jordan notes that adult third culture individuals are more comfortable observing than participating (223). Ann Baker Cottrell and Ruth Hill Useem observe that "90 percent say they are more or less 'out of synch' with their age group throughout their lifetimes." Jordan adds that these adults have site-specific identities based on rehearsed formulae, but often lack ideological commitments because of their perception of themselves as outsiders (219). Thus, among the drawbacks of such mutable, chameleon-like expressions of identity is a potential decrease in individual social responsibility. Feeling like a perpetual outsider results in not feeling responsible to any nation, government or community. More unpleasant still, the combination of privilege and disenfranchisement can produce aloofness: "arrogance isn't an uncommon word when people describe TCKs," write Pollock and Van Reken (103). They repeat this observation, adding, "A 'different from' identity has a certain arrogance attached to it" (104). In third culture literature, this phenomenon manifests in representations of characters who are disenfranchised from local politics and community as a result of their ignorance or lack of understanding of what is actually going on around them. Often self-consciously aware of their privileged position, third culture characters are nonetheless sometimes arrogant dolts, destructively ignorant of the place in which they live.

In philosophical discourse, many have questioned the shortcomings of the *cosmopolitan* individual.[6] Is the cosmopolite's freedom to invent his/her identity conceptually liberatory or indicative of elitism and privilege (Appiah, "Cosmopolitan Patriots" 97)? Is the cosmopolite a parasite, feeding on the cultures s/he visits without civic or political responsibility to them (Appiah, "Cosmopolitan Patriots" 91)? Others ask whether the 1760s definition of the cosmopolite by L'Académie Française ("*pas un bon citoyen*," not a good citizen) still holds (Stanton 635–36). These questions do indicate one specific area in which there is significant overlap between studies of cosmopolitanism and third culture. Is the cosmopolite or third culture individual detached? Arrogant? Socially irresponsible? Third culture literature suggests that for third culture individuals the answer to all three questions might be "yes" but they are also *aware* of their detachment, arrogance and irresponsibility. Third culture characters experience incredible loss. But third culture authors represent in their works guilt for characters' arrogance as well as for the whole history of colonialism and neocolonial exploitation.

Third culture individuals have no specific *national* culture (though they do share a third culture) and their values are (to flirt with the philosophical conundrum) relative. There may be values and ideals expressed in third culture literature, but these tend to be malleable. Similarly, third culture literature may describe inter-cultural problems (such as potentially being devoured by a real or metaphorical "tiger" in *Life of Pi*), but there tends to be no self-assured cultural or moral position. This lack of moral conviction regarding a home nation's norms marks a key difference between colonial literature (in which there is generally a moral order, even if that order is questioned, as it is in Forster's *A Passage to India*, for example) and third culture literature (in which there generally is no single presiding set of moral assumptions, even, surprisingly, in the fiction writings of former missionary kids). In its philosophical use, "cosmopolitanism" strives for a universal order inimical to the moral indecisiveness often expressed in third culture literature.

Replacing a home/away pairing with a more complex web of geographical-cultural connections in fictional narratives is a key feature of third culture literature. Taking this into account will allow scholars to recognize these literatures as different from narratives documenting a single nationality, from those chronicling a "'voyage in' from the periphery to the centre" (Orgun 122), or from those we read as "postcolonial." Third culture literature and its authors do not engage with this kind of center-periphery paradigm (instead, *everything* becomes periphery), for its most important feature is its lack of center. Third culture literature also engages with colonialism's legacies in a significantly different way: its authors and characters often guiltily, secretively, perceive themselves as modern-day colonists, or at least as privileged minorities, rather than descendants of racially, culturally, politically or intellectually derogated citizens of empire.

What to Expect in the Chapters That Follow

My starting point in the work that follows is the task of outlining a new field in literary studies and clearly documenting its characteristics. Social science studies on third culture kids inform effective readings of this body of literature. It is also clear, however, that third culture literature expands what is already known in the social science research. Imaginative truth sometimes rings truer than the "real" story, as Martel argues. Certainly the magnitude of loss and dysfunction in third culture literature suggests that much more emphasis can be placed on the significance of unresolved grief. But there is also more the literature can teach us about identity and shared experiences of displacement. Sidney Werkman writes, "Those who have moved often may find it difficult to form an internal sense of 'narrative' after being shunted between school systems, contradictory national and ethnic moralities, and varying cultural events and role models" (985). What more effective place is there than fiction to narrativize third culture experience, to connect the dots between seemingly incommensurate social, cultural, and geographic experiences? It is a widely recognized truism that literature serves to "open up possibilities for people whose histories have not been taught at school and have been neglected in history books to write their own histories, to give voice to their own experience" (Eckstein et al. 442). It may stick in one's craw to treat such a privileged demographic as one that has been neglected and unrepresented, and yet that is the case. Writers *are* giving voice to this demographic: literary critics could do with an appropriate vocabulary for responding.

My book argues that there is a field of literature that, most simply, shares characteristics reflecting the third culture context out of which it is produced. The term "third culture literature" is an umbrella including any writing produced by a third culture author. In chapter one, I identify some of third culture literature's most typical characteristics. Under the umbrella of "third culture literature," however, there are two subtypes that emerge from such specific and regulated organizational contexts that it is fruitful to examine them as their own categories within third culture literature: the writings that emerge from the cultural context of being raised on military installations (military brat writing) and those that emerge from being raised in a missionary context (missionary kid writing). I treat military brat writing in chapter two and missionary kid writing in chapter three. Characteristics shared by third culture literature generally as well as by the writings of former missionary kids and those of former military brats are as follows: (1) descriptions of multiple geographic dislocations; (2) descriptions of the losses entailed in frequent relocation; and (3) descriptions of perceived disenfranchisement and lack of ownership.

There is also a striking but variable fourth characteristic that expresses with shocking emphasis how the preceding three characteristics culminate in dysfunction. In third culture literature generally, one sees plots in which neocolonial guilt catalyzes a secret action. Characters feel bad for getting away with their privilege and ignorance; as an analogue, those same characters commit some manner of secret crime that they also get away with. In the writings of former military brats, secretive guilt is replaced by flagrant sexual precociousness: neocolonial guilt is superseded by young characters who, placed in the too-adult context of martial conflict, adopt sexual behaviors that are similarly too adult, and they do so quite determinedly, without guilt, thereby challenging the authoritarian military context itself. In the writings of former missionary kids, one sees as a fourth characteristic children who are severely ill (surprisingly, often with malaria). The missionary context requires children be in the service of God, just like their parents, and to rank lower than God and his work within the family; the literature quite vividly suggests that such sacrifices produce suffering akin to severe physical illness.

If we return briefly to *Life of Pi* as an example of third culture literature, it is easy to see how the categories I set up clarify what are in fact the book's key themes. We see *dislocation*— both that of the fictional author (who travels in Canada, Portugal, India, Britain, Siberia, Bolivia and Japan) and of Pi (uprooted from Pondicherry, set adrift in international waters, restored to health in Mexico, and never fully "home" again despite eventually taking up residence in Canada). Pi, a comparatively privileged zookeeper's son in India, *loses* everything. His entire Indian past is left behind and his family drowns, except his mother, who (if one takes the short version of Pi's story to be the factual one) is graphically murdered on the lifeboat. The novel expresses *disenfranchisement* in Pi's contradictory adherence to Christianity, Islam and Hinduism. Pi, explaining himself to his mother, does so in terms that make it clear his encompassing religious beliefs reflect unrooted national identity. Pi's mother says, "Listen, my darling, if you're going to be religious, you must be either a Hindu, a Christian or a Muslim," to which Pi retorts, "I don't see why I can't be all three. Mamaji has two passports" (81). If one can "be" two nationalities, why not two religions, or three, or more? "If there's only one nation in the sky, shouldn't all passports be valid for it?" asks Pi (81).

Martel consistently links religious commingling with national commingling: in both, Pi expresses affiliation to all, and no specific allegiance to any. The flip side to this is that Pi has no specific religious "home" just as he winds up having no specific national "home." Pi's *guilty secret* is that being a castaway turns him into a murderous carnivore and cannibal. Dislocation, loss and disenfranchisement culminate in a taboo dysfunction. The Frenchman on the lifeboat kills Pi's mother, and Pi admits he himself then killed the Frenchman, zealously: "I ate his liver. I cut off great pieces of his flesh" (345). Shocking, yes. But the secret is in an unexplained part of the story involving what is (in the longer, fable-like version) the tiger's gleeful meerkat eating on an island of algae encountered midway through their journey as castaways. The tiger in the long version represents Pi. So what happens if one translates the events on the island into something more realistic? The tiger ate the meerkats that looked "like children self-consciously posing for a photographer" (295). Does this mean Pi ate children? Or something as cute and defenseless as children? Implicitly, Pi himself in the shorter, more "real" version of the story, like a guilty, greedy cannibal/colonist, decimated and consumed numerous innocents. The Japanese inquisitors puzzle over the missing translation of this part of the long story into a shorter reality: "But what does it mean, Okamoto-san? I have no idea. And what about the island? Who are the meerkats? I don't know" (346). We also don't know, for Pi has kept this chilling, niggling detail secret. We can only intimate that the "real" behind the fiction is quite terrible.

My first three chapters follow a similar structure. In each, I use three texts by third culture authors and about third culture contexts to examine dislocation, loss, disenfranchisement and a fourth characteristic (secretive guilt in chapter one, sexual precociousness in chapter two, and sick children in chapter three). What this allows me to do is clearly establish how the field of third culture literature (and its military/missionary subspecies) works. In each of these first three chapters I turn next to an example or two of work by a third culture author that is *not* explicitly about a third culture context. This allows me to show how key themes emerge out of a third culture context even if the texts in question range widely in terms of subject matter. I end chapters one, two and three by considering significant features overlapping all of the texts treated in the chapter.

In chapter one, "Third Culture Reading," I consider Jane Alison's *Natives and Exotics*, Eileen Drew's *The Ivory Crocodile*, Alice Greenway's *White Ghost Girls* and then, as my example of work by an adult third culture kid not explicitly about a third culture context, Joseph O'Neill's *Netherland*. In chapter two, "Adult Situations and Secret Perversions in the Writings of Former Military Brats," I describe military brat (a widely used nonderogatory term for the children of military families) writing as a distinct subset of third culture literature. The chapter begins by making brief reference to perhaps the best-known "military brat" novel, Pat Conroy's *The Great Santini*, but moves on to focus on three works about the military context by Gene Moser (*Skinny Dipping*), Sarah Bird (*The Yokota Officers Club*) and Ann-Marie MacDonald (*The Way the Crow Flies*). My fourth main example in this chapter, showing work by a military brat but not always explicitly about that context, is Ian McEwan (*The Cement Garden* and *Atonement*). Chapter three, "When Your Parents Work for God: The Fiction Writing of Former Missionary Kids," discusses the adult writings of missionary kids as another subset of third culture literature. It opens with a brief discussion of Pearl S. Buck's *The Good Earth*, and then moves to in-depth consideration of Catherine Palmer (*The Happy Room*),

Richard Lewis (*The Flame Tree*) and Paula Nangle (*The Leper Compound*). Chapter three then considers two works by adult missionary kids not explicitly about the missionary context: William Paul Young's *The Shack* and Ted Dekker's *BoneMan's Daughters*.

In chapter four I conclude with a reading of Barbara Kingsolver's *The Poisonwood Bible*. The supposed postcoloniality of Kingsolver's text is frequently contested because, on the whole, Kingsolver's third culture experience is invisible. She *seems* so American. This chapter opens with a discussion of third culture kids as "hidden immigrants" and proceeds to a reading of Kingsolver's novel as being third culture literature rather than postcolonial or American.

My chapters delineate third culture as a field, describe its components, and suggest paradigmatic similarities among a wide variety of fictions. The book includes a broad range of texts, sometimes famous ones, to oblige readers to recognize that even analyses of familiar authors can be freshly revelatory when attentive to the particularities of a third culture context. Obscure works are brought to light, well-known ones are cast in a new light, and essential critical possibilities are revealed by the use of a third culture literary analytical rubric.

CHAPTER ONE

Third Culture Reading

Thanks to Barack Obama, the idea of third culture *identity*, and even the terminology "third culture," have become slightly more widely recognized. Jay Newton writes in *Time*:

> Some would argue that [Obama's] childhood experiences [living in Indonesia], as well as his mixed heritage (his father was Kenyan, his mother from Kansas), give him a better inner compass on foreign policy than most Americans. They cite the pioneering work of Ruth Hill Useem, the late sociologist of Michigan State University, who spent her career studying what she called Third Culture Kids — the millions of U.S. children (an estimated 20 million since the advent of mass air travel) who have been carted abroad by their missionary, diplomatic, corporate or military parents.

Intriguingly, a piece of fiction that made its way to Obama's nightstand and was remarked upon by several journalists was Joseph O'Neill's third culture novel *Netherland*.[1]

In my introduction, I discuss the problem posed by Yann Martel's national indeterminacy for reviewers and critics responding to his work. One sees this again in *The Atlantic*'s interview with O'Neill. The preamble to the interview starts by defining *Netherland* as an American novel, despite the unlikeliness of this characterization: "On the face of it, the story of an expatriate Dutchman obsessed with playing cricket might not seem to have the makings of a quintessentially American novel. *But* ..." (Bacon [emphasis added]). The "but" is telling: Katie Bacon is straining to make an argument that securely locates the novel geographically, despite the plot's confounding British-Dutch-American-West Indian internationalism and the Irish-Turkish-Dutch-British-Americanism of its author. In the interview, O'Neill describes himself as "an exotic American": American, but not. O'Neill considers his childhood a problem in terms of his contemporary identity; its internationality stymies him too. In his literary protagonist Hans, he can "make use of this rather inconvenient upbringing [he] had in Holland." Reaching for a suitable term, he describes Hans as an "international narrator — or this *post*-national narrator, as I've come to think of him" (Bacon). I would characterize Hans, and *Netherland* as a whole, as third culture — not so much "*post*-national" as identified with a "nationality" of expatriate outsiders.

To review from the introduction: first culture (passport home), second culture (local nationals in host country), third culture (fellow expatriates). Experiencing expatriatism as a child is a distinguishing feature of third culture individuals: unlike adults, children have not yet formed a stable national identity. Though all developmental years matter, ages nine to eleven are especially "critical" in terms of identity formation (Fail et al. 324). The objective of this chapter is to expand on and provide examples of what I take to be the four main thematic features of third culture literature: (1) descriptions of multiple geographic locations; (2) descriptions of the losses entailed in frequent relocation; (3) descriptions of perceived disenfranchisement and lack of ownership; and (4) guilt and secretiveness resulting from recognizing privilege relative to the population(s) one lives among. I have elected to focus first on three novels by *and about* third culture individuals (Jane Alison's *Natives and Exotics*, Eileen Drew's *The Ivory Crocodile*, and Alice Greenway's *White Ghost Girls*). These three help clarify what a third culture context is, and how its influence commonly manifests in the four characteristics I list above (dislocation, loss, disenfranchisement, guilt/secretiveness). I then proceed to a reading of O'Neill's *Netherland* to give an example of a third culture text whose plot does not center on a third culture context, but whose characteristics are clearly influenced by the culture out of which the author writes. O'Neill's work lets me show how an author can draw on a third culture background, and how his work might manifest dislocation, loss, disenfranchisement and guilt/secrecy even if the topic he writes about is not explicitly third culture. This chapter will suggest how the existing psychological and sociological scholarship on third culture can facilitate a different understanding of novels written by such individuals; it will also suggest how literature can shed light on the work done on third culture in the social sciences, and establish what I mean by third culture literature in an omnibus sense.

The four novels I treat in this chapter (even *Netherland*, with its recent presidential endorsement) are unlikely to be familiar to many readers, perhaps because of the difficulty of categorizing their authors' national identities, and hence the novels themselves. Third culture literature often "falls through the cracks" because there is not yet an apt and recognizable categorization for it. Not postcolonial, not strictly of a single nation, neither immigrant nor local, foreign nor domestic — these texts occupy an uncomfortably shifting ground for which there is currently no widely used or immediately clear name.

Alison's *Natives and Exotics* spans 1786–1981. It considers British colonial exploration and exploitation using the symbolism of the botanical terms "native" and "exotic" in reference to European migrants who are shown to be out of place no matter where they are (and so, intriguingly, neither native nor exotic). Alison traces several generations of one family from Scotland to Australia (via the Portuguese island Saint Michael) and from there to the United States and Ecuador. The narrative introduces a contemporary third culture kid, Alice (age nine), who finds herself torn between her birthplace (Australia), her passport identity (American) and the country in which she resides (Ecuador). Alice's story occupies one thread of the narrative; other subplots consider her Australian grandmother Violet, and great grandfather George (a Scot who is traumatized by English soldiers, and taken by his benefactor to Saint Michael as a young man, and who finally emigrates to Australia on his own).

Drew's *Ivory Crocodile* is all roughly contemporary, taking place in the second half of the twentieth century. Though it follows the life of its one protagonist and narrator, Nicole (Nickie), this novel, like *Natives and Exotics*, considers distinctly different time periods, and the different locations associated with them. Nickie's American father relocates the family to various parts of West Africa as she is growing up. One thread in this novel concerns Nickie's experiences in Conakry, Guinea, as a child of eight, as well as a second stint in Africa with her father at age twelve, after her mother has died. Another concerns her experiences in returning to a fictional country in Africa (Tambala — somewhere in the vicinity of Angola) as a teacher in her early twenties. The third thread, which frames the novel, concerns Nickie's adult life in New York and her career as an art photographer.

Greenway's *White Ghost Girls* focuses mainly on the lives of sisters Frankie (just entering puberty) and Kate (slightly younger) in Hong Kong during the summer of 1967. The girls and their mother make Hong Kong a home base for their father, an American war photographer engaged in capturing images of the conflict in Vietnam. Greenway structures her narrative so that we jump back and forth in the adult reminiscences of the narrator (Kate) from the beginning to the end of that summer, with very occasional references to a contemporary American context in which Kate refers to herself as "grown up with children of [her] own" (96). The novel alludes to both the Vietnam War and the effect of China's Cultural Revolution in Hong Kong.

Alison, Drew and Greenway all highlight a dislocated, third culture narrator who is, for some parts of the narrative, young (within or close to the nine-to-eleven age bracket considered to be especially significant in terms of the impact of dislocation on national identity). They also all include reflection on that young narrator's experiences from a more mature perspective. All three, then, fictionalize and explore adult efforts to come to terms with third culture childhoods.

Unlike Alison, Drew and Greenway, O'Neill does not write about a child experiencing third culture dislocation in his *Netherland*. Indeed, O'Neill's novel reads, on its surface, like a novel about the immigrant experience of adults who relocate from one place to another. His protagonist, Hans, is Dutch (and parts of the novel reflect on Hans' boyhood in the Netherlands). As an adult he works in London. He then moves to New York with his British wife and their young son, only to be left there alone in the wake of 9/11 after his wife decides that Manhattan is not a safe place to bring up a child. To console himself and pass the time, Hans plays cricket with a team made up primarily of immigrants from the Caribbean and South Asia. More so than the plot of this novel, the way O'Neill characterizes Hans' dislocation, and especially his inability to feel as though he fits in, regardless of where he lives, exposes *Netherland* as third culture.

As in the works of Alison, Drew and Greenway, O'Neill's narrative moves backward and forward in time: in all four of these texts, the shifts from one moment in time to another happen with very sparse narrative bridges, if any. The vignettes are presented discontinuously, as if snapshots of a life presented out of order. That this narrative strategy — disordered snapshot display — is common to all four novels suggests not postmodern play, but rather that the fracturing of linearity is a characteristic of third culture literature, as are symbolically laden descriptions of the snapshots themselves (as I expand below).

Alison, Drew, Greenway and O'Neill have, because of their backgrounds, experiences in common: they share knowledge of a lifestyle, even if their passport nationalities, current homes and places lived do not overlap. They have a similar "place" (condition) of origin. In creating a clear understanding of the shared culture influencing these authors, and thus their works, it is necessary to consider the foundational dislocations of the authors' personal histories.

Jane Alison's history is the most complex of the authors I study in this chapter. She was, for many years, cryptic about her geographical trajectory as a child. Typical of this evasiveness, the biography on her website reads:

Jane Alison was born in 1961 in Canberra, Australia, and until she was eleven grew up in the Australian and U.S. foreign services. She went to public schools in Washington, D.C., and studied classics at Princeton and Brown Universities and creative writing at Columbia ["About Jane Alison"].

Geographical twists and turns are omitted in the conciseness of "grew up in the ... foreign services" (a phrase that crops up often in biographical information accompanying reviews of Alison's work).[2] It is an apt phrase for a third culture kid, for "in the foreign service" indicates not the passport home (first culture) or host nations (second cultures) but a third culture of expatriatism that is not rooted in any particular geography and implies the experience of being an (often quite privileged) outsider. The biography on her website goes on to locate her as currently in the United States, and does not mention a recent seven-year stint living in Germany. In an interview with Ellen Kanner, Alison reveals that she spent childhood years in Ecuador. Catherine Keenan's piece on Alison in the *Sydney Morning Herald* in 2004 observes that "Alison left Australia and went to the United States with [her stepfather] at age of six and, aside from a six-year stint in Washington, they moved every few months, every two years at the outside." In 2009, Alison published a memoir, *The Sisters Antipodes*, which chronicles her childhood relocations in the context of what turns out to be another story of identity-confounding dislocation: her parents' divorce and remarriage. Alison's biological father Edward, an Australian diplomat, made friends with Paul, an American diplomat. In the course of their close friendship, the wives of these men, and their families, all came to know each other well. Each man had two daughters. The youngest daughters, exactly (to the day) one year apart in age, were named Jane and Jenny. Each man fell in love with the other's wife, and they traded partners and children. Alison, then, switched fathers and nations with her doppelganger Jenny. Alison's third culture upbringing is thus accompanied by the vertiginous dislocation produced by the "truth is stranger than fiction" swap of stepfather Paul for her biological father Edward.

Eileen Drew's biography is equally international, though less convoluted in terms of familial relationships. The book jacket of *The Ivory Crocodile* notes that she was "born in 1957 in Morocco as the child of an American diplomat [and] grew up in Nigeria, Guinea, Ghana, Korea and Washington, D.C. In her early twenties she joined the Peace Corps to return to Africa [Zaire] for a two-year stint." Faith Eidse and Nina Sichel write, in their introduction to an essay by Drew in the collection *Unrooted Childhoods*, "Like many children raised internationally, she finds it hard to explain her foreign life to those who haven't lived abroad" (53). Drew herself comments in her essay, "I never felt very American in the States. Each time we returned from a tour in Africa, culturally, we had to catch up" (64).

Peter Gordon points out that "[Alice] Greenway lived in Hong Kong in two stints in the 60s and 70s, attending Hong Kong International School." Adrian Turpin starts his piece on Alice Greenway with this description:

> Alice Greenway is trying to remember where she spent her childhood. "I was born in Washington, then we moved to Hong Kong, then we moved to Thailand, then Boston. And — oh, I'll have to write it down. Then we must have gone to Washington again, then Hong Kong, then Israel, then back to the States. I think I've got that right."

It is a telling feature of some third culture lives that the moves are so numerous that even the individual in question struggles to remember them all in the order in which they happened. (Third culture life is indeed like a disorganized box of travel pictures.)

The book jacket for *Netherland* states that "Joseph O'Neill was born in Ireland and raised primarily in Holland. He received a law degree from Cambridge and worked primarily in London.... He lives with his family in New York City." The two uses of "primarily" hint strongly that there is more to O'Neill's story. An interview with Mark Sarvas reveals abundant complexity. Born in Ireland of mixed Irish and Turkish ancestry, O'Neill describes his childhood travels as a mélange of forgotten languages:

> When I was four years old, or something, I went to pre-school in Turkey and I spoke Turkish like all the other boys there. And I forgot it all. And I also spoke Iranian, or Persian, when I lived in Iran, but I forgot all that, as well. I'm not sure which came first, English or French. Both, I suppose. I'm told by my parents that in Mozambique, when I was a very, very young child, I spoke Portuguese with the Portuguese-speaking nanny. So, I grew up speaking lots of languages and forgetting all of them [*Elegant Variation*].

Just as Greenway needs to write down which place came when in her life story, O'Neill's multiple relocations befuddle even him. O'Neill continues in the interview with Sarvas (a.k.a. *The Elegant Variation*, or TEV) to suggest two intriguing things: (1) that the product of all of this moving was a sense of being alien everywhere, and (2) that for a writer this actually poses problems:

> JOSEPH O'NEILL: I know, I know. When I was growing up, I thought Holland was my home. Then I thought London was my home. And now I think that New York is home. So eventually, you start thinking, well perhaps one is essentially homeless. If I go back to Hol-

land — I'm going to spend seven weeks in Amsterdam this spring — I have no sense of going home anymore. And when I get back to London now, I feel somewhat alien. The only place now I feel like I go home to is New York [where he has lived since 1998].

TEV: I wonder if [it is] slightly advantageous as a writer, from that perspective, being able to slip in and out of all sorts of sensibilities?

JOSEPH O'NEILL: I think traditionally it would be a disadvantage. Because so much of novel writing is concerned with shared memories of childhood and national culture, and *Netherland* was the first time I was able to use childhood memories. I have no deep roots in any culture, no natural allegiance to any particular culture.

One can suggest that O'Neill treats cricket more like home than any actual place. As Philip Sherwell notes in the *Telegraph*, O'Neill "has played every summer since he was 10, and represented Holland internationally at the under-16 and under-19 level."

Clearly all four authors have lives, and childhoods in particular, that can be characterized as third culture: in their formative years, all four lived outside their passport "home," and did not integrate or remain in their host countries, but rather interacted with other internationally mobile individuals like themselves. Kathleen A. Finn Jordan gives a list of eleven third culture characteristics, which includes "a lack of identification with one's ethnicity"; "a sense of elitism"; "a sense of marginality"; "psychological sensitivity to an internalized sense of otherness"; and "issues of separation, grief and loss as a result of frequent transition" (213). My objective is not to seek these characteristics in Alison, Drew, Greenway and O'Neill themselves (though one could do so easily enough on the basis of their interviews and articles about them). Instead, I aim to consider how these authors use their fictions to explore the effects of a third culture context. Alison, Drew, Greenway and also O'Neill each investigate the implications of multiple dislocations on identity, human interaction and nationality. My book establishes a literary category that recognizes third culture as a distinct cultural context (just as postcolonial, diasporic, or migrant literatures are — at least in part — defined by cultural contexts). In this regard, research like Jordan's helps to shed light on the literature. I indicate how studying the ways in which third culture literature manifests and explores the cultural context that influences it adds to and expands beyond sociological studies like Jordan's (or Pollock and Van Reken's, or even the seminal work of Useem). In my analyses of the ways in which these third culture novels contain what I have been listing as four key characteristics — dislocation, loss, disenfranchisement and guilt — I am using sociological and psychological research (included in this chapter, as well as in my introduction) as referents. In my analyses of other literary features shared by these texts (disconnected, nonlinear narratives; photographs used symbolically), I indicate how the literature might enlighten and serve as referent for the sociological and psychological research.

What follows below is an analysis of *Natives and Exotics*, *The Ivory Crocodile*, and *White Ghost Girls* (the three novels *about* third culture identity) in terms of dislocation, loss, disenfranchisement and guilt, followed by an analysis of *Netherland* (by a third culture author, and indicative of a third culture context, though not explicitly *about* it). Despite differences in their novels' plots, each of the four authors explores the *effects* of dislocation; they investigate the implications of being third culture even if they do not employ that specific vocabulary. The chapter will conclude by considering all four novels in terms of their use of discontinuous chronologies and descriptions of photographs.

Dislocation (Alison, Drew, Greenway)

In *Natives and Exotics*, *The Ivory Crocodile* and *White Ghost Girls*, mobility, in terms of many changes of residence, features prominently. Alison's character Alice remarks, as her plane descends into Ecuador, "She was nine and this would be her fourth country, sixth city, seventh house" (12). As a young woman, Alison's Violet muses, "People wandered and wandered, and what did it mean, where on earth did they ever *belong*?" (112). Drew's Nickie thinks, "Everything went too fast, we were always moving. As an infant, an embryo even, I moved. Conceived aboard an oceanliner, born in a boondock country. It went so fast I can barely remember" (4). When people ask "The Question" (why she has come to teach in Tambala), Nickie responds, "I was born in Africa," continuing to give "an edited synopsis of my life: my birth in Cairo, how I'd moved a lot and lived sometimes in the States" (131). Greenway's Kate recalls the following conversation between her parents, indicative of the constellation of places influencing their lives:

> "Just wait til you see it, Marianne, the flame of the forest trees, the jade green sea," my father crowed when he came to collect us from New York two summers ago. Hong Kong would be safer than Saigon; an old-fashioned British enclave, he called it [12].

Kate also examines a picture her mother has on her dressing table, of the sisters dressed for church, including white gloves. Kate remembers those gloves as "the skin my mother wants for me ... the skin I might have, maybe, if I were a real American girl, if we still lived in New York or on my father's farm in Vermont" (19). Kate is not a "real American girl" because of her experience in Hong Kong. The family travels back to America after their stint in Hong Kong and Kate observes, "My mother calls the place we're going home. I don't" (156). However, Kate is not "from" Hong Kong either, and is constantly aware of locals referring to her as "gwaimui"—a white ghost, foreign (18).

Distinctively, the moves in all three of these novels are *not* immigration: first there is no emphasis on assimilation in any location; second there is always the assumption that another move will follow on the heels of the current one; and third there is no clear single home base that is moved away from. A succession of locations, national and international, are invoked: all are temporary, none are fully home. These moves are thus dissimilar to those one might see in diasporic or (im)migrant writing. In Jhumpa Lahiri's diasporic *The Namesake*, for instance, the Gangulis move from Calcutta to Boston: from home to away, with a firm sense of India as home and no expectation of further moves after America. In Zadie Smith's immigrant novel *White Teeth* we see a constellation of places (India, the Caribbean, World War II Europe), all ultimately grounded in a multicultural London in which London-born youths with parents from elsewhere strive to anchor themselves and establish their "black Britishness." They have arrived at a final destination: London. There is neither a final destination nor a place that anchors in third culture literature. The mobile youths in *Natives and Exotics*, *The Ivory Crocodile* and *White Ghost Girls* are also not in exile: they are not refugees, for they experience the comfort of expatriate "enclaves" (Greenway's word) in the places where they reside. Materially, they are replete. All are sheltered under the auspices of international organizations that move their parents around the globe (the American foreign service in Alison and Drew, *Time* magazine in Greenway).

Loss (Alison, Drew, Greenway)

All three novels express loss in terms very much like its expression in postcolonial, migrant and diasporic writing. One sees nostalgia for an unreclaimable past that is both a moment in time and a place. Salman Rushdie famously articulates how a migrant writer's longing for, and effort to write about, a remembered home is tantamount to longing for, and creating, something fictional:

> It may be that writers in my position, exiles or emigrants or expatriates, are haunted by some sense of loss, some urge to reclaim, to look back,

> even at the risk of being mutated into pillars of salt. But if we do look back, we must do so in the knowledge — which gives rise to profound uncertainties — that our physical alienation from India almost inevitably means that we will not be capable of reclaiming precisely the thing we lost; that we will, in short, create fictions, not actual cities or villages but invisible ones, imaginary homelands, Indias of the mind [*Imaginary Homelands* 10].

The key differences between the losses one sees in third culture literature and those one sees in other types of (im)migrant writing are that third culture literature represents the problem both of yearning for something that may not have existed in the first place *and* of mourning a loss that many people fail to recognize as a loss at all because of the assumption that travel, especially for privileged expats, is categorically a mind-broadening, enriching, *good thing*. Ramón Soto-Crespo writes, "Mourning the homeland is one way for the diaspora writer to maintain a connection with it" (342), and Sara Suleri opens her postcolonial/diasporic *Meatless Days* with the sentence, "Leaving Pakistan was, of course, tantamount to giving up the company of women," proceeding on to a narrative that describes and reconnects her to the women she has lost, and the places in which she knew them (1). What one sees in third culture literature is more vertiginous: mourning does not reaffirm connection, but rather emphasizes disconnection and the nonexistence of a homeland.

In *Natives and Exotics*, "Each year for Alice seemed to dwell in its own house and sometimes even in its own country so that you moved through space as well as through time" (16). When friends move away (as she herself will in a few years' time), Alice goes to the housekeeper for solace, knowing that the hug she gets is impersonal, "only kindness, the same Maria would give the next girl who lived there when Alice was gone. Because who could afford or bother, when it was always so brief?" (53). Alice has moved so much she knows the pattern: "friends they'd left behind at the last post, friends they'd never see again and would soon replace" (13). She's aware that her efforts to maintain contact over distance are too fragile: "It would never work, Candi was lost. Everyone was always lost. And the letters didn't really do much" (51). Even the house in Ecuador Alice lives in is lost; it becomes almost like a fiction because of the aggregation of Alice's experiences of constantly moving:

> School ended soon after, and then the house began to do what houses always did [when we moved....] The squares left on walls when pictures came down, the sound of her footsteps loud on the floor once the rugs had been rolled up. Soon this house would dissolve behind them, because nothing, nothing ever stayed [78].

All of the mobility turns even brick and mortar into a fiction. In Alice's memory it will be as if this house was, perhaps, never more than something imaginary.

The Ivory Crocodile's Nickie also describes loss of friendships: "Every time my family moved, I thought I didn't mind. When we moved from Washington to Conakry my best friend up the street vowed to write and wait for me," but

> at that time I was a Pollyanna, faithful that good friendships last and small sins fade, American enough to think anything new is good. As it turned out, the correspondence with my best friend fizzled, and by the time we returned to Washington she had moved away [87].

Friendships in Conakry are equally vulnerable: "Lorraine was my special friend, then Linda, then Cass. With their fathers, they came to Conakry and left" (6). The losses of people drive the adult Nickie's nostalgia for Africa, not as a real place, but an imaginary homeland: "I ... had returned to search soft-focus for that *paillotte* of my past, that vast black family spanning the night" (254). Adult Nickie observes that, as a result of her past,

> I was out of focus myself, and tended to generalize, looking for some idea I had of Africa in everyone I met, digging, defacing, as if for stolen treasure. I gave each potential ally the same part in my personal drama; it wasn't Mpovi I was trying to befriend, nor Bwadi, nor Diabelle. It was Africa [13].

Because of her childhood dislocations, Drew's Nickie recognizes her own destabilized, "out of focus" identity; because of lost childhood friends, she is now trying the impossible (to befriend a continent), even while recognizing that in the process of indulging her nostalgia she is homogenizing and failing to engage with the individual people who are around her. An accurate, un-stereotyped apprehension of the present is impossible for Nickie *because of her past.*

In *White Ghost Girls*, Kate asks a series of rhetorical questions, the answers to which would provide a catalogue of lost places and people. They include the following:

> Can you give me a back alley, a smoke-filled temple where white-hooded mourners burn offerings and wail for the dead? The single chime of a high-pitched bell? The knocking of a wooden fish?
>
> Can you give me hot rain, mould-streaked walls ...? The feverish shriek of cicadas, the cry of black-eared kites? The translucent green of sun shining through elephant-ear leaves? ...
>
> Can you give me my father's hand in mine, Frankie's in the other? [1].

The list Kate provides laments both the loss of Hong Kong and the loss of *who they were when they were in Hong Kong*. It grieves the relationships between them as family, and their lives in an exotic land. It mourns for who her father used to be when he was a foreign correspondent for *Time*, working in Saigon. It also, more literally, mourns the death of her sister Frankie.

Much research in psychology and sociology points to mobile, expatriate childhoods as having profoundly negative effects: "The mobility [third culture kids] experience in their developmental years denies them a sense of home, roots and the stable network of relationships that impart an important dimension of self-definition" (Fail et al. 323). Expatriate children are taken to have had enriched lives; moving about the world is seen as a privilege, and enjoying special "outsider" status also connotes privilege. The adult third culture individual is considered lucky to have had the mobile and often affluent life s/he has experienced. Yet, with each move, everything and everyone is lost, and there are typically several moves in a childhood. Unacknowledged grief manifests in literary expressions of mourning, sometimes startling and hyperbolic ones, as if the grief of such dislocation can only be expressed adequately if magnified into its most superlative and alarming forms.

All three of these novels include significant and graphically described deaths. In *White Ghost Girls*, Kate narrates, over the course of more than a page, her sister's death, including the "loud thump" Frankie's body makes as it hits the speedboat that is unable to alter its course in time so as not to hit her. Kate sees "the blood from [Frankie's] head [run] red all over the boat." She describes her father—"I see him swear, cry out. In his eyes a look of ruin" as he cradles Frankie in his arms, having stopped trying to resuscitate her—and herself screaming: "I don't think it will ever stop" (152). Drew includes a description of young Diabelle's death after the girl has tried to induce an abortion by taking an overdose of anti-malarial medication. It starts with two pages describing Nickie traveling to Diabelle's bedside and hearing the village women wailing their mourning as if the girl had already died. When Nickie gets to Diabelle's bed, she notes that the girl's "skin looked ceramic, glossy and rigid, the contours of her cheekbones and eye sockets exaggerated, her mouth parched and shrunken, her coloring a dark extension of the shadows in the room" (279). At the moment of death,

> All at once [Diabelle] reared up from the spine, her chest bowing out, and when a garbled noise came from her mouth I looked away. The wailing outside hit a narrow note and I bit my knuckles, fighting the urge to run, swerving against somebody's shoulder, and for a moment I

allowed the scent of perspiration to block out the putrid atmosphere [280].

Natives and Exotics includes George, who, in 1822, sees his parents cleared off their land for British "*improvements*" (120). He runs from "the bloody horrors that had leached into his skull and dwelled there ever since: the sound of [his mother's] head cloven, the flames roaring up, the ax sinking into her neck, then the look in her eyes as she fell" (121). The descriptions of death in these texts are operatic; more than vivid, they are unavoidably visible. It is impossible not to keep seeing them (even hearing and smelling them) in one's mind's eye. They function as expressions of third culture grief and loss that has not been recognized.

Pollock and Ruth Van Reken write that "next to sorting out their sense of personal identity, unresolved grief ranks as the second greatest challenge [third culture kids] face"; they continue, "For most TCKs the collection of significant losses and separations before the end of adolescence is often more than most people experience in a lifetime" (165, 166). For third culture individuals, feelings of disorientation are "deepened by feelings of grief and loss" (Jordan 214). Pollock notes that the third culture child's

> grief is *multiple* (it happens over and over again); *simultaneous* (friends, teachers, household staff, places, smells, sounds, foods, languages etc., at the same time); *intense* (because many of these are loved or valued); *unresolved* (unless the grieving process has been acknowledged and permitted to run its course); and *lonely* (regardless of where the child steps off the plane there are few people [with whom the child can share this experience]) [in McCaig 117].

As recipients of such good fortune as to live well and experience many parts of the world, third culture individuals are supposed to feel happy. Barbara Schaetti ("Attachment Theory") observes that third culture grief is "notoriously disenfranchised" (112).[3] Disenfranshisement occurs when "(1) the relationship is not recognized, (2) the loss is not recognized, and (3) the griever is not recognized" (Schaetti 112). Third culture individuals *do* have rich and joyous life experiences; however, they also suffer from the compounding of numerous losses (status, lifestyle, possessions, relationships, national identity, community, etc.).

Recent blogs like "denizen: for third culture kids" include accounts of adults not adjusting to repatriation after their third culture childhoods because of identity crises, and of depression and suicide occurring as relatively frequent consequences. In adulthood, the effects of unresolved childhood grief "kick back in the form of diffused depression, anger, or another dysfunctional expression" (McCaig 117). It is remarkable that so much third culture literature emphasizes not just loss (in the form of death) but also dysfunctional behavior. Often this comes in representations of inappropriately sexualized children, as though the behaviors required by third culture contexts are too adult for children, but the best way to express this in writing is to show these children in situations that any reader — third culture or not — would recognize as too adult.

In *Natives and Exotics*, the adult world of diplomatic parties is mirrored by the parties enjoyed by the diplomats' children. While the adults talk politics, the prepubescent youths kiss, grope and undress each other feverishly, in the quickening intensity of friendships they know will end soon: "in locked pink bedrooms, in closets, in basements, hairless little bodies kissed passionately, frantic now because it was summer and their time was almost up" (45). The father of a boy hosting one of these parties comes to check on the children

> and at first he didn't switch on a light. But he noticed on one of the sofas a blanket that seemed to be moving. He looked down at it a moment, then stepped closer, pulled it away, and stared down in disbelief at a peachy tangle of bare limbs.
> "Like Maggots," he would say later. "What the *fuck*?" [48].

Alison describes sexual precociousness as a result of anticipated losses (summer will end soon, the children will part from one another); it is heightened interpersonal connection to make up for impending disconnection. But it is also a too-quick maturing of children into a sexual context, just as they are too quickly matured into contexts of loss and international conflict (Alison juxtaposes her descriptions of the lewd children with descriptions of American-Ecuadorian violent conflict over fishing regulations).

In *The Ivory Crocodile*, the sexualization of youth also parallels political tension (aid, including Western teachers, and the ambivalence of their actions as they seemingly produce as much harm as good). Schoolteacher Nickie is privately approached by Diabelle, a student she describes in terms of her youth: "girlish," uninformed, "needy as a puppy" (38, 49). She gives Diabelle information about birth control, which is of little use because she cannot provide the girl with condoms or the birth control pill (58–59). Diabelle subsequently becomes pregnant by an American aid worker whom Nickie has also been dating, and then, as cited earlier, tries to self-induce an abortion, and dies (274ff). Here, too, one sees an adult circumstance and consequence imposed on a child, and expressed in terms of sex and its consequences.

In Greenway, Frankie flirts with adult men. Kate notices that their father "doesn't see how Frankie sits too close to Humphries.... How Humphries' hand brushes the tops of her thighs" (88). "Frankie flirts with

Pym" as well, "a large, loud, British detective who laughs and looks at her with surprise" (108). Then she seduces George, and Kate catches her *in flagrante delicto*: "I think she's been crying; her mascara's smudged, her shirt's untied. She looks small, crushed beneath George's large body" (140). Kate, age fourteen, loses her virginity to the Chinese deaf boy on whom she has a crush, as much because she hopes it will mean acceptance and forgiveness as because she likes him: "I feel a sharp pain ... I cling to the deaf boy, clamber up him gasping for air. Cry out. It seems I don't want to drown, I don't want to be punished or killed after all, not the way Frankie was" (166). Kate conflates sex and forgiveness. She frames Frankie's death as punishment for her selfishness in flirting and flaunting rules, for being too expatriate. Kate sleeps with a local hoping it will let her be less foreign.

Sexual encounters — themselves unsettling — are presented as ominous antecedents of death and grief. The far-too-adult losses incurred in multiple dislocations are expressed in representations of youths engaged in sexual activity far beyond their maturity. Impending loss is pathologized as sexual dysfunction.[4]

Disenfranchisement (Alison, Drew, Greenway)

Fail, Thompson and Walker write that third culture individuals "view themselves as cosmopolitan people who feel comfortable in a variety of environments, but lack a sense of belonging in any one" (323). Pollock and Van Reken similarly write that "at the heart of issues of rootlessness and restlessness" is the third culture individual's sense of their "lack of full ownership," which in turn gives rise to a "sense of belonging 'everywhere and nowhere' at the same time" (30). There are two consequences of this adaptability: first, the individual feels that they don't belong anywhere, and, second, the individual is detached from politics and a sense of responsibility to his/her host country (or, upon repatriation, to his/her passport home). As Pollock and Van Reken note, "TCKs are often sadly ignorant of national, local, and even family history" (87), and "although their expanded worldview is a benefit, it can also leave TCKs with a sense of confusion about such complex things as politics, patriotism and values" (80). This is notably different from disenfranchisement in a postcolonial novel like J. M. Coetzee's *Disgrace*, in which Lurie is well aware that he is white, in his fifties, and in a new South Africa in which he is redundant. Lurie's problem is not one of lacking affiliation or political commitment, but rather of having too strong an affiliation with outmoded and unpopular politics.

One sees both a sense of not belonging and political detachment in the novels of Alison, Drew and Greenway, the former often articulated as not having "rights" in a place, or not "owning" any part of it. In *Natives and Exotics*, Alice's mother asks of their residence in Ecuador, and of American involvement in Ecuadorian politics, "Do we really have any right? ... To be here altogether, you know what I mean. To be *involved* in all of this. I don't know. Do we really belong here?" (66). In Ecuador, Alice experiences her past and her connection to Australia as dream-like, intangible:

> It was strange the way some things seemed familiar — a certain shrub with watery blue blossoms; a palm tree with a skinny, scaly trunk and a wild head of fronds at the top. But familiar from where? ... Maybe that palm tree had been in Australia? [22].

Just as the familiarity of the tree is inexplicable, so is her relation to place. Places don't belong to her, nor she to them. Alice experiences a powerful longing for Ecuador: "It's a difficult thing to crave like this, land, especially when your body is so small. And a dangerous thing, too, when you have no business being there, when it's not even where you're from" (43).

Third culture individuals sometimes have an identity shaped by *not* being like a local, at home or abroad: "In trying to proclaim what they consider their true identity, they ultimately form an 'anti-identity,'" asserting to others "I'm not like you" (Pollock and Van Reken 97). One sees this in a proliferation of declarations of what is "not" in these novels. In *The Ivory Crocodile*, Nickie comments, "The United States might be rich, yet nothing there had ever felt like mine" (13). Returning to Africa does not make her feel at home either: "I was in the picture now — yet I was simply passing through, traversing at a snail's pace this Africa that was not mine" (123). In Tambala, Nickie is an outsider — "The fact was, my place was on the fringes" — but she is equally "on the fringes" in the United States (173). Nickie attends a wedding in Tambala and helps prepare the meal:

> Peanuts rained handful by handful into the bowl; I was surrounded by shells like tiny capsized boats. Camouflaged, blending into this tableau of feminine purpose, I felt immaterial: nothing but an empty costume, paler than white. The real Nickie wasn't here shelling peanuts — she couldn't be. Who, then, was fastened in this African dress, and where had the real Nickie gone? I hadn't the foggiest idea who the real me was or had ever been [95].

Nickie does not belong where she is, but cannot call to mind a more comfortable, more "at home" vision of herself. Neither African aid worker nor American versions of her identity strike her as authentic.

White Ghost Girls' Kate is aware that people native to Hong Kong, like the family's gardener, consider herself and her sister "strange foreign vermin infesting Chinese soil" (43). She describes her sister as out of place in American clothing, "in a white cotton dress with puffy sleeves and a bow around the back. You can tell, just from looking at her, these are not the clothes she would choose" (21). American dresses, and American identity, do not fit, and yet the naked pose Kate imagines Frankie would choose ("Gaugin's Tahitian native") is the enactment of an incongruous fantasy of impossible indigeneity (21). Kate sees herself as "underexposed" and "camouflaged": her understanding of her own identity is as something blurred, shadowy, hidden and ultimately unaffiliated (21).

The politics of their host countries are obscure to characters in all three novels. For instance, in *Natives and Exotics* Rosalind (Alice's mother) wonders about Western involvement in Ecuador's coup, without really understanding how the coup connects with American-Ecuadorian conflicts over fishing and American sanctions against Ecuador. She argues with her diplomat husband:

> "So where would you like to be, Rosalind?" Hal said.... "Is there a place you would rather be?"
> "Oh stop it. I don't know. I just don't understand who has a right to be where."
> "It's not a matter of right, it's a matter of responsibility."
> "A responsibility to take what's under other people's feet?" [65].

Rosalind's "I don't know" is perhaps the most salient part of this exchange: she has a shadowy sense that America is exploiting Ecuador but she doesn't *know* and, aside from arguing with her husband, she takes no action to remedy that problem. Drew's Nickie similarly withdraws from political imperatives into ignorance when she responds, "I refuse to feel responsible for someone else's poor judgement," after Bwadi asks if Afric Ed is, as rumored, sponsored by the CIA (71). She realizes the extent of her obliviousness late in the novel. When the military comes to the village Nickie lives in, she's not sure why they are there, what is going on, or whether to be afraid. She can't figure out an explanation; the fingerprinting of the villagers, including herself, is a mystery no one will talk to her about and that she cannot comprehend: "For the next few days I strolled, sweating in the shade of the bounteous *petit marché*, chatting with people in the road. And nobody said a thing. Disoriented, I was circling, vividly blind" (273). In Greenway's novel, Kate and Frankie slip away from their *amah* (nanny/housekeeper) into a Red Guard protest that they do not know much about and fail to recognize as genuinely dangerous. In the midst of shopkeepers closing their stalls, and Red Guards facing off against a phalanx of police officers, Frankie is "grinning, her eyes ablaze" (57). Kate observes, "This is the real thing.... It's what we want, to get close, to see the Red Guards, all the things our father doesn't tell us about Vietnam" (57).

Interestingly, despite characters being uncertain at best in their experiences of local politics in their host countries, all three of these novels include strong anti–American sentiment. Alison's Hal (Alice's American father) is characterized as pro-exploitation; he notes that American concessions over Ecuadorian fishing regulations are just for show: "They'll lose a lot more than we do when we take it all back" (47). Drew's Nickie is disillusioned at discovering herself to be just another American in Africa: "I'd wanted so badly not to exploit. I'd thought I was better than missionaries and their white God ... better than the dumb diplomats" (285). She adds, "I wax paternalist again, American to the core" (286). In Greenway, the backdrop to life in Hong Kong is the war in Vietnam. Greenway does not need to rehearse the anti–American sentiment accompanying contemporary understandings of that war: having the children's father be an American photographer, documenting the war for *Time*, is allusive enough. The resolute anti-Americanism of these novels is, given their dates of publication (*Natives and Exotics* in 2005, *The Ivory Crocodile* in 1996, and *White Ghost Girls* in 2006) and the context of the Bush (father and son) years, remarkably *safe*. The United States was not popular internationally. Indeed, the stereotypical liberal, internationally-minded view of America was, and continues to be, critical of the United States and what are perceived to be its neocolonialist, strong-armed tactics. Taken together, the anti–Americanism of these novels appears to be the iteration of merely standard political views. Jordan notes that third culture individuals often rely on models of political behavior they think appropriate for a specific context, the model standing in for a "genuine" response the dislocated individual is unable to give: they have "myriad formulas and conventions that worked country by country or school by school, appropriate configurations, handles.... They appear to have site-specific identities and often disappoint the ideologically committed" (219). Intriguingly, for all three, the model performed in the novels positions characters as self-condemning. Alison's characters (Rosalind, and her ancestor George especially) perceive themselves as colonists, Drew's Nickie condemns herself for being just another American aid worker and Greenway's Kate is an American white ghost in the midst of war (Vietnam) and revolution (China).

Guilt and Secrecy (Alison, Drew, Greenway)

The guilt and self-condemnation in Alison, Drew and Greenway's novels stem from characters deducing that their privilege relies on exploiting others. In the world outside fiction, "historically, many TCKs' parents are part of what others consider a special, elite group (such as diplomats or high-ranking military personnel).... Their standard of living is usually well above the mean for that particular country, and their lifestyle may include servants, drivers, and other special privileges such as extensive travel" (Pollock and Van Reken 99). In *Natives and Exotics*, we meet Alice, the daughter of a diplomat, and George, effectively a nineteenth-century colonist despite his blinkered, botanical life; in *The Ivory Crocodile*, Nickie, also the daughter of a diplomat, returns to Africa as a teacher paid by an American aid organization; in *White Ghost Girls*, Frankie and Kate are the daughters of a war photographer working for *Time* magazine. The fictional characters are explicit about, and ashamed of, their privilege. Coetzee's *Disgrace* once again provides a useful contrast to these third culture novels. In *Disgrace* Lucy is raped on her farm and Lurie's face disfiguringly burned by the rapists: South African whiteness is abject, punished. The injuries sustained by Lurie and his daughter are punishments for their whiteness and are meted out by their black neighbors. Lurie does not self-punish, and neither does Lucy. Though Lucy is secretive about the rape and feels shame, it is more because of what others have done to her than what she has done by virtue of being white and privileged. Lurie feels no shame and keeps no secrets. *Natives and Exotics*, *The Ivory Crocodile*, and *White Ghost Girls*, however, present characters who perceive themselves as the agents of their own guilt and punishment. They are ashamed enough that they are secretive about what they think they have done.

In *Natives and Exotics*, Alice lives in a palatial diplomatic mansion, behind white walls that conceal "another world" in which "the street smelled of urine, dogs sniffed in the gutters" (24). The international school she attends similarly encloses her "within white walls, on the other side of which Ecuadorian children their own age were herding cows with sticks" (25). When Drew's Nickie is a child in Conakry, she watches her brother Benjamin drive a VW into the sea to see if it will float: the excess, frivolousness and irresponsibility of the act, especially in comparison with local living conditions, makes her ashamed:

> Benjamin waved at the fisher boys, at me. An eerie sibilance sounded in response, murmurings and whispers that seemed confined inside my head, wary, imprecise. But then I looked around. A flank of little kids had gathered at my back.... I'm sorry, I wanted to say. Children like these often laughed at us, at how we cut oranges rather than peeled them with our teeth, at our Band-Aids, our swimsuits. They were not laughing now [33].

In *White Ghost Girls*, Kate and Frankie circulate in an expatriate world that involves private school and a yacht club as well as household help in the form of Ah Bing and a gardener. They visit one of their mother's friends, and the contrast between her house on the hill and the town below is stark:

> Miss Tipley's house, her garden, her pool perch at the top of the world like a bird's nest high in the jungle of the Peak. Hong Kong throbs beneath us. Its packed apartment blocks, its busy harbour streaked with boats and white wakes, are framed by a balustrade dotted with potted pink coral plants.... Chinese were forbidden to live on the Peak before World War II. The English enacted a law to prevent overcrowding and outbreaks of cholera and tuberculosis and other diseases that raged in the Chinese city. But also to protect themselves from too intimate contact with [the Chinese] [34].

All three novels carefully present contrasts between the expatriates with affluence and the locals outside. By doing so in such detail, all three novelists imply that privilege is something to be ashamed of, even punished for (despite the fact that, for these characters, privilege is something they have inherited). The novels ask what right these people have to be so much better off than those around them, and then present plots in which privilege allows people to make grand mistakes and get away with them with only secret shame as their punishment. They also get away with being privileged, with only secret shame as their punishment for that too.

There are in these novels subplots in which nonchalantly undertaken transgressions transpire in secret, and give rise to unexpectedly terrible consequences. Characters perceive themselves as culpable for something terrible *that they did not intentionally do* (just as they are privileged and exploitative of their host countries in spite of themselves and their good intentions). Privilege lets characters unobtrusively break rules in ways they do not at first see as exploitative, but the ramifications of their actions are so much bigger than expected that the characters are shamed into continued silence. They get away with mistakes they have made, even though they know they should not.

In *Natives and Exotics*, it is George who is a secret transgressor. Aiming to create a haven, a garden to feel at home in, and a bountiful crop of oranges to sell, George and his friend/protector Mr. Clarence plant an exotic garden of imported plants in the Azores, and breed a new species of orange. The imported plants bring with them a disease that "colonizes" and ravages the island's flora (just as colonists brought diseases and oppression to the indigenous populations); the new orange tree they create is infertile and does not bear fruit. George and Mr. Clarence find themselves complicit with empire. Mr. Clarence says of the exotic garden, "This is nothing but empire's plunder," and of the blight and infertility their plants have introduced, "We, too, with all the clearings and the cruelty.... We're as deep in it as anyone" (168–69). Mr. Clarence punishes himself by not eating fruit, and thus dies of scurvy. His demise is met with little fanfare and, significantly, no public acknowledgment of the ecological damage he has wrought (182). For George, the result is paralyzing disorientation and recognition of his dislocated homelessness: "For the first time George understood he was a man, like any, wandering lost upon the earth. Something like homesickness ripped at his chest" (169). George, quietly and without reparation, leaves the island, guiltily and knowingly complicit with a horticultural imposition akin to other savageries wrought by the British Empire in the nineteenth century.

Just as George intends to do something good (create a special garden and a new type of orange) but actually devastates the island, so, too, in *The Ivory Crocodile*, Nickie intends to do something good when she tells Diabelle about birth control, explaining, with diagrams, how the different methods work, despite the unavailability of condoms or the birth control pill and the unreliability of rhythm or withdrawal methods. Nickie makes Diabelle her co-conspirator in the business of knowing about birth control in the first place (which the villagers would have disapproved of): Diabelle was "as practiced as any, I knew, in the art of keeping a secret, and her African solidarity now lay with me" (59). Nickie feels she has "connived with Diabelle" and that as a result she is "duplicitous, yet stuck," adding, "I felt like a rat" (61). Diabelle then becomes pregnant, Nickie's teaching having led to secretiveness and complicity rather than useful supplies for the girl. Only later, after Diabelle's demise, does Nickie begin to think that her role in teaching Diabelle about sex set in motion the events that led to the girl's death. Nickie begins to see herself as the one to blame for teaching Diabelle something that should have liberated her, but did not. She blames herself for being another American trying to satisfy some need of their own at the expense of Africa: "I was American, I told myself. I was white. I was stupid and guilty and possibly insane" (269). And yet Nickie never explicitly owns up to her conversations with Diabelle about birth control, weeping instead on the shoulder of the dead girl's sister the cryptic "*Kiadi. Je regrette*" (283).

In *White Ghost Girls*, Kate and Frankie elude their *amah* on the streets of Hong Kong during an anti-imperialist Red Guard protest. Amid the throngs of people and firecrackers, the two are grabbed by men who split the girls up. The first gives Kate a bag of "lychees" to carry back to town. She is afraid, though, and drops them in a garbage can, where they — clearly not lychees at all — explode, hurting people in the surrounding crowd, including a young boy who utters a seemingly unending "high scream" (63). The second man either molests or rapes Frankie in an incident that takes place behind closed doors. The girls don't tell. Frankie's behavior becomes more and more erratic; it is "the important story ... even though no one speaks of it. Even later, we never say it out loud. The lychees, the bomb at the market, become my secret" (95). Though victims, the girls behave secretively, as if perpetrators, precisely because they are foreign *gwaimui* (white ghosts) (62). They perceive themselves as guiltily laying claim to a place not theirs in presumptuously playing in the streets — as George and Mr. Clarence do in "playing" in their gardens, and like Nickie "playing" in her nostalgic fantasy of Africa — and as causing destruction as a result.

Joseph O'Neill's *Netherland*

In *Netherland*, O'Neill explores issues of dislocation, loss, disenfranchisement and even guilt, just as Alison, Drew and Greenway do in their novels. He contends with the same third culture issues even though his plot seems to be about other things (9/11, cricket, failed marriages). *Netherland* works well as an example of third culture literature because, with attentive reading, it is clear that O'Neill uses his text to investigate third culture concerns. Fascinatingly, *Netherland* seems at first to be a novel about immigration (akin, perhaps, to Smith's *White Teeth*). One expects the interaction between "immigrants" and cricket teammates Hans and Chuck to show the similarities and discuss the overlap between white and black experiences of immigrating. Significantly, O'Neill's text does something much more puzzling: it shows Hans as utterly disconnected, Chuck as happily rooted in his new American-ness, and the two as opposites, not doppelgangers. This is a confounding maneuver unless one reads the novel as third culture, and O'Neill as grappling with one of the questions I have been answering in this chapter: What makes "third culture" different from "immigrant"?

O'Neill's novel shares with Alison's, Drew's and Greenway's works the four key elements that I take to be characteristic of third culture literature: dislocation, loss, disenfranchisement and guilt. In terms of mobility, the novel opens with protagonist Hans reflecting on international moves ("The afternoon before I left London for New York") and proceeds to his descriptions comparing places and implying movement ("It was the kind of barbarously sticky American afternoon that made me yearn for the shadows cast by scooting summer clouds in northern Europe") (3, 7). In addition to movements in real space, Hans feels himself traveling between "unsettlements that cannot be located in the spaces of geography" and as residing in a state of perpetual dislocation tantamount to an isolated "small country of fog" (120, 38). After 9/11, his family moves into a hotel, which itself suggests transience and incipient movement. Donald Albrecht writes, "Hotels house communities of strangers who gather outside their normal environments for brief periods" (29). The hotel is both indicative of mobility and an apt representation of third culture in that it contains a group of people whose main similarity is the experience of staying temporarily in a place in which they are all outsiders. Albrecht adds, "Hotels also represent a fluid sense of personal identity" (33). By the time Hans is living in the Chelsea Hotel, he finds his own identity too fluid. He muses that he is

> given to self-estrangement. I find it hard to muster oneness with those former selves whose accidents and endeavors have shaped who I am now. The schoolboy at the Gymnasium Haganum; the Leiden student; the clueless trainee executive at Shell; the analyst in London; even the thirty-year-old who flew to New York with his excited new wife: my natural sense is that all are faded, by the by, discontinued [49].

Hans considers the selves of different eras and locales to be, ultimately, different selves that have little to do with his present identity. This idea that the self is reinvented in each location is typical of third culture (see, for instance, Drew's Nickie, imagining that the mistakes of her American self will be left behind when she reinvents herself in Conakry).

As in *Natives and Exotics*, *The Ivory Crocodile*, and *White Ghost Girls*, in *Netherland* loss is explicitly the result of multiple moves. Hans remarks: "In all my time in America, I had not received a single social call from those I'd designated as my London friends; and neither, it's true to say, had I called them" (105). Hans also loses his mother, wife, son and eventually his cricket friend, Chuck Ramkissoon. Hans grieves when his mother dies not just because she has passed away but also because the geographic distance between them had been so great for so long that she had been absent from all but his imaginary life for some time already:

> Mama was barely less present than she'd been during the many years in which, separated by an airplane journey, we'd spoken once or twice a month on the telephone and seen each other for a week or two in a year ... a still more disquieting idea took possession of my thoughts —
> namely that my mother had long ago become an imaginary creature [85].

It is Hans who has left his mother behind, just as he left childhood friends behind, only to realize, decades and continents later, that "to leave is to take nothing less than a mortal action. The suspicion came to me that they were figures of my dreaming, like the loved dead: my mother and all these vanished boys" (89). People are left behind in the novels by Alison, Drew and Greenway, and what distinguishes these losses as third culture ones is that they are absolute: the individuals that are left behind will not be seen again, and no contact will be feasible. It is as if moving away amounts to the death of what is left behind. One sees that same absolute loss in O'Neill's description of his "mother and all those vanished boys": reconnections are presented as simply impossible. These characters might as well have died when they were left behind.

Just as loss is emphasized in Alison, Greenway and Drew, so it is in O'Neill's novel. In the work of Alison, Drew and Greenway, third culture loss and grief are reenacted in extremes of losing (death, sexual dysfunction). In O'Neill, loss and grief are expressed in the extreme context of 9/11. The attacks precipitate the family's move from their condo near the Twin Towers to the Chelsea Hotel and portend their subsequent international movement (London–New York), providing a context ridden with fear and uncertainty. In reviewing *Netherland,* Zadie Smith observes that it is "only superficially about 9/11.... It certainly is about anxiety, but its worries are formal and revolve obsessively around the question of authenticity." Her observation is apt: The novel uses 9/11 to express the anxiety resulting from loss, grief, and dislocation; it is not about 9/11 per se.

Concern about authenticity is a quintessentially third culture problem, and a facet of what I have been referring to as third culture literature's preoccupation with disenfranchisement. Hans, like characters in the novels of Alison, Drew and Greenway, feels himself to be perpetually an outsider. He is the man at dinner parties irritated by references to a friend "everybody but me knows," and still more irritated to be reduced to his passport nationality (180). At a London dinner party, despite his time in New York, Hans is not invited to comment on Manhattan as a holiday destination: "This isn't because I've been back for a while but, rather, because I'm precluded by nationality from commenting on any place other than Holland — one of those parochialisms, I am pissed off to rediscover, that remind me that as a foreign person I'm essentially of some mildly buffoonish interest to the English" (181). Hans is not English, nor is he a New Yorker, and, though Holland and its inhabitants are mere "figures of [his] dreaming," he is pigeon-holed as Dutch (89). This is another quintessentially third culture moment: passport nationality being given precedence despite the individual's quite passionate conviction that they are not really, or not simply, of that nation; this conviction comes paired with an inability to effectively challenge the assumption because they cannot lay claim to nationality in the many other locations that have shaped their identity. This is thus a third culture bind: you are your passport nationality because that is what you can lay claim to; you are not of the other places you have lived because there are no legal or rhetorical ways to legitimate or make permanent your relationship to them.

As in the novels by Alison, Drew and Greenway, in *Netherland* third culture disenfranchisement leads to a distinctive detachment from — or noncommittal attitude toward — local politics, and thence to a standardized default political mode: America-bashing. An anti–American tirade appears in the mouth of spouse Rachel, who spends three pages asserting that "the U.S. has no moral or legal authority to wage this war [on Iraq]" (97). Hans says of his own contributions to political discussions, "my orientation was poor. I could not tell where I stood. If pressed to state my position, I would confess the truth: that I had not succeeded in arriving at a position ... I had little interest. I didn't really care. In short, I was a political-ethical idiot" (100). Hans' comic summary captures the point that Pollock and Van Reken make that "some TCKs who flip-flop back and forth between various behavioral patterns have trouble figuring out their own value system from the multicultural mix they have been exposed to" (93). Hans also characterizes himself as taking the path of least confrontation, or the one that lets him keep the most friends, which is revealingly third culture given that friends are so hard to retain in the context of multiple national moves: "I have a temperamental disposition to pardon that simplifies things for me and is certainly a symptom of moral laziness or some other important character weakness" (238).

As in Alison, Drew and Greenway, O'Neill presents privilege as prerequisite for a subplot that involves guilty, secretive self-condemnation. Hans works at a bank as an equities analyst specializing in "large-cap oil and gas stocks.... Inside the business, I had the beginnings of a reputation as a guru" (26). Published in 2008, just as the severity of the economic crisis was becoming apparent, *Netherland* anticipates the unpopularity and perceived culpability of wealthy financiers in such fields as equities. Hans is well recompensed, able to afford a Manhattan condo *and* accommodations at the Chelsea Hotel indefinitely *and* fly to London on alternate weekends to visit his estranged wife and son *and* join them on a luxurious beach holiday in India at the last moment. He is on the side of the world's great exploiters. He comes from privilege too: "The conservative, slightly stuck-up stratum of society in which I grew up, especially loves cricket.... Dutch bourgeois snobbishness and Dutch Cricket are, not unrelatedly, most concentrated [in The Hague]" (42).

Chuck Ramkissoon is the something-from-nothing immigrant foil to Hans' privileged third culturism: he provides a contrast (the immigrant identity he enjoys makes it clearer that Hans is neither immigrant nor local) and he is also Hans' guilty secret, the one exploited and damaged (just as third culture individuals exploit, do damage and are secretive about what they have done in Alison, Drew and Greenway). Chuck identifies himself as from New York, though his American mistress insists that he is from Trinidad (17). Unlike Hans, Chuck is committed to his new nation: "I love it here," he says (72). Hans listens to Chuck's rant about the bald eagle's fishing habits and deduces that "Chuck's fascination with this phenomenon — his interest in naturalism, birds especially, went back to his youth in Trinidad — was, I was to understand, heightened by knowledge gained from his enthusiastic and successful studies for the U.S. citizenship exams" (75). Chuck enthusiastically reshapes his Trinidadian identity into an American one; Hans' identity remains that of an outsider in New York, unable to integrate his current and younger selves. Chuck is also involved in various shady business deals ranging from selling kosher sushi to gambling, with plans for a cricket club somewhere in between. He is a character whose "deviousness was ... transparent"; he winds up dead "in the river with his hands tied up" (71, 230). Chuck befriends Hans, inducting him into the world of New York cricket, sharing with him the dream of building a cricket arena. The cricket connection is significant, the game of cricket being a familiar space to an assortment of outsiders (akin to an expat community for a third culture kid): it is an answer to "unsettlements that cannot be located in spaces of geography or history" (120). Chuck also spends time teaching Hans to drive (which, as it turns out, is Chuck's way of getting Hans to drive him around town to collect bets in the illegal numbers game he runs)(171).

Hans drifts into association with Chuck after his wife and son leave New York. Although Chuck has secret criminal dealings all around Manhattan, Hans is the guilty one: he uses Chuck to fill a vacuum left by his wife and son, is nonchalantly noncommittal about the friendship, *and then leaves.* Despite even the filiative connection implied by playing cricket with Chuck, Hans abandons the man who effectively took care of him in the midst of his marital crisis. He realizes that "Chuck merged, in my mind, with these other West Indians and Asians I played with" and "it was only after the fact that I figured out they'd already been looking after me" (174). Hans moves back to England, after which "we never spoke. Every once in a while, in the grip of an affectionate curiosity, I'd search the web for a mention of Chuck Ramkissoon. I found none" (236). When Chuck is murdered, Hans' actions are cryptic (he stands in the rain deliberating about going to Chuck's funeral in Trinidad and then heads home to call the New York police). He doesn't know what to say: "What is the declaration that is in order here?" (237). Could it be "that, although I may not have missed him for two years, I now miss Chuck terribly? Do I declare that I loved Chuck?" (237). Hans feels guilt, and loss, when he hears of Chuck's death, as though he were somehow to blame for not protecting the man. Only near the end of the novel does Hans identify himself openly as "a personal friend" of Chuck's, no longer secretive about their association (250). Hans invests months trying to figure out what happened to Chuck after he hears the investigation into the man's murder has stalled. When he can find out nothing more substantial than theories, he looks up the cricket field online:

> There's Chuck's field. It is brown — the grass has burned — but it is still there. There is no trace of the batting square. The equipment shed is gone. I'm just seeing a field. I stare at it for a while. I am contending with a variety of reactions and consequently with a single brush on the touch pad I flee upward into the atmosphere and at once have in my sights the physical planet, submarine wrinkles and all [252].

Is there a more consummate third culture resolution than this? If place represents people lost, the solution is to move further away.

Through Chuck's death, O'Neill implies that rooting oneself, as an enthusiastic immigrant like Chuck might do, is a "dead end." Hans story— of irresolvable dislocation — is the primary one in the novel. Chuck's — of connection — is a cautionary tale. O'Neill seems to be saying, "You can't actually do what Chuck wanted to do — you can't actually make yourself belong": bleak, but O'Neill is also, perhaps inadvertently, revealing his own quintessentially third culture attitude in the plot he writes.

Time

Obviously the four texts I study in this chapter (and, indeed, in subsequent chapters) share thematic features that I have chosen to reduce to four categories in order to prove a point: literature produced out of a third culture context is influenced by it in distinctive ways. However, it is important to go beyond a diagnostic reading of these novels. They are not merely symptomatic of a cultural experience that has been explored in the social sciences. They also bring literary form and technique to bear on third culture experiences, going beyond the *real* to do what literature can do so well: present what can be understood as *true* using the liberties afforded by fictional narrative. Thus, when Barbara Schaetti writes that the third culture individual's "life experience is typically fraught with change —

changing places, people, pets, possessions.... It is possible to say that *the primary source of continuity for the global nomad* [her synonym for third culture kid] *is, in fact, discontinuity*" ([emphasis added] 109), we can look to characters in these novels talking about discontinuity, as I have done above, but we can also consider how literature is equipped to express discontinuity in other ways.

All four of these novels write about time explicitly: "I was lost in invertebrate time" (O'Neill, 30); "For how could you remember if you kept wandering on? Everything, the whole past, drifted off behind you, it fell away and sank and was gone" (Alison, 227); "I missed my father and brother the way you miss the past" (Drew 24); "This summer ... is the only time that matters. It's the time I'll think of when I'm dying, just as another might recall a lost lover or regret a love they never had" (Greenway 2). However, all four also express third culture discontinuities by juxtaposing disparate moments in time, using very discontinuous narratives, and so creating the effect for the reader of lives composed of pastiches of divergent experiences (the effect, in other words, of third culture life).

O'Neill presents moments in time from 1999 to 2006, told in narrator Hans' retrospective. Following shifts from one time to another is a dizzying challenge throughout the novel, but take, for example, the abrupt transitions in a mere eight pages of text: "One afternoon" over the Christmas holiday in India in 2005, followed by "the next day" in that same year (222, 223), and then a "damnably sunny day six months earlier" in London during 2005 (224), then "after the holiday, one Sunday afternoon in February [2006]" and "six months later," both in London (228), then a return to the Indian vacation when "Jake and I spent the second day of our Indian expedition at a nature reserve" (229) and, finally, "Marinello is the name of the ice-cream shop, or *ijssalon* in The Hague where, after a shopping eternity at the Maison de Bonnetrie, my mother would sweeten me with two scoops of chocolate ice-cream" (230). This syncopated time line reads, perhaps, as a postmodern challenge to teleologically driven narratives. However, to read it as such is to miss an important, and profoundly third culture, point: for third culture individuals, life happens in episodes, with each episode taking place in a discrete geographic location, and these episodes are seemingly disconnected, as if each is a card in a player's deck and can be shuffled or reshuffled into any sequence. There is no connecting story to thread through the gaps between episodes, so they are not like beads on a necklace, one following the next, always in the same order. O'Neill's jumping around in time shows us that the narratives which constitute third culture subjectivity are a jumble of separate incidents-in-places; it is difficult to keep an accurate chronology — and *irrelevant.*

Unruptured chronology implies continuity while the third culture story is, as Schaetti notes above, "in fact, discontinuity." The point is to juxtapose disconnected moments and places: that is how Hans feels, and how third culture experience feels.

Time lines are discontinuous in Alison, Drew and Greenway as well, for the same reasons: discontinuity expresses third culture experience. Alison's novel has five parts and a preface of sorts about Sir Joseph Banks set in the late 1700s: Part One shows Alice in Ecuador as a child (presumably during the early 1970s); Part Two is the story of Alice's grandmother Violet as a young woman in Australia in 1929; Part Three tells of George and Mr. Clarence in the Azores in the 1820s and 30s; Part Four shows Violet on a cruise around the world (1980 or so); Part Five finishes with Alice visiting Scotland in 1981. Within the first thirteen pages of *The Ivory Crocodile*, Drew's Nickie describes an episode in the 1990s (3–4), her birth in Cairo in the early 1960s (4), Conakry in the late 1960s–1970s (5–11), another stint in Africa with her father in the 1970s, and Tambala in the 1980s (13). As in O'Neill and Alison, episodes in time are discrete, and each is clearly linked to a specific geographic location; as Drew's novel continues, episodes cease to come in chronological order. Greenway's Kate narrates from a "present day" sometime in the early 2000s and focuses on the summer of 1967. Within her telling of what happened that summer, she reaches backward to earlier incidents in the United States (such as her parents' meeting) (81), forward to her teenage years in Venice (167) and further forward to her own adulthood "many years later" in someplace that is implicitly no longer "the Far East" (96, 98). Thus the incidents of that summer are interspersed with other episodes in time in other places. Greenway takes a time period that lends itself to teleology (the span of a single summer and its culmination in Frankie's death) and purposefully interrupts the chronology, jumbling it to reflect the shuffling card deck of episodic third culture memory.

Snapshots

Pollock and Van Reken write, "What we have also discovered, however, in doing seminars around the world, is that because theirs is an intangible world, not tied to one visible place, most TCKs have lived their experience without words to define it" (72). This description is interesting. Yes, most third culture individuals lack the vocabulary to describe their background, just as there is not yet an established term that covers third culture literature (hence the writing of this book). And also no, the problem is not the lack of "visible place"; instead, the problem is a proliferation of vividly visible and yet also incompatible places. The way O'Neill, Alison, Drew and Greenway write it, third culture individuals rifle through their memories as if looking at an assortment of photographs: it is striking that narrative discontinuity in each of these four texts is indicated by photographs, and that the symbolic import of photographs is discussed in each novel. Photographs freeze memory and place in time, they can be shuffled like playing cards, and there is not necessarily a thread that connects each to the next: they are an ideal way to express the nature of third culture life experience and memory, and all four novels feature them prominently.

In each novel, photographs are used to suggest that third culture individuals cannot turn their geographically scattered memories into a contiguous narrative. O'Neill's Hans observes that he takes pictures of his son and then tosses

> the packets of photos into a cardboard box that held all of my photographs, including black-and-white shots dating back to the mysterious blankness of the sixties and seventies.... I never went through the box properly, had no idea what to do with any of these so-called mementos. There were, I knew, people who organized such things into files and folders, cataloged hundreds of examples of their kids' schoolwork and paintings, created veritable museums. I envied them — envied them for their faith in that future day when one might pull down albums and scrapbooks and in the space of an afternoon repossess one's life [129].

Hans cannot turn all of the different memories and locations of his life into a narrative that makes sense. He envies those who can, for he cannot claim his life out of the disordered box of snapshots at all. He implies that because the episodes are jumbled and seemingly unconnected, he is disenfranchised from his own experiences. He takes the box to a professional album-maker, but that is no solution either, for the story she makes of the photos is "one that begins continuously until it stops": the album accurately shows repeated "self-cancellations," in which new versions of self cancel out old ones, but it also puts things in one order, leaving Hans to bristle, "Is this really the only possible pagination of a life?" (235). The one order, a chronological one, pretends that episodes (snapshots) are connected and follow on one from another, when a third culture experience indicates that that is not the case.

O'Neill writes about photographs failing to tell the story of a (third culture) life because of insurmountable discontinuities; Alison writes about this same inadequacy, but explores it in discussing a single photograph, or, more accurately, the half of this photograph that has been preserved (the other half is mysteriously torn away). This photo's interpreters strive to explain and connect to the narrative of an internationally dispersed family tree — and they do so inaccurately. Violet looks at the ripped image of her ancestor George and his benefactor, Mr. Clarence, and misconnects what evidence the photo seems to give her:

> All that was left of him was a ripped old photograph: a large man with a shattered face standing by a tree. It might have been a she-oak, part of the picture seemed to be swaying, blurred. He stood among its boughs as if for protection, and there was an idea that he had been deaf. His big trunk was packed into a tight, faded coat, and he had close-set eyes, uncomfortable large hands. His arms were clenched by his sides, one tightly gripped by a bird-like hand. A woman, his wife? But the rest of her had been torn away, leaving a furred, dirty edge of paper. Even her name on the back was torn off, there were just a few words, mostly smudged. Violet's father had studied this document again and again, as if one day the words would come whole. All it said for sure was *George Clarence*, then the tear and a smudge that looked like *Salt* or *Saint* something, then *Scotl*; even the rest of that word was gone [106].

This picture depicts George and Mr. Clarence (the latter, presumably, the misleadingly effeminate claw-like hand). Perhaps, given the she-oak and the "*Scotl*," it shows them on their departure from Scotland to Saint Michael in the Azores ("*Salt* or *Saint*"). Of course, photographs, whether third culture or not, produce distortion by freezing moments in time and limiting what is represented so that important things might be omitted from the frame (as Mr. Clarence is here). As Maryanne Garry and Kimberly A. Wade write, "We know that the saying 'the camera never lies' is not true.... Photographs have long been used to alter collective memory. Stalin, for example cut the out-of-favor from official photographs.... Not only can doctored photographs alter collective memory; new research shows they can distort our personal memories" (Garry and Wade 359). What's significant in a third culture context is that over repeated moves, the past starts to feel like a fiction. The desire for photographs to authenticate memory is especially strong as a result, and the disappointment of their inadequacy and inaccuracy is consequently especially significant: if even the photograph creates a fiction, what was real? What if the individual's disconnected, displaced life cannot be meaningfully (to use O'Neill's word) repossessed, even in photographs? The inaccurate reading of the photograph of George indicates the profound unrooting (as in the description of George's "trunk" as he stands next to a blurry tree) of a third culture background.

Drew's Nickie is a photographer, drawn to the hobby, then profession, as a way of answering the discontinuities of her life. Nickie states with optimism, "My own love of photography was, I think, connected to my aimlessness; my pictures recorded where I'd been and who I'd been, establishing chronology. Like Hansel and Gretel's bread crumbs, my photos showed me the way back ... my photos were my map" (80). However, the novel is riddled with evidence to the contrary. Photographs preserve neither people nor "the way back" to a fantasy of home. Nickie brings her portfolio with her to Tambala:

> Determined to take myself seriously, I was a bit melodramatic then about what I thought of as "my art." The prints were black-and-white five-by-sevens, mounted on heavy bond, each adrift within white borders, bound together as a spiral book.
> They didn't work.... Figures jogged ahead, tossed shoes into a corner, voices skated, refusing to flow along this line of tension, to blend into that shadow. My photos reduced my friends to flat abstractions. I missed them very much [25].

Nickie tries to exert agency, imposing art and narrative on the subjects of her pictures, and they resist, not cooperating with her vision. In fact, the effort to impose her vision effectively obscures her subjects, rendering them "abstractions" rather than portraits of her friends, "the little stand-in family" she has "most recently left behind" (26).

Drew concludes *The Ivory Crocodile* from the perspective of the adult Nickie:

> I'm in love with Africa. It's a chronic, impossible devotion ... it's an exquisite loss. It's like a perfect photograph printed big enough to claim a wall, mounted behind glass, black and white, an uninhabitable moment in someone else's life. My handprints on the glass are as close as I can get [288].

In these lines, Africa sounds like a homeland she yearns for but is unable to penetrate: it is a picture of someone else's life (huge, imposing, not to be overlooked), and she can only touch the glass. Yet adult Nickie "left Africa out of the pictures in my show" (4). If photographs are meant to provide a map "back," she does not provide herself with a map back to Tambala or Conakry. If they are meant to provide a chronology, she has, with the omission of those places, omitted swathes of time to create an inaccurate one.

Through Nickie, Drew also introduces the problem of photographer-voyeur: s/he who photographs watches and shapes what s/he sees, but is not a participant. It is an effective iteration of the paradoxical benefits and losses of being third culture in a host country: third culture individuals are outsiders, but empowered; they are in locations that let them see wonderful things, but are positioned as voyeurs, not participants. Nickie is openly bossy when photographing, as when she takes pictures of Mpovi: "Before today, I'd never attempted to order her around; normally she instructed me and I submitted, an apprentice on her turf" (64). Nickie is arrogant with "numb invincibility" behind the camera, patronizingly rubbing lipstick off Mpovi's cheek (63). The camera makes her more of an expat, more of an outsider, more of a first world exploiter of the third world; it gives Nickie power and authority. At the same time, the camera interposes between Nickie and the Africa she badly wants to experience (and even be part of).

Greenway includes both photographs (which fail to capture an accurate narrative) and a photographer (the girls' father). Frankie and Katie are depicted in a photo that their

> mother keeps on her dressing table. In it, we're wearing light cotton dresses with sashes that tie round the back. The dresses look too young for us, too innocent. They contradict our faces and bodies. They are dresses my mother makes us wear. If you could see our backs, the bows would be crumpled, half-undone, creased with sweat from the hot drive [19].

Kate analyzes the photograph, explaining how it both captures contradiction (the dresses "contradict our faces and bodies") and deceives the viewer (who cannot see the crumpled, sweat-creased bows). Despite knowing from this image that photographs do not tell all, and cannot sum up the essence of a person, Kate strains to believe there is truth in photographs. Like dislocated individuals in *Natives and Exotics, The Ivory Crocodile*, and *Netherland*, Kate wants photographs to explain who she is in relation to her disjunctive memories and the places in which those memories happen. She prizes a photograph her father takes of her, believing it reveals "the warm wet, a slight wind. You can smell Ah Bing's steamed rice, her joss, the rotting damp of the garden, hear fishermen heading in, hurrying now because of the typhoon." Obviously a photograph cannot evoke the smells and sensations Kate attributes to it, nor can it really show that she is "quiet, secretive" (21). Although Kate wants place and identity to be encapsulated in the picture, it is evident that no photograph can do all that she hopes. Kate confronts photographic misrepresentation on her fourteenth birthday. He father tries to take a picture of Kate, but Frankie interrupts and there is an argument. The photograph their father finally gives to Kate as a present shows the younger sister wearing "Frankie's hat, with Frankie's arms around [her]": there seems to be no conflict between the sisters, no evidence of that evening's disagreements and certainly no inkling that, as Kate acknowledges, Frankie hates her ("She hates me for keeping her secrets, for being her confidante, her alibi, her sister, without being able to help or protect her") (130, 142).

For Kate (as for Hans, Violet and Nickie), photographs provide more aporias than explanations. In addition, in *White Ghost Girls*, as in *The Ivory Crocodile*, the photographer imposes a perspective on his/her subject. Kate looks at photographs taken by her father for traces of his personality:

> My father knows about dead people. He photographs the war for *Time* magazine in New York.
>
> In the morning, I spread the newspaper across the living-room table. There's a black-and-white photo of American soldiers wading through a stream lined with mangrove trees. The soldiers walk thigh-deep through muddy water, equipment hanging off them, face alert, guns bristling. I look for my father [11].
>
> My mother removes the papers if the pictures are too gruesome, the stories too violent, but usually she's too late. I study the photograph of Vietnam. I think I see my father.
>
> "He's in the Mekong," I tell Frankie. "He's walking down a river lined with trees. There are fish in his trousers. Leeches in his socks."
>
> "How do you know?" she asks, pulling the paper out of my hand [14].

In terms of revealing the photographer, photographs are also inadequate. Kate imagines where her father must have been in order to take those photographs, and what it must have been like for him. However, as Frankie's "How do you know?" makes clear, we don't *know*. One can imagine photographers behind cameras, but their presence is spectral. Neither what is in the pictures, nor who is behind the camera, are completely disclosed by photographs, regardless of how much desire and hope is superimposed upon them.

In writing this chapter, I was surprised by how much these works are about loss and also surprised that a box of jumbled snapshots provided a way, not to reclaim losses, but rather to acknowledge the unreal brightness of what snapshots might depict and the inevitability, in a third culture context, of there being no way to put images in a "logical" order. These novels explore issues hitherto invisible to most readers: what it means to lose places and people if you are privileged enough to have had access to a wide range of places and people; what it means to be disconnected from politics because of too much cultural exposure and too little national commitment; what it means to know, and feel guilty about, your own privilege. These authors recognize that lives are made of stories rife with disconnection, but that third culture lives in particular juxtapose seemingly inconsistent events. My point throughout this chapter has been to identify third culture literature as a distinct category. My aim has been to show that works by authors like O'Neill, Alison, Drew and Greenway have specific features that may be attributed to them, and which distinguish their work from national literatures, immigrant literatures, postcolonial literatures, the literature of exile, and so forth. In these four novels, photographs reveal discontinuities, gaps and misrememberings. Narratives shuffle episodes in time, juxtaposing disparate moments and the places in which they happen. These techniques and images make manifest the elusiveness of third culture as a shared experience not grounded in specific nations or specific moments in time, but rather in similar experiences of what it is like to grow up as a privileged outsider living in and moving through a series of locations.

CHAPTER TWO

Adult Situations and Secret Perversions in the Writings of Former Military Brats

Pat Conroy's well-known novel *The Great Santini* chronicles an American military family and their travails. It presents the perspective of that family's children, and of the oldest son, Ben Meecham, in particular. Bull Meecham, Ben's father, is as much a Lieutenant Colonel Marine at home as he is at work, goading his family aggressively, abusively, just as he might a young recruit. The film version of *The Great Santini* (1979) stars Robert Duvall in the role of Bull, Blythe Danner in the role of his frequently intimidated wife, and Michael O'Keefe in the role of Ben: Duvall and O'Keefe won Oscars for their performances (imdb.com). Several scenes enjoy long-lasting infamy. One in particular (alluded to in *Austin Powers 2* as well as *The Simpsons*) has Bull playing basketball with Ben in a one-on-one game in which whoever scores first wins. Ben scores, and Bull suddenly changes the rules, insisting that the winner must score twice. Ben refuses. Bull bounces the ball repeatedly off his teenage son's head, asking, "You gonna cry?" The novel and movie affirm significant stereotypes about the "tough-love" military man at home, a man insistent that his children be as good as his best recruits despite their youth and vulnerability, and despite the fact that he is their *father* rather than someone who outranks them.

Starting this chapter with a reference to Conroy evocatively grants access to some of the issues and stereotypes this chapter will address, key among them the effects of growing up in the military, something Conroy himself knows about intimately. The website "Away from the South" suggests that Conroy's stories

> have been heavily influenced by his upbringing. His father, a U.S. Marine Corps pilot, was physically and emotionally abusive toward his

children, and the pain of a youth growing up in such a harsh environment is evident in Conroy's novels. Military assignments also caused the family to move frequently, and Conroy claims to have moved 23 times before he was 18 ["Pat Conroy Biography"].

It is difficult to shake off the memory of a terrifyingly pugilistic Duvall in thinking about the autobiographical story Conroy tells in *The Great Santini*. It is also hard to forget that after the book's publication, Conroy's mother divorced his father, citing the novel itself as evidence in divorce court ("About Pat Conroy").

Though military family dysfunction is a key (perhaps *the* key) issue to ponder when one ruminates on Conroy's work, for my purposes it is equally significant to consider the transience Conroy evokes in his novel, and its effect on the community life of the military base as well as on military personnel and their families. The Meechams, like many military families, are mobile; they relocate extremely frequently in response to decisions made by their government:

> So often they had moved, shuffled on a chess board by colonels in the Pentagon, that it had become ritual; they moved though it all mindlessly, relying on spirit and experience, and with the knowledge that it was all the same, that the air bases were interchangeable, that mobility was the only necessary ingredient in the composition of a military family. The Meechams were middle class migrants, and all of them were part of a profession whose most severe punishment was rootlessness and whose sweetest gift was a freedom granted by highways and a vision of America where nothing was permanent and everything was possible [25].

This text provides an iconic example of military life leading to displacement and dislocation for military families, and children in particular. Sometimes these displacements take place internationally, and sometimes within the confines of a single nation, but the experience of rootlessness is analogous to that which characterizes third culture literature, and it results in similar descriptions of inter- or intranational dislocation, the losses entailed in mobility and characters' perceived inability to claim any place as "home." The quotation above describes mobility first as a "punishment" and then as a "gift": it is loss and privilege all at once, but, first and foremost, it is loss. It also gives us the image of a chess board manipulated by players. This is significant, for though the writings of former military brats[1] share displacement with third culture literature in general, military families operate under the aegis of a strict and hierarchical organization. Military families have little, if any, choice in terms of where they live and when they move.

This chapter marks a shift toward third culture literature that reflects a specific organizational culture. Military and missionary families are often referred to as "organizational." Morten G. Ender, for instance, groups the two together to assert that "adult children from organization families share a collective form of behavior" ("Beyond Adolescence" 84). In this chapter, I suggest that the organizational context of the military produces a third culture, and consequently a third culture literature, that fits under the umbrella of third culture and its literature generally, but also has significant characteristics that seem attributable to a specifically military context. In chapter three, I consider the literature of former missionary kids, also showing how these writings fit under the umbrella of third culture literature while having, in addition, their own particular characteristics.

This chapter will follow the "three plus one" structure of chapter one in order to describe a paradigm (with three authors) and then apply it to a perhaps unexpected example (the "plus one"). Thus, I will first discuss three texts in order to establish the characteristics of third culture literature in a specifically military context. These texts are by authors raised in a military context and are also explicitly about military contexts: Gene Moser's collection of linked short stories, *Skinny Dipping*; Sarah Bird's novel *The Yokota Officers Club*; and Ann-Marie MacDonald's novel *The Way the Crow Flies*. I will then turn to Ian McEwan, my "plus one," to provide an analysis of work not explicitly about a military context and yet clearly influenced by the third culture, military upbringing of its author: I focus on his novels *The Cement Garden* and *Atonement*.

If there are, as I argued in chapter one, four key features of third culture literature (dislocation, loss, disenfranchisement and secrecy/guilt), these emerge with new nuances in a culture derived from a military upbringing, for military installations are enclosed, highly monitored, and rigidly conducted communities in which families (particularly children) relinquish the possibility of making their own choices to those with authority: higher-ranking individuals, or, for children, the deployed adult in the family.

The first of the four characteristics is dislocation. In third culture literature, one sees the hallmarks of repeated moves, including descriptions of many relocations, and of the isolation resulting from individuals perceiving themselves as adaptable but ultimately out of place everywhere they go. In the writings of former military brats, one sees the same combination of relocation and isolation. In the case of McEwan, images of closed, isolated communities (like bases) are emphasized so that dislocation is apparent even if changes in geographical location are not.

The second characteristic is loss, or loss despite privilege. In third culture literature generally, this is loss of friends, pets, homes and other markers of family, familiarity and stability. The writings of former military brats share these characteristics. In third culture literature generally, as we have seen in chapter one, death becomes an expression of the emotional severity of loss. This is also true in military brat literature, but death is more anticipated in a military context than in a civilian one. In addition, in military brat literature one often sees one parent already absent or "lost" due to his (rarely her) duty to the country, while the other parent is overwhelmed by sacrifices she (rarely he) has made for family and country, often to the point of his/her own dysfunction.

Third is disenfranchisement. In third culture literature on the whole, this results from feeling like one does not belong anywhere (and so overlaps with isolation in the "dislocation" section); despite one's expatriate privilege, one has no claim anywhere. A result is political detachment or ignorance. The writings of former military brats, like other works of third culture literature, often suggest that characters are ignorant of local politics. However, in military brat literature, the ignorance arises amid heightened commitments to the passport nation. In a military brat literary context, patriotism fosters an *excessive* attachment to and performance of national identity. "Performance" is key, for characteristics of identity are exaggerated by efforts to assert and maintain them in an unfamiliar context, and they are often inwardly recognized by the characters as performances, paradoxically indicating dislocation and disenfranchisement rather than home and national belonging.

It is the fourth characteristic (secrecy and guilt) that is most altered in the writings of former military brats (and, as I will explore in the next chapter, those of former missionary kids). In third culture literature generally, secrecy and guilt are the result of perceiving one's privilege and feeling bad about it, which usually manifests in plots about secretive wrongdoing that individuals get away with (much as they have gotten away with their good luck in enjoying privilege). These plots are often disturbingly sexual. In military brat literature, one sees even more dysfunctional sexual plots catalyzed by something different: not guilt, but instead hierarchical domination (typical of military structures). Adults are overbearing authority figures. Children respond by becoming vicious sexual predators or by challenging authority, however futilely, by engaging in prepubescent consensual sex. Military children are required to comport themselves according to adult rules lest they shame their parents or damage their parents' military careers; children are also required to confront death, and the possibility of their own parents dying. Called upon to be adult in these disempowering ways, the fiction writings of former military brats show children trying to claim some of the more empowering agency of adulthood by misguidedly, and generally disastrously, choosing to engage in sexual activity. In the work of Moser, Bird, MacDonald and McEwan, the representation of children having sex, and of children as shockingly aggressive sexual predators, is a metaphor: one kind of inappropriately adult context in which a minor participates (sex) stands in for another (war).

So, in this chapter, my categories of analysis are dislocation, loss, (patriotic) disenfranchisement, and juvenile sexual precociousness. In the section on McEwan, the fourth category includes both "secrecy and guilt" (typical of third culture literature generally) *and* "sexual precociousness" (typical of a challenge to rigid hierarchies and the repudiation of the powerlessness of children).

As with third culture literature in general, the effect of a formative (childhood) cultural context is a key part of the dislocation reflected in military brat literature, though that literature itself need not be by or for juvenile readers. Pollock and Van Reken write, "Although the length of time needed for someone to become a true [third culture kid] can't be precisely defined, the time *when* it happens can. It must occur during the developmental years—from birth to eighteen years of age" (27). During the years when most individuals form their identity and sense of home, third culture kids relocate frequently, forming an identity based on frequent transitions and a sense of home based on a connection not with their passport home (first culture) or host country (second culture) but rather a community of transient expatriate outsiders like themselves (a third culture). For military children who relocate frequently, but not always internationally, this paradigm is only slightly changed. First culture is the hometown of the parents, second is the town they move to, and third is the transient culture of the military itself. There is a two-fold significance to this information regarding developmental years. First, in all chapters of this book I study authors who were mobile during their developmental years and can be considered third culture kids. I am keen to show that third culture, as a culture, influences the literary preoccupations of these authors when they become adults, just as any culture (Indian, Maori, British, Fijian, etc.) might. Second, third culture authors reflecting upon the details that have made up their own lives and cultures often use child characters in their novels.

In chapter one, texts I used as examples had both child and adult protagonists, but in this chapter the protagonists are generally children or adolescents. There is little literary criticism on *Skinny Dipping*, *The Yokota Officers Club*, and *The Way the Crow Flies* (none, in fact, on any of these except for the author of the last, MacDonald, and then none on this particular novel). There is an abundance of criticism on McEwan, some of which observes that McEwan often uses adolescence as his narrative voice. For instance, Katherine Dodou aptly notes that McEwan's repeated use of children and childhood images "is rooted in [his] interrogation of a mythologised narrative of Englishness" (74). Her argument is that childhood is supposed to connote innocence, as Englishness is supposed to connote propriety. McEwan's work offers a challenge to both notions. But what if the repeated trope of child characters in his work is actually rooted in the effect of a military culture (isolation, loss, disenfranchisement and overweening authority) on children's autonomy? What if it is an exploration of children's identities out of a context that pretends they have none beyond being appurtenances of their families (who are, in turn, appurtenances of the state)?

In "Military Families Under Stress," Amy Reinkober Drummet, Marilyn Coleman and Susan Cable summarize key developmental difficulties that arise for children raised in the military:

> Recent moves coupled with five or more lifetime moves were associated with lower adolescent self-esteem. Additionally, international moves geographically isolate children from family and close friends, increasing their vulnerability, a vulnerability that can be exacerbated by the challenge of having to deal with an unfamiliar culture [Vercruyse and Chandler 1992]. The stress of relocation might be adequately dealt with if that were the only stressor facing military families; however, relocation usually consists of an aggregate of stressors [281].

Other "stressors" include the military context itself: armed forces exist in preparation for conflict and conflict can result in fatalities; the military installation is a strictly run environment in which adherence to rules is both essential and potentially oppressive. Military culture also emphasizes stoicism and heroism: one is expected to be uncomplaining and resilient, especially in the face of difficulty (in other words, one is expected to repress one's emotions).

Some psychologists argue that the "aggregate of stressors" results in what is known as "military family syndrome," "which characterizes military families as consisting of authoritarian fathers, depressed mothers, and out-of-control children" (Palmer 205). The credibility of military family syndrome has been hotly debated: many conclude there is not enough concrete evidence to assert that it exists as anything more than a stereotype. In 1992, the *Journal of the American Academy of Child and Adolescent Psy-*

chology published a debate between psychologists who affirmed the notion of military family syndrome and those who denied it. Sidney Werkman, on the affirmative side, and speaking of the hazards of military life for children in particular, observes that "chronic restlessness, nostalgia, inability to make firm life commitments ... seem particularly prevalent in this highly specialized population of youngsters" (985). Influenced by "heroism, parades, medals, uniforms, danger, dedication," these socio-economically privileged youngsters nonetheless experience "unease, isolation and poor self image" (985). These may not be "acute symptoms" of psychological dysfunction, but they are evidence that "military life leaves an imprint on character structure and pathology" (984). The fiction of former military brats suggests that though these psychological symptoms are not acute, the effect of their nonrecognition may be. In other words, if only the privilege of a mobile upbringing is acknowledged by the world at large, it is the work of fiction to show (often graphically, exaggeratedly, and metaphorically) the "hazards," "stressors," losses and griefs of a military upbringing.

Although Phoebe Evelyn Price suggests in 2002 that "in the last 20 years [there has been an] increase of women in the military" (35), women are still far outnumbered by men. The number of women actively serving in the U.S. Armed Forces in 2010 was 14.5 percent of the total population ("Statistics on Women in the Military"). Of the total enrollment in Canada's Armed Forces in 2008, only 16 percent were women ("Canadian Forces Gender Integration" 5). In 2006, women made up only 9.1 percent of the British Armed Forces ("History of Women in the British Armed Forces"). In all five of the fiction texts analyzed in this chapter, one sees the representation of regressive gender roles in the family: women are mothers, wives and homemakers; men are warriors and authority figures. Donna Musil's 2005 documentary *Brats: Our Journey Home* describes bases as rigidly gendered societies in which expectations of parents in particular are clear: fathers fight (and bring their military ethos home with them, often dictatorially imposing rules and structures), while mothers mother. Though the representations in my five chosen texts are perhaps simply representative of the period just after World War II (as well as before and during in *Atonement*), they also reflect a military context in which it is still more typical for the father to be the "warrior" and the mother the one called upon to create (and repeatedly *re*-create) a domestic idyll, often while the father is himself absent for days or weeks at a stretch, for

> even under the ordinary circumstances of the peacetime military, absence of the father is a condition of the military childhood — a condition imposed by that invisible, unchallengeable member of the family, the Military Mission. Warrior fathers are continually leaving, returning,

leaving again, or working such long hours that their children can never count on seeing them. Part of the training every military child receives is that one is expected to handle this disturbing fact of life in true stoic warrior style [Wertsch 66].

The texts I consider all engage with what the effect of these gender expectations can be for the military child, particularly the child required to behave as an adult (and so adopt adult gender roles) prematurely.

Allen Frances and Leonard Gale observe the distinction between "father" and "mother" dysfunctions resulting from exaggerated gender roles and transience in military families:

> He may be a drill instructor, mess sergeant, or brigade commander who has difficulties with heterosexual intimacy and playful regression with children. He uses his work setting and all-male recreations as the only source of gratification. The wife's needs, by default, must be met in the extended military family or with her children, both of which can be adaptive responses or may lead to the following pathology. She is frequently seen in medical clinics, pathetically pleading for relief from a loneliness she cannot articulate. She may become symbiotically involved with her children, forcing them into premature adulthood to care for her or keeping them in a perpetual state of childhood so that she can continue to care for them [in Wertsch 83].

Drs. Frances and Gale adopt a condescending tone ("pathetically pleading") but what is alarming is the extent to which the fictions I study here bear out their descriptions: the father who militarizes his son's Scout troop in Moser, or wants children in formation in McEwan, or is insufficiently attentive to the traumas of his children in MacDonald. One sees, in addition, a mother who is lonely, depressed and dysfunctional in Bird, and one who forces her children into premature adulthood in both of McEwan's novels.[2]

Turning to the fictions in this chapter, the linked stories in the collection *Skinny Dipping* (Moser) follow the life of Phil, an Army brat (his father an Army pilot), from his time in Japan to his life on post in Virginia. At age thirteen, he becomes the "steady" of El, a civilian. Conflict in their relationship arises from his being a "brat" and her unfamiliarity with life on a military installation. Phil's parents decide that Phil will attend a military school when he is fourteen. It is this impending change (a departure — and it is typical for third culture kids to generally be on the brink of leaving) that catalyzes the two young teens' decision to have sex.

Bird's *The Yokota Officers Club* describes the Root family, stationed first in Yokota, then at a number of locations in the United States and subsequently in Okinawa. The novel reflects on the effects of a military upbringing on the six children (Bernie, Kit, Bosco, Buzz, Abner and Bob).

When in Yokota, the family lives off base, employing/sheltering a maid (Fumiko) who is also the commanding officer's secret mistress. Fumiko is sexually involved with Major Wingo from the age of fourteen on (285). Bernie, the oldest Root daughter, discovers and accidentally reveals the affair to the commanding officer's daughter, which, presumably, is the means by which his wife finds out. The result for the Roots is their speedy transfer out of Yokota and the reduction of the father's successful career as a pilot to a series of short, grueling postings on inglorious Air Force bases in the United States.

MacDonald's *The Way the Crow Flies* chronicles the McCarthy family's life at the Centralia Canadian Air Force Base, featuring the pedophilic fondling of nine-year-old girls (including Madeleine McCarthy) by the grade four teacher at the base's elementary school. Claire, one of these girls, is molested and murdered in the countryside. As readers, we assume Mr. March, the pedophilic teacher, is to blame. But the police blame and wrongly arrest a teenage boy for the murder. Only in adulthood does Madeleine discover that, in fact, Claire was murdered by two of her classmates, fellows in Mr. March's "after three exercise group." Abused themselves, nine-year-olds Grace and Marjorie are responsible for the graphic sexual abuse and strangulation of their peer.

These first three texts obviously have much in common: set on military installations[3] and explicitly engaged with post–World War II calm and concern about the Cold War, they also focus on children's perspectives: Phil and El narrate their story in *Skinny Dipping*, Bernie tells the story of her family in *The Yokota Officers Club* and Madeleine is the primary voice in *The Way the Crow Flies*. In this one respect, McEwan's work is clearly in concert with the others: pubescent Jack narrates *The Cement Garden*, and young Briony is the main voice in large portions of *Atonement* (perhaps all, if we take the novel to have ultimately been "authored" by her)—though Briony grows up, the story is persistently concerned with what she saw as a youth.

On the surface, McEwan does not engage with his military brat past in *The Cement Garden* or *Atonement*, but my contention is that these novels exhibit third culture tropes, even if their settings and plots are neither explicitly third culture nor military. In *The Cement Garden*, a family lives in a neighborhood that itself is somewhat isolated: suburban British drab. The father dies early in the novel; the mother sickens and dies a short time later; the four children bury the mother in the basement and struggle on, parentless. The novel culminates in the oldest children, Julie and Jack, having sex. In *Atonement*, the family lives on an isolated estate: rural British posh. The father is generally absent, working "in town" (or having an affair), while the mother languishes with headaches. Thus the children (two daughters and a son, as well as three cousins), like those in *The Cement Garden*, tend to be unparented. This allows the oldest daughter, Cecilia, to have a sexual liaison with Robbie, the son of the housekeeper, and the youngest daughter, Briony, to misunderstand what she sees and frame Robbie when one of the cousins is raped. The novel follows Briony's life (spanning World War II) and her efforts to atone for the wrong she has done Robbie and, by damning Robbie, her own sister Cecilia.

What brings all five of these texts together are the elements of culture shared by their authors and the way those cultural elements emerge as literary tropes in the works of fiction. Each of the authors I study in this chapter is a military brat (though not all identify themselves as such). *Skinny Dipping*'s jacket declares that "Gene Moser grew up as an army brat, living in Oklahoma, Wisconsin, Japan and Virginia, among other places," adding that, as an adult, Moser "served 27 years in the army, active national guard and reserve." Moser is also behind Operation Footlocker, a project intended to help American military brats enjoy a sense of a shared culture. The project has three regional branches (Virginia, Texas, and Arizona). In each there is a footlocker full of memorabilia donated by military brats. Any organization can borrow a footlocker to display and enjoy its contents ("Military Brat Registry"). Military brat culture clearly has been, and continues to be, a focus in Moser's life.

The Yokota Officers Club jacket says only this about Bird: she "is the author of four previous novels [and s]he lives in Austin, Texas." But Bird herself says, "I grew up in an Air Force family, frequently stationed on overseas bases" ("Interview with Saray Bird"), and the American Overseas School Archives state that "Sarah Bird is an Overseas School Alumnus and an Air Force Brat. Her father was an Air Force Lt. Col. She attended school overseas at Yokota in Japan" ("Bird, Sarah"). The transcript of a conversation between Bird and her family, included in the 2002 paperback edition of *The Yokota Officers Club*, also makes it clear that her family is similar to the Root family described in the novel in terms of being a military family relocated many times and living in, among other places, Japan.

As award-winning authors, MacDonald and McEwan have garnered substantial critical attention in both the academic and popular press.[4] Both writers are celebrated "national" talents (in Canada and Britain, respectively) but both are also former military brats whose childhood experiences can be read as the catalysts for their fictions' isolated families and the extreme losses and hardships endured by their child characters. Given that McDonald's and McEwan's works often deal with isolated youths, it is surprising that no one has seized on their military upbringings as important in understanding the kinds of loss, loneliness and dysfunction they describe.

MacDonald's book jacket biography reveals her publishing history, the Governor General's Award she won for drama and that "she lives in Toronto," while in the *Literary Encyclopedia* MacDonald is "a self-described 'Air-Force brat' ... born on a German airforce base, the child of a Scottish father, who served as an Air Force accountant, and a Lebanese mother" (Scott). If "self-described," MacDonald's brat upbringing is also something she doesn't dwell on, even in interviews about *The Way the Crow Flies*, in which she says she "drew on her childhood experiences" living on Air Force bases, but almost self-protectively chooses not to elaborate (Blake 3). Indeed, one has to persevere through the pages of "sources" at the end of the text to reach, at page 818, an "author's note" that includes the following: "Thank you for your generous help: Theresa Burke, Louise Dennys, Honora Johannsen, *Malcolm J. MacDonald (Royal Canadian Air Force retd.)*, Alisa Palmer, Clay Ruby and the Ruby-Sachs family, Lillian Szpak and Maureen White" (emphasis added). The reference to her father is hardly foregrounded, and though MacDonald clearly identifies him as a retired member of the Royal Canadian Air Force, she does not invite us to read her family into the McCarthys of the novel. Reading her novel as *autobiography* is not my object either. Instead, I aim to establish that a specific cultural background influences this text, and the others described in this chapter, in order to posit that reoccurring patterns and tropes are based on the cultural similarities of the authors.

As with MacDonald, McEwan's biography on the jacket of *The Cement Garden* is focused on his publication record and states simply that "he lives in London." In *Understanding Ian McEwan*, David Malcolm observes, "The early years of McEwan's childhood were spent on military bases in England, and then Singapore and Libya," even noting that "it was in Libya that McEwan claims to have had his first sense of the force of history and politics," before proceeding to readings of McEwan's corpus that do not take this internationalized and mobile background into consideration (2). McEwan himself remarks, in trying to situate himself relative to the class- and society-focused writings of postwar British authors like Kingsley Amis and Angus Wilson, "I think I was trying to make a strength out of my ignorance. I didn't know that world. I was a very déclassé sort of young man. I'd been tucked away in a country boarding school ... I was there because there was a small intake of army brat kids" (Childs 1). This comment suggests McEwan's perception of himself as an outsider, and as a misfit. It is especially revealing that he thinks of this as he discusses his place among British writers of the 1970s: though not emphatic, he clearly, nonetheless, associates the features of his writing that distinguish him from other British writers with his unusual positioning as a former "army brat."

In Moser, Bird and MacDonald, military brat culture emerges explicitly. In McEwan, it emerges implicitly. In all of these works, one sees characters suffering dislocation, loss, and disenfranchisement and also enacting alarming sexual precociousness.

Dislocation (Moser, Bird, MacDonald)

In the United States Armed Forces, "The length of a typical accompanied tour of duty — in which the family goes with the service member to the new assignment — is theoretically three years," and in practice is often much shorter (Wertsch 251). In Mary Edwards Wertsch's study, the average number of schools attended by a military brat (a truer reflection of "the number of times [a third culture kid] had to establish a new identity and a network of friends") is 9.5 (251).

In *Skinny Dipping*, El's friends tell her not to get attached to Phil because "Army Brats and Gypsies are almost the same thing": they are always moving (85). Phil remarks that "it seems like all [he ever does] is pack or unpack" (147). He has moved often enough that he knows how important it is to, as Wertsch has it, "establish ... a network of friends" (ideally ones that raise your social cachet): "he'd learned a long time ago that it was good to make popular friends quickly" (20).

In *The Yokota Officers Club*, Bernie reflects on moving with her sister Kit:

> It got kinda hard after the first half-dozen or so moves though, didn't it? ... I mean growing up military sort of makes you a Buddhist from a very early age. Like, you have to detach. You know it's all transitory. None of it is permanent.... Like when we'd start at a new school, I could never believe how seriously everybody took everything. Like it really mattered who was in and who was out? Who was Homecoming Queen and who was going to the prom and who wasn't? It was already too late to care. I mean, I already knew that this particular microcosm I just happened to be inhabiting was being duplicated millions of times over all around the world. The same in-out, popular-outcast stuff was going on in Hap Arnold Elementary and General Chenault Junior High and Kubasaki High School [83].

Every place is just another place that will be left: investing energy in being popular may or may not pay off, and may or may not really be worth it given the shortness of any particular stay. As Bernie adds, "I went to five schools in the fifth grade"; getting invested in or attached to any one of them would have been waste of energy (355).

MacDonald describes military wives in *The Way the Crow Flies*: "Their ability to march in and out on a dime and a blaze of home-baked, fully accessorized glory is legendary" (173). For Madeleine McCarthy, frequent moving means "home is a variation on a theme" (6). Home is ever-changing and encompasses even the moment when "home is this sky blue 1963 rambler station wagon" transporting the family across Canada (6). She notes, "It's hard to move into a new house without thinking of the day you'll be leaving" (13). On one hand, each new place is an opportunity to re-create a new self, a "fresh self" (MacDonald 138). On the other, each new place makes it harder to figure out what kind of new self that might be, and where that self can claim s/he is "from."

Moving is routine. The military families set up house quickly, repeating oft-practiced patterns. When the McCarthys first visit their new house in Centralia, Mimi is already "mentally arranging the furniture" into its usual places: "couch under the window, framed painting of the Alps over the mantelpiece, reproduction of Dürer's Praying Hands on the kitchen wall" (40). In *The Yokota Officers Club*, Bernie "assume[s] that the house was arranged in the way every house we'd ever moved into was arranged, in accordance with Moe's philosophy that 'Even if you're only going to be somewhere for three weeks you should set the place up like you're going to be there for three years. We're not Bedouins'" (34). In *Skinny Dipping*, El sees Phil's room: "Bed. Dresser. Desk and bookcase. Long shelf on the wall, full of [aircraft] models" (120). It's a stark room, almost like a barracks, in which the primary adornments are reminders that this house is a military one — the house itself is standard issue.

Bird and MacDonald both describe moving itself — not an edifice of any sort — as feeling "homey": "moving, the part after the packers left but before I became the new girl, a spot I tended to occupy until the packers came again, was always the coziest time of my life" (Bird 6); "there is something so full about those suspended times. When it's just [the parents] and their little family on the road between postings" (MacDonald 16).

When Moser's Phil starts public school, after having spent time in Japan as well as on various installations in the United States, he says he is from "Massachusetts" — which is true in that it is where he has *just* come from, but not true in that it does not indicate his origins. His peers are immediately frustrated with him for not identifying himself clearly and for proceeding to claim he is also "from" Louisiana (where he was born) and Japan (17–19): "being an Army brat caused him to think that Japan was as much home as Louisiana" (109). Extreme mobility can result in identifying numerous places as "home," as Moser's Phil does, or in feeling out of place everywhere, as does Bird's Bernie, who notes, on arrival in Yokota, "I wanted to go home but could no longer think of where that might be" (183). Mac-

Donald's Madeleine ruminates on the places her family has been stationed, remembering the "welcome to" signs on highways and at airports — "*Welcome to Paris, Welcome to Brussels, Welcome to Dublin, New Hamburg, Damascus, Welcome to Neustadt and Stratford, and London....* Welcome to Ontario" ([*sic*] 23). Like Moser's Phil and Bird's Bernie, she experiences extreme mobility as a problem in identifying herself in terms of location:

> If your father is in the Air Force, people ask you where you are from and it's difficult to answer. The answer becomes longer the older you get, because you move every few years. "Where are you from?" "I'm from the Royal Canadian Air Force." The RCAF. Like a country whose citizens are scattered across the globe [12].

"I come from a country that has no name," Conroy writes of his national identity in his (nonfiction) introduction to Wertsch's *Military Brats* (xx). He speaks as though he did indeed come from a "country whose citizens are scattered across the globe," a nation of dislocated military kids (MacDonald 12). Even "at home," he writes, "we are an undiscovered nation living invisibly in the body politic of this country" (xix). Conroy's observation — that the legacy of a military childhood is being part of a hidden "nation" of dislocated brats like oneself— provides a link between the explicit military contexts of Moser, Bird and MacDonald.

A fascinating commonality in these fictions is the prevalence of jargon. Dislocated personnel and their dependants speak an equally dislocated patois. Each base is a peculiarly prefabricated and homogenized territory with its own distinctly organizational, rather than local, lingo. MacDonald's Madeleine observes that if you know the usual buildings and their acronyms, "you can go to a base ... anywhere in the world and understand it" (6). When visiting the Army post in *Skinny Dipping*, Phil's civilian friend Sam asks, "What's in a PX [Post Exchange, similar to a department store]?" mere moments before El, scandalously, fails to stand for (or understand) Retreat (the lowering of the flag) (56, 59). In *The Yokota Officers Club*, the Root family is well practiced in "PCS" (a permanent change of station, meaning any assignment that lasts for more than six months) (4) and terrified that a misdemeanor will result in their father being "RIF'd." Bird's Bernie explains:

> One day Donna Ingram was sitting next to me coloring in the route Vasco de Gama discovered to the New World, and the next she was gone, RIF'd. RIF'd was one of those terms like "reconnaissance" that we knew for years before finding out their meaning. We always knew that reconnaissance meant something you weren't even allowed to ask about, and we knew that RIF meant your father lost his job because of a bad family. Learning later that the letters stood for Reduction in Force

added little to our elemental understanding that if the lawn wasn't mowed every week the life we knew would end in the time it took the Housing Officer to report our transgression [42–43].

When the Root family is finally RIF'd, it happens suddenly, at four in the morning: "We weren't allowed to speak to anyone. We were each permitted to bring only one small bag apiece" (350). In MacDonald's novel, the McCarthys also shop at the PX and live in the PMQs (permanently married quarters) (12). They are well aware of the importance of rank: the CO (commanding officer) and his implementation of SOP (standard operating procedure) are paramount (43).

Like all third culture kids, military brats experience mobility and dislocation as a result of their parents' career choices, and without the benefit of a grounding "home" identity such as might be enjoyed by their parents. The child is "somehow secondary to serving parental needs" (Wertsch 60). Musil's film *Brats* describes military families as, in this respect at least, dysfunctional enough to be pathologized: the emphasis on a parent's military career overshadows all else. Musician Kris Kristofferson (who narrates the film, and is himself a military brat) suggests the relevance of Stephanie Donaldson-Pressman and Donald Pressman's *The Narcissistic Family* in understanding military families. The Pressmans write about family environments that are, for the children in them, quite abusive. The comparison of military life and *The Narcissistic Family* is shocking to a viewer of Musil's film, underlining that this is a family system gone wrong because of the organization that controls it.

The fictions give examples of the extent to which military control is part of household living: the organization is in charge of both the parent's career and the domestic sphere. In Moser, Phil's father "equat[es] Scouts to the Army" (112). In Bird, the father puts a monthly duty roster on the fridge (42), and the Root children's bedrooms ideally look like "miniature barracks, with beds made the instant they were evacuated, sheets and blankets tucked in under the mattress so that the entire waxed and gleaming floor was visible" (41). In MacDonald, the father (unusually for these fiction texts) allows his wife some authority and *she* wields it militarily: "Madeleine and Mike know better than to squabble over the choice of bedrooms. Maman is the commanding officer at home and she will assign quarters" (40). As Wertsch's study of military brats indicates, adherence to rules and obedience, as inculcated in the service parent, makes its way home into families in which "white glove" inspections for cleanliness and dust are enforced (with militant punishments for lapses), as are duty rosters, hospital corners on the beds (even those made by young children) and a rigid schedule for mealtimes (7–9).

Children of military families learn that their family's nation controls the family, and that children do not typically contribute to, or factor into, decisions about where the family will live. Military brats learn that the enlisted parents are responsible first to their country, and second to their children. This creates a "dislocation" or displacement of parental responsibility from family to state, as well as a distance between parents' obligations and childrens' needs. For instance, Moser's Phil knows his time in Virginia with his girlfriend El is limited because of his father's career. Phil's own desires will not be taken into consideration when the family finds out about their next posting: "How long would he stay around her neighborhood? He'd been here a year and a half. When would his dad move? Transfer" (74). Bird includes governmental letters at the start of many chapters to emphasize the status of "dependants" as secondary (they do not influence state decisions) and yet inseparable from the state's decision (they move where and when they are told). "Dear Dependants of the United States Airforce: Welcome to your new duty assignment, Kadena Air Base, Okinawa," begins one such letter (3). And in MacDonald, military responsibilities overshadow Madeleine's repeated efforts to tell her father she is being molested by her teacher. Jack McCarthy is more concerned with reading about the Cold War than Madeleine's distress the first time and the second time she tries (170, 183). He plans to go to her school one day and nearly finds out about the "after three group" himself, but is preoccupied with his intelligence work and the nuclear scientist he is helping to smuggle into Canada from East Germany, and so forgets (258).

While the needs of dependants are secondary to those of the military (making them inconsequential), their behavior is closely scrutinized. Military children are expected to represent the country — or, more specifically, the *organization*— they are from by comporting themselves with excellent manners, behavior and cultural sensitivity. Any transgression or disobedience could, in addition, reflect poorly on their military parent and damage his/her career. In *Skinny Dipping*, Phil's father reminds him that in Japan he is "a guest and an ambassador" (9). Phil tells El, "Mom always reminds me that I could hurt Dad's career if I get into bad trouble, especially on post" (117). In *The Yokota Officers Club*, the letter to dependants stationed in Okinawa referred to above concludes by reminding families that "the serviceman's family is just as much a representative of the United States Government as the serviceman himself" (3). Mother Moe's depression means the lawn goes un-mowed for far too long. It is a relief to the children when she perks up and they clean the house and yard: Bernie observes that "we quickly achieve a level of hygiene adequate to avoid being RIF'd"

(113). In *The Way the Crow Flies*, Mimi (wife and mother) feels pressure as she watches the wife of the commanding officer welcome a new family with the heightened diplomacy and comportment required of a high-ranking spouse:

> Mimi observes Vimy closely. Her manners, her ability to put others at ease; that is the definition of breeding and a must in a CO's wife. Mimi learnt a lot from her mother and her twelve siblings back in Bouctouche, New Brunswick, but she didn't learn what women like Vimy can teach her. Jack will one day be in Hal's position and Mimi knows she will have to entertain "wheels," as Jack calls them [dependants], in her own home. She will be promoted too. The men all have to take exams and pass courses in order to qualify for advancement; the wives have to train on the job. Mimi notes how Vimy smiles graciously, and doesn't take Sharon's whole hand, but instead lightly presses her fingers [174].

Mimi is watching and learning how to play the role of the dependant wife whose spouse is ascending the ranks on base, aware that the wives are as much under scrutiny as their husbands. Under the military microscope, the comportment of spouse and children matters as much as that of the "serving" family member.

It is Bird's neurotic young Bosco who reminds us, in *The Yokota Officers Club*, of how entangled all these issues are for children: military culture (with its jargon), the fear of adversely affecting one's parent's career, and the fear of more dislocation (another move) are all bound together. When Bernie returns from her freshman year at an American university, Bosco sobs at her, updating her on their mother's depression and her sister Kit's delinquent behavior:

> [Mother] never gets out of bed. I thought she'd get up when you got here. Kit is going to get us RIF'd. Her best friend Sandra Muller, they RIF'd her. She was taking drugs. She went up to the north end of the island with some GIs. I heard Kelly Kulchak's Mom talking about it. OSI came and her whole family was gone overnight. Her hamster, Snerd, was in a cage in the carport and they just left him. He was mummified when the next family moved in and found him [79].

Their mother isn't comporting herself properly, and neither is Kit. This puts the whole family at risk of an RIF that will punish them (another move) and damage their father's career. The reference to the mummified hamster in the Mullers' garage also reminds us that with all the dislocation comes loss. Left behind, the hamster (one of the markers of home) is here quite literally dead to the Muller family: there is no going back. No wonder Bosco cries at the thought of it. And when the Roots themselves are RIF'd, they, too, leave everything behind, "even Chisaii," the song bird that had been the family's pet (350).

Loss (Moser, Bird, MacDonald)

As Kristofferson describes it in *Brats*, military subculture leads to a privileged and painful childhood. It is privileged in its exposure to numerous overseas or regional cultures and in the protection and guardianship provided by the military.[5] It is painful in its enforcement of rules as well as in the effect of repeated moves to new homes: there are inevitable losses (people and places, always temporary, get left behind and the fostering of a meaningful connection with "home" is extraordinarily difficult). Though the benefits of "growing up global"[6] are many, third culture literature brings to light the disadvantages and the difficulty of expressing loss from what even adult third culture individuals themselves generally recognize as privileged positions, particularly of class and education. As in third culture literature in general, military brat writing tends to dwell on negative effects that might be unexpected for someone who has lived a more rooted life. Indeed, one explanation for the extremes to which Moser, Bird, MacDonald and McEwan take their fictional plots may be that it is only in representing shocking losses of sexual innocence that the losses and anxieties experienced by a military brat can be translated into terms a non–third culture civilian can imagine. In military brat writing, severe losses due to mobility are even *more* severe, as military families are among the most transient of third culture families. An "on-base" environment provides an exaggerated form of interstitial community as well. A child on a military base is a child asked to serve a "home" nation they may or may not have actually ever lived in, is constantly aware of the possibility of war, and is, as a military dependant, aware that sudden changes of residence and location are non-negotiable and beyond their control.

In *Skinny Dipping*'s stories, we see privilege and some of what has been lost. El notices that Phil talks "like he'd been lucky to live in places she'd only read about and seen pictures of" (49). Indeed, Phil does *feel* lucky to have lived in Japan. However, he has also, by age thirteen, "lived in six states and Japan" (74) and garnered for himself, simply by virtue of being so transient, the reputation that military brat boys have for being disloyal and mercenary in their advances on girls. El asks if it's true "[a]bout brat boys. Not really caring about a girl? Just wanting, wanting, uh, to sort of see what she'll do?" (75). The implications of her comment are troubling: for most military brats, of *course* it might be true. Think back to Bernie Root, who knows she must "detach" from the cliquishness of high school because "it's all transitory" for the ever-mobile military brat (83). How much loyalty or interpersonal consideration *can* be expected of the military brat? Subject to circumstance, and generally unable to control the decisions of the organization for which his/her parent works, *any* brat might wind up in the position of not caring very much about relationships.

In *The Yokota Officers Club,* Bird explores a variety of possible results for transient military brats and their ability to socially engage. She has Bernie highlight the touted privilege of mobility and concomitantly outline how it can backfire:

> There is a common belief about military brats that all the moving around makes us very adaptable and we end up becoming sort of social geniuses. The only person in our family that this is true for is Kit. The rest of us are class–A social retards. The best we can hope for is not to be noticed, to survive the purgatory that is any place outside our front door.... Kit's ability to relate to humans outside of our family awes us [36].

A complex and paradoxical situation emerges from the many moves occasioned by military life: children are secondary to their parents' "home" government (a "home" that may not feel like "home" to the child at all) but, because of the repeated transitions, children are also more than usually reliant on the family (parents and siblings) for all of their social interactions. In *The Way the Crow Flies,* the McCarthy family is first and foremost connected to each other, as it is with each arrival in a new place when "the four of them stand in their new living room. The empty smell. Fresh paint and cleanser. The white echo of the place" (40). They stand as a family unit amid all that has been stripped away, just "their little family" with "no outside world" (16).

Yet, though Madeleine is "at home everywhere and nowhere, there is the occasional sense of having misplaced something, someone. Sometimes, when the family sits down to dinner, she has the feeling that someone is missing. Who?" (65). In chapter one of this book, characters like Jane Alison's Alice (*Natives and Exotics*) miss buildings and places left behind. In this military context, perhaps because housing and facilities (PXs, etc.) can tend to be quite similar from base to base, more emphasis is on people left behind, or on the process of leaving behind itself. As Bird's Bernie emphasizes, when she returns to Yokota after many years,

> This is not my *hometown*. A hometown is where you go back and they remember you from when you were a kid. This is like being Jewish and going back to Krakow or something. All the buildings are the same, but

everyone you ever knew is dead or PSC'd, which amounts to the same thing [265].

Her equating of death and PCS sounds hyperbolic, but here, as in the texts analyzed in chapter one, the fiction strives to make clear the enormity of what the military brat loses: she does not simply fall out with a friend or two, but rather is ripped from an entire community of individuals whom she will never see again. It is as if they have all died. *Skinny Dipping*'s Phil is most motivated by his desire *not* to leave El behind, as others (like his friend Jason in Japan) have been left. Madeleine of *The Way the Crow Flies* feels the spectral presence of those she has left, made additionally unsettling by the fact that she can't quite put her finger on what, or who, is haunting her, as if the people left behind have, in fact, already been almost forgotten.

In *The Yokota Officers Club* Bosco mourns vividly and is "impossibly bereft," contemplating losses she hasn't even experienced yet:

> Think of all the last times no one ever notices. You think you'll play with your troll dolls forever, but one day you get a horse and you never play with them again, and you can't even remember the last time you played with them. You just do and then you move and your Mom throws them away because you're over your weight allowance and you get to the new base and you don't have your horse so now you want to play with your troll dolls, but they're gone. They're gone, and you can't even remember the last time you played with them. They're just gone [76].

Bosco's grief is vertiginous: she anticipates a succession of losses in which the most devastating feature is that one only realizes what has been lost in hindsight. One does not get a chance to prepare, much less say goodbye. This also makes the military context different from some of the contexts I explore in chapter one or chapter three. Military brats are used to having to move *without warning*. They relocate suddenly. They leave significant things, sometimes even household pets, behind (which is as ruthless as any third culture kid's move might be), but they are requested to do so with even less time to grieve than the typical third culture kid. Only months or years later might they remember that they didn't tell someone to get the hamster out of the garage. Only months or years later might one even notice that one's treasured troll dolls were gone. Their loss is all the more significant for the fact that it is unheralded, unremarked upon, and invisible except to the belatedly devastated child.

Though it sounds terribly cliché, one of the big losses for a military brat is innocence, especially if "innocence" includes the good fortune to be able to disregard mortality or the physical misery of humanity when engaged in conflict. Moser's Phil observes, "Brats knew about war and danger; it was second nature to them" (91). He is knowledgeable about nuclear explosions because of living in Japan after the bombing of Hiroshima: he knows what happens to buildings and human bodies in the miles around an explosion's blast site. El asks him, "How can you know about all that stuff and not be sad?" (95). Military brats on the whole know something of the potential for death and destruction. This emerges in the fictional texts in the form of children fixated on the possibility of the death of one or both parents. In a civilian context, children with such preoccupations might be considered neurotic. In a military context, however, the death of one or both parents is in fact possible.

In *Skinny Dipping* there is a helicopter crash in which two people die. El remarks to Phil, "That could have been your dad," a comment that Phil, being heroic and stoic, brushes off until much later that evening when, tucked in bed and cuddling his toy "Bun Rabbit" like a much younger child might, he cries (64). For it *could* have been his dad: "The pilot wings and medals [his father wears] were for what he had done. They were not protection" (65). In *The Yokota Officers Club* there is an explosion on Okinawa and Bernie describes the Root family's reaction as their father leaves to report for duty: "'Where's Daddy going?' Moe [the mother] lifts Bosco up without answering. My little sister's face is glazed with tears and snot, and she is gasping in hiccupy breaths. 'Is the Island sinking? Are we all going to die?'" (94). Moe is not allowed to know where her husband is going, but he may not come back, which is perhaps why she gives no response. She does not know what the explosion is either, which is why Bosco's overwrought question is not as ridiculous as it might seem. The island most likely is not sinking, but on a military base it is indeed possible that they may all die. MacDonald's Madeleine repeatedly asks her father if he is going to die, and requests as a bedtime story a recitation of the story of the plane crash that once nearly did kill him:

> "What would have happened if you had died in the crash?"
> "... I didn't die."
> "But what if?"
> "I don't think you'd be anywhere."
> What is worse? Being dead? Or not being born? [133].

Madeleine even intentionally "imagines her mother dead in order to appreciate her better" (57). All of this preoccupation with the possibility of death is indicative of both a third culture context in which impermanence is the norm and a military brat context in which death is a real possibility, not an abstraction of other anxieties. If, above all, a child needs his/her guardians to be alive to preserve the life of the child him/herself, then the most dramatic demonstration of a child's needs being secondary to those of their parents' country is the parents' willingness to die in service of that country and/or to jeopardize their children's lives.

(Patriotic) Disenfranchisement (Moser, Bird, MacDonald)

In chapter one, I discussed how third culture authors reflect on the experience of feeling as though they have no home, or that there is no single place in which they belong. Indeed, for characters in third culture literature, the experience of transience, or of being an expatriate or outsider, is sometimes more "homey" than any particular location, and certainly more like home than their official passport nation. A perhaps unexpected flip side to feeling nationally disenfranchised is that characters in third culture literature tend to be, at best, noncommittal about and, at worst, destructively ignorant of the politics of the places in which they reside. For military brats, and the fictions they produce, there is a key difference in terms of whether characters feel out of place: military bases, thanks to sharing many characteristics with each other (movie theaters, schools, certain kinds of housing, parade grounds, etc.), *can* feel somewhat like home. But, though superficially home-like, such installations are profoundly impersonal, institutional spaces in which most of the population is transient. There is also a difference in terms of what characters in the writings of former military brats know of local politics: characters technically know something of the interaction between their host nation and the passport country that the base represents; *however*, what they know is influenced by patriotic rhetoric and by a military chain of command that profits from servicemen and -women and their dependants not knowing as much as they could. As Wertsch describes it, people on base, especially enlisted members, are part of "a [military] culture in which secrecy is second nature" (Wertsch 40). What one sees in the fiction writing of former military brats is both patriotic and, paradoxically, disenfranchised. Characters "belong" to the military organization, but are transient, like other third culture kids. Because they "belong" to a military organization, they are limited in terms of what they are able to know of their host location and its politics.

Thus military children inhabit contexts that are simultaneously intensely patriotic and dislocated; military installations are expressly of and for the home nation, and yet are isolated enclaves in a host environment. Bases are also familiar places and yet consummately temporary. Bird's Bernie describes her first arrival in Yokota as familiar, even though she has not been there before: "We drove onto Yokota Air Base and my lungs expanded with the first full breath I'd taken since we left Travis. Everything that was wrong with Japan was right here ... an American flag snapped overhead. A barbed wire fence with a guard at the gate embraced it all. This was home. This was where I wanted to stay" (187). The best thing about Yokota is that it is a base, and very much like the Travis base she has recently left. For Bernie, arriving at an American base means arriving at the predictable: barbed wire, flag, guards. For a child who has already moved many times as a military dependant, predictability, even if impersonal, feels very comforting, even homey.

Similarly, in *The Way the Crow Flies*, the McCarthys relocate to the Centralia Air Force Base after their assignment in Germany. The novel starts as they drive across the country from visiting Mimi's family on Canada's eastern coast, and yet the first time Madeleine feels she has returned home is when she reaches Centralia. After one slowly driven tour of the base, and a brief stop for Madeleine and her brother Mike to look through the windows of what will be their new school, Madeleine muses that "it's funny how this is the first time since they've arrived in Canada that [she] has not felt that she's climbing into the new car in the new place. It's just the car. It's just Centralia, where we live" (38). Like Bernie, Madeleine experiences the base as home. As Bernie notes of Yokota, this base is one among many, "a prototype" (260). For *Skinny Dipping*'s Phil, Army life is a comforting norm. When he arrives at military school, he thinks at first that it is just like being on post and feels reassured: "There was a flag flying high overhead, some old machine guns on display, an obvious parade field at the base of the hill the school sat on, uniforms both gray and army, papers posted in glass cases. At first it looked almost homey" (152). Phil's description of the school would perhaps only connote "homey" to a military brat raised on military installations; to civilians, the guns, uniforms and glass cases would likely sound off-puttingly, not comfortingly, institutional.

When Phil takes El to the post for the first time, the military police manning the gate salute the car. El asks why, to which Phil responds, "The bumper sticker. He saw an officer's sticker, so he saluted" (55). They are in Phil's father's car. Phil's father is an officer. The officer sticker on the bumper warns the military police to salute someone who outranks them. Phil "felt proud of that and at the same time a little embarrassed. He'd seen so many times when civilian kids just didn't understand" (55). What civilian kids "don't understand" is the significance of rank, but what Phil's comment reveals most forcefully is that life in the military has rules and norms that differ significantly from those of the civilian world. In *The Way the Crow Flies*, MacDonald also uses bumper stickers, but to different effect. In this novel there is a botanical garden with an amusement park on its grounds called "Storybrook Gardens," which puts a bumper sticker on each car in its parking lot as a way of advertising: they do this to the McCarthys' car when they visit, and they do it to Oskar Fried's car too. Their bumper sticker is "bright yellow, etched with the silhouette of a castle. Storybrook Gardens" (343). The sticker is significant evidence when police try to discover who murdered young Claire, but it is also a fascinating device in the way it connects with the bumper sticker in *Skinny Dipping*. In the Moser text, a military bumper sticker informs anyone on post of the rank of the car's owner. In MacDonald, the military bumper sticker one might expect is replaced by the image of a castle: "Storybrook Gardens." If a sticker is a synecdoche for military rank, then MacDonald's use provides a reader attuned to military bases and their hierarchical trappings a little mocking joke to enjoy: rank and the base on which it is so important are like an amusement park and the characters that populate it. They are artificial constructions, and the base is a world unto itself that is not entirely real.

Military installations are, in a Baudrillardian sense, a bit like Disneyland in its offering of a "miniaturized pleasure of real America, of its constraints and joys" (Baudrillard 12). As Bird's Bernie observes of a festival on base in Okinawa, the "Kadena Karnival," "it was Americana in a concentration known to few who have not experienced the overseas military base" (120, 122). Hyperbolic Americana is distorted by a military context and strains under foreign influences. The vehicle pulling the carnival's hay ride is a tank; the carnival's concession stand sells American snacks in a Japanese idiom: "Fry Chicken $1. Fry French 50 cents. Yakitori $1. Yakisoba $1. Spagheti $1. Squid $1" (122). Where, for Baudrillard, Disneyland is actually presented as a fiction in order to establish the putative reality of the rest of America ("The imaginary of Disneyland is neither true nor false, it is a deterrence machine set up in order to rejuvenate the fiction of the real in the opposite camp" [13]), for Bird the fiction is that there is a "real" America back home: for military brats in particular, the exaggerated Americana makes the "real" America recede ever further into the realm of the unimaginable. The result is that, for American military brats like Bernie or Phil, or Canadian military brats like Madeleine, the fictionalized version of their home nation as represented by military bases becomes home, not America or Canada themselves.

A base has an influence, often colonial, in the country in which it is located. Catherine Lutz asserts that, in places like South Korea, American military presence is perceived as "an invasion" justified by the supposed "advance of political and economic freedom." Joseph Gerson goes so far as to describe America's network of overseas military bases as an "imperial infrastructure." He writes of Okinawa in terms that echo Bird's fictional depiction (above):

> The "soft" side of military colonialism expresses itself in food, cultural tastes and markets. Inexpensive and plentiful food on and around U.S. bases in Okinawa — especially during the 25-year formal military occupation (1945–72) has permeated Okinawan culture, changing tastes — especially for the young — and has created markets for companies like McDonalds, Burger King, and Mattel Toys, and these foreign forces exact their costs.

Military bases are strategic, politically motivated settlements in which servicemen act according to the wishes (and in the interests) of their home country. For a child "at home" in a foreign place, this poses a problem. When s/he becomes aware that the "local" culture and the parents' culture may be at odds, where do a child's loyalties lie? This pressing question occurs far less often than one might think: more than missionary kids, more than third culture kids in less organizationally constrained environments, military brats are kept separate from the host country. Brats who live on bases in their home nation are likewise kept relatively separate from the civilian community (even if, as Moser's Phil does, they attend civilian schools). Military brats are encouraged to meet their educational, physical, social and entertainment needs on base as much as possible. This effectively makes them quite ignorant of the country and culture beyond their base's barbed-wire perimeter fences, even if that country is their passport "home."

But the fictions of Moser, Bird and MacDonald have in common the fact that the *fathers*, not the children, are revealed as less savvy than they should be regarding what is going on in the world. In these texts that investigate what it is like to grow up as a military brat, what is emphasized for critique is *not* how little the children know, but rather how ineffective parents, especially fathers, are in their efforts to keep certain information secret for the good of their country — their efforts fail, often to their families' detriment. In addition, fathers in these texts are presented as troublingly limited in their understanding (and misunderstanding) of international relations and politics. Both the failure of fathers to keep privileged information effectively secret and their failure to accurately understand what is going on mean that these fathers inadvertently expose their children to experiences and consequences that are far too adult for them.

MacDonald's Jack McCarthy is perhaps the most vivid example of this phenomenon among these three fictions, for he not only manages to remain oblivious to how Madeleine is being abused by her teacher (in spite

Two: Adult Situations and Secret Perversions 87

of her efforts to tell him) but he also completely misunderstands his role in helping a German World War II scientist/defector and, in his misunderstanding, sets in motion a process that culminates in the death of one of his own friends. Jack is asked to help "Oskar Fried" settle into his anonymous flat off base and to babysit the man until he can cross over from Canada to the United States. It is a secret job, and Jack is excited by the subterfuge. He wrongly assumes that "Oskar Fried is a scientist from the winning side"; he thinks the assumption he has made is "crystal clear" (156). But Fried is actually an engineer who didn't make the first cut when the United States was recruiting talented defectors to help develop NASA's space program. He is a second-rate, bitter, demanding and petulant defector, it turns out, and is from the losing, not winning, side.

Jack also has a neighbor on base named Henry Froelich. Froelich is the elementary school's math teacher and father to several adopted children, including teenage Ricky, who is wrongly framed and arrested for Claire's murder. Froelich becomes Jack's friend, despite the fact that it takes Jack far too long to realize that Froelich is German, Jewish, and in Canada recovering from life in a concentration camp. Froelich, coincidentally, encounters Fried on a civilian street one day, and recognizes him as one of the engineers for whom he had worked in the camp in Germany. He is appalled, and later tells Jack. Jack, being far less savvy than he should be, reports what has happened to his superiors in the secret scientist-transfer scheme, with the following result:

> In the morning [Jack] picks up the newspapers from the front step.... In the bottom left-hand corner of the front page is a reproduction of Henry Froelich's school board photo and three inches of print. *The father of convicted sex killer Richard Froelich is missing and feared dead. Henry Froelich's station wagon was found parked on the U.S. side of the Peace Bridge yesterday morning by New York State troopers. No suicide note was found, but ...* [sic]. [586–87].

Implicitly, Jack's American counterparts have killed Henry Froelich after hearing from Jack that Froelich had recognized Fried. Wrongs and tragedies agglomerate around Jack. To summarize a complicated and lengthy part of the book's plot quickly and overly simply: Ricky is wrongly accused of rape and Henry Froelich dies. The latter death is certainly Jack's fault, but Ricky's situation is, after a fashion, Jack's fault as well — if Jack had not been distracted by his subterfuge, had paid attention to his own daughter and found out about the abuse, Mr. March would surely have been investigated and Ricky likely would not have been accused of murder. What all of this means for Madeleine is that she has been abused, her classmate has been killed, her teenage neighbor has been wrongly arrested for murder, and his father has died. These would be traumatizing experiences for the most grounded of adults, but Madeleine is only nine and, the way MacDonald writes it, all of these disasters stem from decisions made by Madeleine's father.

In *The Yokota Officers Club*, Bernie's father Mace responds to demotion by taking correspondence courses: he indulges in the pursuit of knowledge irrelevant to his current situation in order to distract himself. As Bernie observes, "It didn't used to be my father's choice to rise before dawn, back when he was still flying and had to be at the flight line for early missions" (58). Now that he isn't required to be at the flight line, he studies art history, the Civil War, and bonsai gardening in the wee hours of the morning. The effect is that Mace "lives in a different time zone from ... his family, which is why he goes to bed to read at seven-thirty every night" (57). Mace makes himself unknowable to his family, and is determinedly oblivious to as much of what is actually going on around him as possible. His desire to be ignorant is compounded by the military's desire to reveal as little strategically significant information as possible. Thus, when a plane explodes on Okinawa, and Mace is called in for a TDY (temporary duty assignment), he has this argument with his wife:

> "I know TDY, Mace. I want to know where and for how long."
> "That's classified."
> "Is it because of the plane blowing up? Are you going to SAC? Were there nuclear weapons? *Are* there nuclear weapons?"
> "Classified. Classified. Classified. And classified. Any other bright questions?"
> "Mace, for God's sake, you're leaving your children on this goddamned island. Should I try to get us emergency leave?"
> "Emergency leave? Emergency leave! Why don't you just send Ho Chi Minh a nice note and alert him to *all* of our strategic circumstances?" [101].

Mace himself doesn't really want to know what is going on with either the war or his family. In addition, he is not allowed to tell his family what little he does know. The manner in which Mace rails at Moe suggests that he is defensive, that he perhaps doesn't know himself exactly what his TDY entails and that he may actually be scared because he does not know, but cannot bring himself to show any vulnerability. Of course, Mace's demotion and RIF out of Yokota years earlier had much to do with information and efforts to keep it secret: he was supposed to "employ" Fumiko as a housekeeper so that Major Wingo, his commanding officer, could continue to have an affair with her. Wingo tells Fumiko classified things and Fumiko consoles young Bernie during one of her father's TDY absences by revealing details about her father's mission. Then Bernie tells one of her friends, and eventually the information gets back to Wingo's wife, LaRue. With the revelation of the affair comes Mace's dramatic and inglorious demotion, and a succession of short, soul-destroying postings.

Bernie is a teenager when she figures out that when she was a little girl in Yokota, she destroyed her father's career, her family's financial prospects, and her much-loved Fumiko's life: "I realize for the first time how I handed Fumiko to LaRue Wingo on a platter.... I was the one who told. That everything that happened after that happened because of me" (342). As a young girl, Bernie knew too much adult information. As a military brat, a misstep on her part meant she was indeed responsible for destroying her father's career, which in turn seriously affected the rest of her family, and, of course, utterly ruined Fumiko's prospects.

The case of what military fathers know and try to keep secret is not as prominently developed in Moser's stories, and yet even here the father puts the son in a position of experiencing too much. Phil is nine when his family lives in Japan. His parents take him to Hiroshima, and show him a bridge that hadn't been destroyed by the bomb. As he describes it, "There was a woman walking across the bridge when the bomb went off," and you can tell she was there because "[y]ou can see her shadow on the side of the bridge. The bomb made all of the side much lighter, except where she was. You can see her body, up to the rail. It's not paint or nothing. It's like a shadow that's always there" (94–95). Perhaps death itself is not a terrible thing for a nine-year-old to know about, but Phil's description of the "shadow" is haunting, as is the absence of the woman's body. She has simply disappeared, meaning that anyone can simply disappear, leaving an evocatively violent shadow behind: she is gone because she was bombed, the shadow indelibly reminds us. Women (and children) die when nations fight wars, even if they are just minding their own business and crossing a bridge. Though Phil initially doesn't think that "we [the American military] hurt kids and parents," he discovers that indeed they do (13). Military actions can and do kill civilians, which means that Phil and his family are vulnerable *and* that, as a military family, they are culpable: they destroy lives. These might be disturbingly adult insights for a nine-year-old.

What appears in these texts, then, is a critique of what fathers do not know (but should). The ignorance that, in chapter one, I argue is indicative of national disenfranchisement, emerges here as indicative of both national disenfranchisement (too many moves, making it hard to feel especially committed to the politics of any one place) *and* a military context in which the idea of "privileged information" (who has the need and/or right to know) predominates. These texts suggest that for dependants in a military context, both not fully knowing what is going on *and* stumbling upon information they should not know can have terrible results. Children in the military wind up experiencing things far too adult for their years, and being responsible for far more knowledge than might be age-appropriate. They have no choice. However, it is not a major leap from unsolicited exposure to adult experiences to children *choosing* to dabble in other adult activities and responsibilities — specifically, sexual ones. If treated as more adult than their years in some respects, why not choose to be adult in some of the (ostensibly more empowering) others as well?

Sex (Moser, Bird, MacDonald)

In chapter one I discuss the frequency with which plots involving guilt and secretiveness appear in third culture literature. What one sees in the writing of former military brats is a little different. There are sexual acts that one would expect to occasion guilt (and might perhaps arise from secretiveness), but they do not. The acts themselves are reveled in, and rather than arising from secretiveness or repression, they stem from a context in which children quite openly have too much knowledge regarding mortality, human vulnerability, and the inevitable losses that come with frequent relocations. Precocious sexual activity, in all three of these texts, represents children trying to wrest control away from the adults and military organization to which they are generally required to submit. It is a challenge to the circumstances a military brat is required to accept, including the assumption that military brats can handle themselves as adults when required to move, confront mortal danger, or reckon with the possibility of the death of a parent. Feeling that life is out of control manifests in plots about that most adult context of all (intercourse), in which children try to take control and so assume some vestiges of adulthood.

Moser's Phil and El plan to have sex. They are thirteen. It is their summer vacation. Their plan comes in response to both Phil's and El's families requiring that the children spend less time together, and also to the announcement that Phil will be leaving to go to military school in the fall. Phil complains, "They're treating us like children" (116). "We'll show them we're grown up," says El (118). "Yes," Phil thinks in assent, "We'll show them" (118). Their sexual activity is explicitly prefaced by a desire to prove that they are more adult than their years. It is first a challenge to the adults, and only second a physical pleasure. In addition, there is Phil's impending departure, which to the children feels like a deadline: if they are going to do it, they have to do so soon. As El later explains to her mother, "No ma'am. He's going off to school. We wouldn't have if he was [going to be] at Mount Vernon this year" (132). Urgency drives their need to act more precociously than they otherwise would (this is like Alice's fooling around under blankets with her friends in Ecuador in *Natives and Exotics*, discussed in chapter one). The children (Phil and El, but also chapter one's Alice) have a very third culture imperative driving them: "act now, for you may have to move soon and that will mean you never see this person again."

Phil's mother is out, he and El are in his house alone, they have a condom, and have selected a classical radio station. Everything between them is measured and happy: "He pulled off his shirt, exposing his hairless chest. She lay on the bed in her thin panties and sexy bra and smiled at him. He lay next to her and they hugged, kissed while thoughts stopped and experiences began" (121). They are both "nervous yet ... eager" (119). In the isolated universe of Phil and El the couple, their encounter sounds like loving sex between young people who care for each other. But then Phil and El are caught by Phil's mother: "El desperately pulled the sheets over her breasts, which she knew Mrs. Boydon could tell were small and immature, no matter what Phil might believe. They were visual evidence that they were too young for this" (123). Immediately Phil and El are children again. El thinks of what her "Mommy" will say when she finds out (125). Phil is effectively put in a "time-out," as one would if punishing a very young child: "Phillip Mathew, you will not get out of that chair until I tell you that you may," scolds his mother (126). Whatever agency the two children claim in having sex is very quickly lost when an adult intrudes, and reminds them how powerless they really are. El is, in fact, sent away to a relative for the rest of the summer, and when she returns Phil is at military school. Parental and organizational authority crushes their resistance effort.

The trope of young sexuality being used as a challenge to adult and military authority appears in *The Yokota Officers Club*, but is split between two characters: Fumiko and Bernie. Fumiko is, throughout the novel, Bernie's foil. We see through Bernie's eyes, and Bernie's key preoccupation is what happens to Fumiko. In some senses the novel is a detective story: Bernie tries to discover her role in ruining Fumiko's life. Perhaps more intriguingly, though, Fumiko is a manifestation of what a military brat like Bernie would most hope for in trying to rationalize, explain and challenge the circumstances of life as a military dependant. Bernie "translates" Fumiko's story: in an egregiously false-sounding chapter, Bird has adult Fumiko speak with teenage Bernie about what happened to get the Root family RIF'd:

> "Fumiko, I was ten years old. I don't remember."
> "Ten? Ten not so rittoe."
> "Fumiko, tell me."
> "Okay but you hear stupid *pan-pan* girl talk or you hear what Fumiko mean?"
> "I'll hear what you mean" [280].

And again:

> "You risten Fumiko or risten what Fumiko mean?" Her voice is as high and babyish as it was that first time [in other words, when Bernie first met Fumiko when she was ten years old].
> "I'll hear what you mean. I promise" [281].

The clumsily constructed conceit means that Bird can have Bernie narrate Fumiko's entire life story without struggling to re-create flawed, Japanese-accented English. However, it also means that Bernie (and even Bird?) finesse this supposed "authentic" Japanese narrative — projecting, inserting, and shaping so that perhaps a bit of military brat desire inflects the story that is told. Bernie can, both in her imagining of Fumiko and in her role as Fumiko's translator, do two things: first, she can imagine for herself a stronger personal connection with Japan, and with a Japanese person, than would typically be possible for a military brat; second, she can project onto Fumiko some of her own fantasies, perhaps most significantly the desire to challenge adult and military authority.

In the narrative of her life story as "heard" by Bernie, fourteen-year-old Fumiko is sold in prostitution to Major Wingo. For him, the appeal is that Fumiko, starving in postwar Tokyo, looks so much younger than she really is. Despite the fact that their relationship is a business transaction (she is sold to him), she gains security, shelter, food and, eventually, also love. Oddly, the situation between the two of them seems somewhat reciprocal. Despite the age disparity, Bernie/Bird narrates this relationship so its tone is similar to that of Phil and El's sex: nice for them, disturbing for a reader. Apparently, Wingo

> took a girl he thought was twelve into his bed. What had to happen happened. I was glad I was not really twelve, and I was glad the officer did not have a penis like a beer bottle. I was like a kitten to the officer, a doll, a playmate.... I squealed with delight when he brought me presents from the PX: Baby Ruth candy bars. Tootsie Rolls. Tinkerbell bubble bath. Superman comic books. We shared the same secret: I wanted to be a child as much as he wanted me to be one.... In short I was happy. I had nearly starved to death in a cave.... I came to love the officer. It seems a strange thing to say now; it didn't then. He gave me my life back. Yes, I loved him [298–299].

Fumiko is "happy," though she (unlike Phil and El) has not chosen this. She, according to the story, gets to live, and even experiences love, thanks to Wingo. The image is of a child, with comics, candies and bubble bath, in a military man's bed. If Fumiko is a projection of Bernie's desire, or perhaps of a military brat desire more generally, then her sexual activity does indeed challenge military authority in the sense that it reveals a succession of flaws in a member of the military: first, the affair represents impropriety and the breaking of many rules (Wingo is married but has an affair, *and* he buys a local girl, effectively enslaving her); second, it is pedophilia (taboo); and third (perhaps most treacherous in an Air Force context), it is through the affair that Fumiko discovers that Wingo is actually afraid of flying (310ff). Her sexual activity undermines the myth of the fearless fighter pilot. Fumiko's story enables Bernie's critique: through Fumiko, Bernie can see flaws in the myth of military heroism.

Fumiko's affair allows her to survive, but beyond that it offers her no agency. However, it is Fumiko's sexual activity that gives ten-year-old Bernie the "power" to have her family RIF'd. Because of what Bernie knows of Fumiko's liason, Bernie reveals too much by accident. The military organization and hierarchy reasserts control, so that, just as Phil and El are reminded of their youth, Fumiko loses Wingo's protection and the Roots are sent away: Wingo has Fumiko and the Root family removed from Yokota, saving himself, his position of authority, and the reputation of the military in keeping his pedophilic affair relatively secret.

Fumiko's affair represents only half of the sexuality-as-resistance-to-authority trope in *The Yokota Officers Club*; teenage Bernie's dancing represents the other half. Bernie's dancing is sexual, and offers a challenge to adult authority, military structure, and the social hierarchy of teen life on base. She prefers to dance to music the base radio station won't play: Van Morrison and his ilk (151). Bernie wonders "if Okinawa is haunted by the ghost of all the songs [she's] ever hated and never wanted to hear again. The Oldies Undead" (65). On base, the music selection is "safe" and "clean": the Monkees, the Association and similar groups (no Doors, no Jimi Hendrix, no sexually explicit or drug-laden lyrics). At the Kadena Karnival, there is a local band playing current songs, "the first non-sanitized music" Bernie has heard "since arriving" at Okinawa (128). The band plays adjacent to another "act," which involves an old Okinawan woman in a bikini, Lovely Assistant, putting a python's head in her mouth and miming a blow job while the snake's tail curls provocatively around her crotch. Over near the band, Bernie starts to dance: "I ... drop into a deep-bobbing Monkey, climbing the vine with ferocious arm swings that Moe clucks and smiles at. Just to make her laugh more, I break into an impersonation of Lovely Assistant complete with excessively low crotch-drop" (129). The sexuality of Bernie's dancing challenges the military base's propriety as much as Lovely Assistant's act, and it challenges parental authority too (Moe is amused but also "clucks," gently scolding her daughter).

Still dancing, Bernie finds herself facing Kit, and Kit's well-dressed, popular entourage with their "aura of blond American perfection" (130). Bernie has drawn an enthusiastic audience, overshadowing Kit and overturning a social order in which Bernie is normally unpopular and invisible. But having her sister actually see her dance is, for Bernie, much like El's experience when Phil's mother walks in — she feels exposed: Kit "turns away before her friends can associate her with what [Bernie realizes] suddenly is a crude copulatory performance" (130). The dance offers a celebratory challenge to the normal order (and so fits well with the theme of Karnival/carnival), but only for a few moments before Bernie recognizes that in challenging norms and authority she has effectively prostituted herself, selling a "crude copulatory performance" for a scant moment of release from military, family and social hierarchy.

After Bernie's dance, the Roots move on to see another Kadena Karnival "act" in which a mongoose kills a snake, leading Moe to finally realize her children shouldn't be seeing or doing things that involve death and sex. "This is what you consider fit entertainment for children?" she rails at no one in particular:

> "This? One creature eating another alive? No child should see this. Any of this." She swings her hand in a wide gesture that takes in the old woman giving a python a blow job, children dangling from a Huey [helicopter], GIs cursing bar girls, runways with B-52 bombers taking off every three minutes. "You should all be ashamed of yourselves" [137].

Moe conflates the rule-breaking inappropriateness of the Karnival acts with the routine work of the base (B-52s "taking off every three minutes"). All of it is inappropriate for children. All of it is too adult. Though Moe can't physically gesture to it, Bernie's dance clearly belongs on the list of things that are too adult and consequently not suitable for her children to see or do.

In *The Way the Crow Flies*, it is not Madeleine who challenges authority sexually, but rather two other girls in her class: Grace Novotny and Marjorie Nolan. The former seems to be largely neglected by her parents, smells as though she probably wets the bed, is repeating fourth grade, and is having trouble "flying up" from Brownies to Girl Guides with her peers. Marjorie Nolan is left to her own devices too often as her mother suffers "headaches" and is perhaps an alcoholic. "Margarine" responds by becoming increasingly bossy, and, eventually, by becoming friends with outcast Grace. Both are part of Mr. March's "after three exercise group" along with Madeleine and a rotating selection of other grade four girls. As Madeleine summarizes in later years, "he raped us [and] he played games involving strangulation" (791). Though Ricky Froelich is imprisoned for the murder of nine-year-old Claire, it turns out that Grace and Marjorie were responsible: in a field they rape Claire with an ear of corn, and then Marjorie instructs Grace to strangle Claire just as Mr. March has strangled both of them. Grace, disturbed at the best of times, strangles too long and too hard, and Claire dies: "Grace looked bewildered. She reached for Marjorie's sleeve.... 'Marjorie ... ?' Her voice trembled, tears filled her eyes and she asked, 'What happened to her?' 'You killed her, Grace, that's what happened. Now go home'" (802). The grotesque incident reminds us insistently of more than one layer of tragedy, for Grace and Marjorie are victims first, perhaps, of a type of "military family syndrome": their fathers work, their mothers slide into dysfunctional behaviors, and they themselves run wild. The military organization has rendered them invisible and unimportant. Then the two girls are abused by Mr. March with no one to notice, and no one to advocate for them: an adult has imposed himself upon them. Their sexual act with the corn cob is a way of posing as adults: they pretend that they are like Mr. March, taking what power from the pretence they can. The strangulation is intended to be part of their playacting, but goes too far, resulting in Claire's death.

Years later, when Madeleine tries to investigate, she discovers that Grace has been missing since she was fourteen: "There was no song to soften or explain where some girls went. Grace had gone to snuff" (784). Grace, in other words, is likely dead. Her brief act of confused empowerment leads to a guilt that in turn leads to her complete self-effacement.

These books present plots in which children are traumatized by situations far too adult for them. Moser, Bird and MacDonald contrast military brat experiences of impermanence, isolation, loss and lack of control with the futile efforts of military children to assert adult authority. In each of these three instances, children engage in sexual activity strategically, believing they can thereby gain a measure of adulthood (or a measure of control over their circumstances). In each case, however, trying to claim adult security, and even adult agency, through physical intimacy fails. The empowering fantasies that these child characters try to make manifest with a sexual act are revealed as flimsy, impermanent, even grotesque aberrations. It is at the far extreme (grotesque aberration) that we meet Ian McEwan, especially in his early work.

Ian McEwan's *The Cement Garden* and *Atonement*

McEwan's impressive, often disturbing corpus is considered definitive of a postwar British literature typified by morbid unpleasantness. Kiernan Ryan writes of McEwan, "The caricature still haunting [him] is that of novelist obsessed with the perverted, the depraved and the macabre" (203). Ryan adds that McEwan's work is characterized by "the freezing of his moral faculties and his refusal to react as decency demands to the shocking scenes staged by his own morbid imagination" (203). But what if the extremity of violence, perversity, isolation and even amorality in McEwan's work has more to do with a third culture context than a British one? I contend that reading novels like *The Cement Garden* or *Atonement* in light of third culture literature, and military brat literature in particular, makes more sense of McEwan's disturbing imaginings than reading his work as indicative of postwar Britishness.[7] What is disturbing, especially regarding his portrayal of children and adolescents, arises at least in part from the isolation and disenfranchisement of a military brat cultural context as well as the redressing of the rigid power hierarchies of military life.

I have chosen these two novels because they represent both early and more recent work by McEwan: *The Cement Garden* was first published in 1978, and *Atonement* in 2001. In this way I can use a third culture, military brat reading to show that his later work is not "haunted" (as Ryan would have it) by early atrocities but rather that early and later works are both indicative of the cultural context out of which McEwan writes. Thus McEwan is not the "king of macabre" who chooses a "radical shift in stylist posture" in the 1980s (James 81), but rather a quite consistent writer. These novels are very different in terms of content (children who encase their mother's dead body in cement in the basement versus an adolescent who wrongly accuses a young man of rape and spends her life rewriting the events of that day, and its consequences, in order to atone for what she has done) and yet they share hallmarks of military brat writing: in both one sees dislocation, loss (including death), disenfranchisement and sexual perversity.

Reading McEwan as a military brat allows for a new interpretation of the omnipresence of these themes in his writing. My analysis of sexual perversity as a response to adult authority in McEwan — as with the readings of sexual perversity in the novels by Moser, Bird, and MacDonald — responds and adds to extant sociological and psychological studies of military brats. The hierarchical nature of military life (in tandem with parental commitment to the nation, dislocation resulting from frequent moves, and the enclosed environs that are the bases themselves) makes children feel isolated and disempowered: the trope of inappropriate sexual activity in these novels is indicative of the extent to which youths might react against a context in which they can feel themselves as simultaneously preyed upon and lacking in advocates by claiming sexual agency and thus a semblance of adult autonomy.

Dislocation

McEwan spent his years up to age eleven in "Germany, Tripoli and Singapore" as the son of a Scots sergeant-major (Ricks 19). After this he went to an English boarding school that took "mostly working class lads from broken homes in central London [and] a handful of kids from the military" while his parents remained in North Africa (Hamilton 3; Remnick 156). Life on military bases entailed residing in isolated, dislocated bubbles of faux–Englishness. McEwan describes "army places abroad" as "like small council estates anywhere in England" (Hamilton 4). In McEwan's description of his experiences, these places are, then, not unlike the isolated estate of *The Cement Garden* or the more elite isolation of the Tallis home in *Atonement*. Indeed, Ryan observes that McEwan's protagonists are "frequently housed in some suburban deadzone and sealed inside a situation from which the oxygen of emotion has been pumped" (209). "Suburban deadzone" is one way to translate the artifice of military base culture into fiction, so we could read McEwan's repeated use of this type of setting as invoking an isolated, dislocated base context. Ryan goes on to add, "This is what creates the obscure sense of menace" in so many of McEwan's works (209): dislocated settings like isolated suburbs generate a claustrophobic intensity (one is "sealed inside a situation from which the oxygen of emotion has been pumped") and this results in a sense that something is amiss, or about to go amiss. The dislocation produces menace and suspense. This, too, seems apt as a fictive re-envisioning of military base life: also claustrophobic, with the reminder of war (and fatality) continually foregrounded. In *The Cement Garden* and *Atonement*, we do not see repeated moves (as one typically would in third culture literature, or in military brat writing like that by Moser, Bird or MacDonald). We do, however, see isolated residences and claustrophobically close families.

In *The Cement Garden*, Jack notes:

> Our house had once stood in a street full of houses. Now it stood on empty land, where stinging nettles grew round corrugated tin. The other houses were knocked down for a motorway they never built.

> Sometimes kids from the tower blocks came to play near our house, but usually they went further up the road to the empty pre-fabs to kick the walls down and pick up what they could find. Once they set fire to one, and no one cared very much [28–29].

The family's house stands alone near an empty clutch of prefab houses, in the midst of an area cleared for an unfinished motorway. In *Atonement*, the Tallises live in a house that is a new reconstruction of an old manor house on a large plot of land that isolates it in the midst of a winding driveway with two bridges (75), an artificial lake with an island and a temple (76), a bungalow for the housekeeper and her son, and enough space to accommodate, decades after the family's departure, a golf course (363). Its rooms seem to stifle their inhabitants, as in the dining room where the "effect of suffocation was heightened by the dark-stained paneling reaching from the floor and covering the ceiling" (125). In the rooms there is generally "a quality of stubborn silence that occasionally smothered the Tallis home" (145). In this house, "the walls, the paneling, the pervasive heaviness of nearly new fixtures, the colossal fire dogs, the walk-in fireplaces of bright new stone referred back through the centuries to a time of lonely castles in mute forests" (145). Though at opposite ends of the socioeconomic scale (suburban poverty, rural aristocracy), both environments are remote from the world around them and isolate the families who live in them, intensifying their interactions and, indeed, creating a stifling atmosphere of impending catastrophe.

Conroy's observation — that the legacy of a military childhood is being part of a hidden "nation" of dislocated brats like oneself— provides a link between the explicit military contexts of Moser, Bird and MacDonald and the implicit ones of McEwan's novels. *The Cement Garden*'s family is a "hidden nation." The novel is not given a specific setting but rather is indeterminate (somewhere in Britain, sometime after World War II). What is revealing is the extent to which McEwan creates these children as extremes of military brat life, even of military brat pathology. Jack says that he "felt isolated from everyone [he] knew" (107). "No one ever came to visit us," he notes, indicating that even when alive the parents were devoid of friends and immediate relatives, and though the youngest sibling (Tom) has friends he plays with in the street, according to Jack no non-family member has come inside the house since "the ambulance men who took my father away" (28). Only Jack's insular family is part of his "hidden nation," as he suggests when wondering why they concealed their mother's dead body rather than telling an outsider she had died: "It was not at all clear to me now why we had put her in the trunk in the first place. At the time it had been obvious, to keep the family together. Was that a good reason?" (98). When things are going well for the orphaned children, Jack, tellingly, describes this "hidden nation" as "a secret army," a description that hints at McEwan's use of military brat dislocation in this text's depiction of children who are moral and national outsiders: the children clean house and Jack notes, "I saw my sisters ... moving all the furniture into the center of the room and for the first time in weeks I was happy. I felt safe, as if I belonged to *a powerful, secret army*" (emphasis added, 95).

In *Atonement*, the Tallises provide shelter for three "outsider" children: cousin Lola and her twin brothers Jackson and Pierrot, described in revealingly military terms as "refugees from a bitter domestic civil war" (8). The outsider children illustrate how tightly the rest of the children close ranks around their mother. The three cousins are "without love ... in a strange house" (100), while the rest of the Tallis family, even those returning from the outside world like Cecilia and Leon, "slip into old roles" and enjoy (or suffer) close "connections [that] had never been broken" (103). Even in daydreams, characters are unable to really leave the tight weave of the nuclear family. Cecilia says, "I'd love to come up to town," but "[e]ven as she said the words she imagined herself being dragged back, incapable of packing her bag or making the train" (110). The estate is so isolated and the familial connections so strong that Cecilia perceives herself as unable to escape. This nuclear family is also a hidden army from which defection is impossible. When outsider cousins Jackson and Pierrot do run away, Emily (the mother of the house and their aunt) does not call the police, instead believing the family can handle the situation themselves, as if they can be their own closed community and mete out their own justice, just as a military base might (146).

Wertsch writes, "The rootless children of warriors grow up with confused and incomplete notions of what it is to belong—but they know all too well what it means to be an outsider, and that in fact becomes as much of a social role as they are likely to experience" (Wertsch 309). The family in *The Cement Garden* is, above all, isolated from the potential support of friends or family: they may as well be in a foreign country due to the insubstantiality of their connections to people or even to the place in which they live. *Atonement*'s Tallises similarly live isolated on their estate so that the rape of young Lola, when it happens, feel like a rape in an Agatha Christie novel: it is an event within what seems to be a closed community, cut off from stabilizing external influences and perspectives.

Loss

In Moser, Bird, and MacDonald, characters describe the loss of home (meaning houses as well as human connections) due to repeated moves.

In *The Cement Garden* and *Atonement* one sees houses that are presented as facades; they are mere edifices that do not supply a sense of being at home in the first place. Home is already lost. McEwan takes the impermanence that Moser, Bird and MacDonald attribute to the houses that accommodate military families who often move and applies it to houses *without* the precondition of frequent relocation. In other words, Moser, Bird and MacDonald explain the connection between houses that seem impermanent and the many moves families make, while McEwan focuses on the sensation of impermanence so typical of a military family context without describing the accompanying relocation. In the work of all four authors, impermanent houses are a product of military cultural contexts; McEwan writes from, but not explicitly about, that context in *The Cement Garden* and *Atonement*.

The Cement Garden's Jack visits an abandoned "prefab" house, gutted by fire and observes:

> Most houses were crammed with immovable objects in their proper places, and each object told you what to do — here you ate, here you slept, here you sat. But in this burned-out place there was no order; everything had gone. I tried to imagine carpets, wardrobes, pictures, chairs, a sewing machine, in these gaping smashed-up rooms. I was pleased by how irrelevant, how puny such objects now appeared. There was a mattress in one room, buckled between the blackened, broken joists. The wall was crumbling away round the window, and the ceiling had fallen in without quite reaching the ground. The people who slept on that mattress, I thought, really believed they were "in the bedroom." They took it for granted that it would always be so [48].

Jack, with a consummate third culture sensibility, implies that he does not take "bedroom," or indeed any construction of "home," for granted. He suggests that furnishings and the order they impose are temporary: believing otherwise is foolish. His rumination on this ruined house is poignant (his family — his "home" — has fallen apart with the orphaning of the children and their inability to look after themselves). It is also extremely evocative of a military brat's experience of living in uniform military housing: the uprooted individuals living amid carefully organized furnishings meant to demarcate different features of home nonetheless recognize that everything has once again changed, and that the furnishings are ultimately insufficient to enforce permanence. As McEwan's Jack would have it, this arranging and staging of permanence (of the sort one sees the mothers perform repeatedly in Bird's *The Yokota Officers Club* or MacDonald's *The Way the Crow Flies*) is merely a charade, and one that a military brat would almost certainly see through.

In *Atonement*, the house represents an "intention ... to create an ambience of solidity and family tradition" from a "baronial structure" with "squat presence" (145). McEwan implies that this plan has failed. No matter how sturdy the walls, and how weighed down with paneling and portraiture,[8] the building does not provide an anchor for the family. It lends them neither solidity nor permanence. The house itself paradoxically symbolizes groundlessness, impermanence and the family's disenfranchisement from place. The house, a replacement for "the original Adam house," shares its grounds with a mock temple:

> The temple was supposed to embody references to the original Adam house, though nobody in the Tallis family knew what they were.... More than dilapidation, it was this connection, this lost memory of the temple's grander relation, which gave the useless little building its sorry air. The temple was an orphan of a grand society lady, and now, with no one to care for it, no one to look up to, the child had grown old before its time, and let itself go.... The idea that the temple, wearing its own black band, grieved for the burned-down mansion, that it yearned for a grand and invisible presence, bestowed a faintly religious ambience [73].

McEwan's description of the temple suggests that continuity and permanence happen at a remove: the family home connotes impermanence; the temple endures, though increasingly dilapidated, but it is at a distance from the house, and at a distance from the Tallis family. The Tallises are ignorant of how the temple's architecture refers to the old house, the one their current home has replaced. Their ignorance indicates their lack of roots in, and connection to, the estate on which they live. They have neither memory nor understanding of the past in this place. Unlike them, the personified temple, even in its rundown state, does have memory and even filiative connection with the place and what used to be there. Fascinatingly, the temple is also "an orphan." Its mother, the old house, has died, leaving it to fend for itself, and it still mourns her. The temple is another child left with inadequate parental guidance, like the children in *The Cement Garden*, and like Briony, Cecilia and especially outsider Lola in *Atonement*. In *Atonement* McEwan thus describes the house as an edifice that evokes the provisional homes military families re-create in location after location and the temple as characterizing a child orphaned or neglected by parents with stronger commitments outside the home, as can be true in military families.

Military bases are distinguished by the frequent absence of the deployed parent (most often the father) and the resulting closeness of the mother and children. In *The Cement Garden*, the father dies; in *Atonement*, the father is always "at work" (having an affair) in the city. Military mothers can be overwhelmed and isolated by the combination of parenting in the absence of their spouses, too frequent relocations and strict expectations of military obedience and propriety. It is unsurprising that, if one reads McEwan's writing as military brat literature, one sees not only absent fathers but also mothers so overwhelmed that they become ill, and then absent. The mother in *The Cement Garden* becomes ill and dies; the mother in *Atonement* habitually absents herself when she takes to her bed because of migraines. Both novels, though not explicitly about military contexts or military bases, evince military brat contexts by presenting isolated settings seemingly detached from the world around them, domineering but absent fathers, withdrawn (or ultimately dead, as in *The Cement Garden*) mothers and, though they live in strictly ordered settings, children with more covert sexual autonomy than mature understanding of how to use it judiciously.

McEwan describes his own father as an outsider who disrupts quotidian routines when he returns from duty, reminding us that "even under the ordinary circumstances of peacetime military, absence of the father is a condition of military brat childhood" (Wertsch 66):

> He was something of a stranger to me. He would go off all week to work and only come back at weekends ... when I saw him, I'd run behind the settee and call to my mother to send him away. As far as I was concerned, he was an intruder into my rather intense, pleasant relationship with my mother [Hamilton 4].

Wertsch points out that military brats often feel they experience two lives: one (typically more relaxed) when their father is away, and another (typically dominated by militaristic rules, schedules and strictness) when he returns: "The family dominated by mother and the family dominated by father [are generally] two very different worlds" (Wertsch 68). McEwan describes his father as "quite terrifying" and "a stickler for the spit and polish of traditional army life" (Begley 89). He adds, "My earliest recollections are of weekday idylls with my mother interrupted at weekends by the loud appearance of my father" (Begley 89).

If one takes McEwan's own background as his cultural context, one can see the absent/overbearing father aspect of a military upbringing developed in the novels too. *The Cement Garden* includes a father obsessed with order: the unsatisfying garden, for instance, prompts him to plan covering the whole thing in concrete, because "it will be tidier" (21). His behavior at children's parties is similarly militant: "He liked to have the children stand in neat lines waiting to take their turn at some game he had set up. Noise and chaos, children milling around without a purpose, irritated him profoundly. There was never a birthday party during which he did not lose his temper at someone" (41). And then, while Jack, the oldest son, obliviously masturbates upstairs, the father keels over dead, face-first into the still-wet concrete, "the smoothing plank in his hand" (23). The father is, for obvious reasons, absent thereafter from the text. In *Atonement*, it is expected that the father will "work late and ... stay up in town," and that he will, as he always does, have his "department" phone home to inform the mother of this fact (102). His paternal responsibilities tumble down the hierarchy: "Leon, who had the pure gift of avoiding responsibility, would not assume his father's role. Nominally it would pass to Mrs. Tallis, but ultimately [to] Cecilia" (102). In the absence of her father, concern for militaristic rigidity seemingly falls to Briony, for whom even the possibility of others having internal thoughts filled with the chaos of a stream of consciousness "offended her sense of order" (36). The Tallis parents are, from the start, *both* "absent in their different ways": the father because of his "work" in town, and the mother because of her migraines (103).

McEwan also sets the stage for the kind of maternal dysfunction Wertsch describes as typical of military mothers: they become too physically and/or emotionally dependant on their children as a result of their own isolation: in McEwan's work, one sees how this may be represented as children being catapulted into "premature adulthood," or else frozen at an idealized childhood age[9] (83). After the father in *The Cement Garden* dies, the mother suffers from an unspecified malaise. "No Doctors came to see mother," and yet Julie, the oldest daughter, takes a prescription to the chemist to be filled every Saturday (49). The mother becomes "bedridden so gradually we hardly commented on it" and "her bedroom became the centre of the house" (49). The children accept her inertness without demur: "'When Mother gets up' became a vague, unsought-for time in the near future" (50). The children bring her food and drink; they even perform at her bedside for her: a joke by Sue, cartwheels by Tom, a handstand by Julie and a rendition of "Greensleeves" by Jack (45). She requires the children to look after her, and they do. She wants them to circle around her, and they do. She prevents them from seeking outside help, telling them that if people found out she was not looking after them, they might be "put into care," and the house might stand empty so "it wouldn't be long before people would be breaking things, smashing everything up" (59). As the dysfunctional center of the house, she misguidedly, mildly and yet megalomaniacally prohibits outside intervention. Then she dies (59), and after a heartbreaking incident in which Tom, six years old and the youngest child of the four, tries to climb into the bed in which her corpse still lies (64), the older children submerge their dead mother in a trunk full of cement in the house's basement (73) and then try to proceed with life without parents altogether.

In *Atonement*, Emily's migraines frequently leave her bedridden. She recognizes that, because of this, she has been too absent from her children's lives. When Briony's attempt to rehearse her play with the twins and Lola goes awry, Emily lies in her bed downstairs listening and musing that "if she were not so ill, she would go up now and supervise or help, for it was too much for them, she knew. Illness had stopped her giving her children all a mother should" (66). Emily goes on to acknowledge that her children perceive her role as something other than "mothering" because she is so often unavailable to them: "Sensing this [i.e., that she didn't give all a mother should], they had always called her by her first name" (66). Contradictorily, Emily is also determinedly convinced that she oversees her family; she is certain of her ability to perceive them at all times: "over the years, many hours of lying still on her bed, had distilled from [her] sensitivity a sixth sense, a tentacular awareness that reached out from the dimness, unseen and all-knowing" (66). Emily is protected from fully realizing how little parental authority she has by her own children: "Whenever Mrs. Tallis exercised authority in the absence of her husband, the children felt obliged to protect her from seeming ineffectual" (128). *She* is as a child to the children, who shield her from seeing the full extent of her ineffectiveness. Paradoxically, the children's careful maintenance of their mother's perception that she has authority *does* make Emily the family's central figure, but as someone vulnerable and needing their collective care instead of someone who is the family's presiding *caregiver*.

In *Atonement*, Briony, left too much to fend for herself and revel in her own imagination, represents the potential for unchecked children to destroy adult lives (in the same way that—as Bird explores—unruly children on bases can destroy the military careers of their parents). Briony "commit[s] her crime"—blaming the wrong man for Lola's rape—and Robbie, accused, goes to jail, losing the life he may have had as a medical student, and as Cecilia's lover. Robbie is conscripted into the war from prison. While fighting in France, Robbie hears that Briony may recant her testimony against him and "merely tasting the possibility reminded him how much had narrowed and died. His taste for life, no less, all the old ambitions and pleasures" (227). Briony tells tales as a child, but persists in literary invention as an adult: part three of *Atonement* reveals that perhaps what we have read in part two about Cecilia and Robbie's reunion is merely another one of Briony's fantasies and that instead "Robbie Turner died of septicaemia at Bray Dunes on 1 June, 1940 [and] that Cecilia was killed in September of the same year by the bomb that destroyed Balham Underground station" (370). McEwan gives us layer upon layer of loss: Briony lost to her own fantasies because she is left too much alone,

Robbie's life lost to young Briony's inaccurate testimony, and then the accurate story of Robbie and Cecilia's romance lost to adult Briony's rewritings of it.

It is as if in these fictions McEwan is describing the worst-case familial scenarios military life could provide, especially for children (and their victims). In *The Cement Garden* and *Atonement*, the father is absent, the mother becomes the center of the family, and then the mother is physically incapable of playing the role thrust upon her. The children are thus adrift without a center. In *Atonement*, parents absent themselves, leaving children to make consequential decisions on their own, and make them badly.

Both parents die in *The Cement Garden*, allowing McEwan to fully explore the ramifications of parental mortality (the flip side of a child's mortality or disappearance, which he explores in another of his novels, *The Child in Time*). They do not die in the service of their country, which makes their deaths seem disappointingly futile or "insignificant" (*The Cement Garden* 13). Nonetheless, McEwan depicts the scenario that the military children in Moser, Bird and MacDonald imagine: what it would be like if they were left to fend for their own needs.[10]

(Patriotic) Disenfranchisement

In chapter one, I consider the ways in which a third culture context can result in individuals who imagine that no place belongs to them, and that they have no right to claim affiliation with any place; in third culture literature, images not just of rootlessness but also of *rightlessness* proliferate, and this sense of having no right to lay claim to a place as "home" can, in turn, come with a sense of neither being required to take responsibility in any place nor to be a good citizen. In considering Moser, Bird, and MacDonald in the preceding part of this chapter, it becomes clear that military brat fiction represents a different spin. Characters are supposed to feel extremely responsible to their homeland, but identify instead with the parodies of "home" presented in the hyper-nationalist contexts of military bases: they "belong to" a construction of home they recognize as a fantasy while engaged in the defense project of protecting a "real" homeland with which they have a tenuous connection. In McEwan's novels, "patriotic disenfranchisement" manifests in two distinct ways. First, *The Cement Garden* and *Atonement* present faux–Englishness: in being English *qua* English, they suggest a simulacrum of national identity as one might find it on military bases. Second, and paradoxically, they present isolated characters who are detached from their nation, from *moral* responsibility to it, and from the *moral norms* that their nation might favor.

In the first section of *Atonement*, the Tallis family lives on an estate that evokes a quintessential English nineteenth-century gentility the family strives to embody in the twentieth century. In the second section, Robbie is a soldier at war in France: *dulce et decorum est*, as Wilfred Owen might have it. How patriotic it *seems*. Also in this section, Briony becomes a nurse tending to wounded soldiers in a London hospital—again, this *seems* like patriotism. And yet, Robbie is only at war because he has negotiated "an early release [from prison] in return for joining the infantry" (203), and Briony nurses to crowd out her own guilt: "She was happy to have little time to think of anything else" (277). Though the signifiers of patriotism are in place, these characters are neither motivated nor particularly enfranchised by it. Robbie wishes not to *win* the war but "to survive" it so that he can return to Cecilia (203); Briony unsuccessfully tries, not to save soldiers, but to keep herself from thinking of the lives she has already ruined (Robbie's and Cecilia's), for "when she stood on her landing in her dressing gown, last thing at night, and she looked across the river at the unlit city, she remembered the unease that was out there in the streets as well as in the wards, and was like the darkness itself. Nothing in her routine, not even Sister Drummond, could protect her from it" (277).

The Cement Garden's children don their very English school uniforms (including crisp white shirts) and head off to sports meetings, seeming Enid Blyton–esque in the model of English childhood they present. Popular and influential in terms of shaping in their young readers' minds the ideal models for being an *English* child, Blyton's *The Famous Five* and *The Secret Seven* (in which children have adventures and solve mysteries without adult help or oversight) had a vast readership. In fact, as Amy Rosenberg notes:

> British children had been devouring Blyton's work since the early 1920s. A poll recently conducted by one of the United Kingdom's most prestigious literary prizes, the Costa Book Awards, identified Blyton—who produced more than 700 books and 5,000 short stories during her 45-year career—as Britain's most beloved writer of all time, ranking her above Jane Austen (fourth), William Shakespeare (fifth), and Charles Dickens (sixth). (Two other children's writers, Roald Dahl and JK Rowling, ranked second and third, respectively.) Judging by sales figures alone, Blyton is adored not just by Britain, but by the entire world.
>
> Her books still sell more than eight million copies a year worldwide, for a running total of over 600 million copies sold. She's the fifth most translated author in the world (behind Shakespeare and before Lenin).
>
> What that means, of course, is that the majority of the kids reading Blyton in the second half of the 20th century were not British. In fact, most of them were the children of former British subjects.

Two: Adult Situations and Secret Perversions 107

Blyton's work creates and models a highly desirable Englishness enacted by small groups of children for overseas readers. Perhaps, once upon a time, young expat McEwan in Libya or Singapore was himself one of those readers. So, seeming to emulate Blyton's model, what one might call *The Cement Garden*'s "Secretive Four" solve mysteries (like what to do with their mother's corpse) and have sexual, incestuous *mis*adventures. In being Blyton-esque they seem, superficially, *very* English. McEwan takes a performative Englishness and quite literally perverts it. As in *Atonement*, then, *The Cement Garden* presents Englishness and what seems at first like enfranchisement (willingness to participate in English societal norms), only to reveal the detached isolation and disenfranchisement of its characters.

In these two novels, characters are motivated by personal, not national, concerns. *Atonement*'s Robbie is *de facto* leader of the remnants of his troop but contemplates abandoning them to save himself: "Perhaps it would make sense to leave now, before it was too late.... Slip away, leave the corporals to their fate" (203). He only stays because it is too dark to leave, not because he feels responsible to them or to the war: he "thought better of it. He could barely see the ground in front of him. He would make no progress in the dark and could easily break a leg" (203). Nurse Briony, despite tending grotesquely mutilated soldiers, remains obsessed with retelling the story of Cecilia and Robbie and submits a manuscript (*Two Figures by a Fountain*) narrativizing it for publication (311). In the helpfully editorial rejection letter, Briony is reminded of her own cover letter, sent with the manuscript, in which she must have acknowledged the detachment implied by writing about a summer day in the midst of an international conflict. The rejection letter notes, "You [Briony] apologise, in passing, for not writing about the war" (311). "In passing" is especially significant: though the war is mentioned, it does not overshadow Briony's insular, familial preoccupation.

The insularity and selfishness of *The Cement Garden*'s children is unmitigated by pretences of national service. What is most striking in this novel is the rejection of the nation's moral norms. Caught with a cadaver in the basement, and *in flagrante delicto*, siblings Julie and Jack are unrepentant. As police cars pull up outside, they unconcernedly discuss the last birthday party before their mother died, happily reminiscing: "We were not sad; we were excited and awed" (153). Tom, the youngest, who had been feigning sleep while Jack and Julie experimented with sex, "wakes up" as "the revolving blue light made a spinning pattern on the wall": "We crowded round the cot and Julie bent down and kissed him. 'There!' she said. 'Wasn't that a lovely sleep?'" (153). Tom's false sleep is celebrated, his witnessing of incest between his siblings is not a subject of concern, and the arrival of English law in the form of the police is unremarked upon, as though these children are simply not part of the legal and moral world outside their home.

Dodou argues that McEwan chooses to use children in his fiction in order to examine

> "English innocence" as an alibi in a spiral of increasing brutality. At stake here is partly what Robert Young calls "the idea of Britain as a moral nation," whose "particular power, responsibility and burden was the creation of global order and the administration of an impartial justice, based on a belief in fundamental English decency" [75].

In this construction, youth is supposedly analogous to innocence, just as Englishness is supposedly analogous to decency. Youthful Englishness *should* result, then, in guileless, responsible and moral behavior. However, McEwan — writing from a military childhood overseas in which children can find themselves in both adult and falsely hyper-nationalized military contexts — responds by giving his youths a preternaturally adult (self-) destructive agency and by making his nation's purported decency simply irrelevant to the pantomime of Englishness performed by his child characters. Jack and Julie challenge expectations: they repudiate the oft-reported powerlessness of children in military contexts (see MacDonald, Bird or Moser for fictional representations of powerless children responding in adult ways to their situations), and they stymie expectations of national identity by acting "English" while being demonstrably unfazed by the moral rectitude reputedly demanded by that national affiliation.

Zadie Smith observes that McEwan's stories do not include a "narrator who guides your judgement as you read"; there is no "judging consciousness" ("Ian McEwan" 118). In his characters, McEwan cultivates a national/moral remoteness typical of a third culture, military brat context. As in the work of Alison, Drew, Greenway and O'Neill (in chapter one) and also Bird, MacDonald and Moser, McEwan's cultural context fosters fiction in which his characters are notable for feeling that they don't belong, and that they don't owe anything to the place in which they live or people whom they live among. The fictional characters find themselves detached from nationality, as well as from the moral obligations that pertain to nationality.

McEwan notes that young voices in particular allow for "detachment," which is "useful rhetorically" in his fiction (Ménégaldo and Fortin 67). This explains some of the prevalence of young voices in his work. But if third culture and military brat contexts are remarkable for the effect they have on *children* in particular, and the maturing of those children into (patriotically) disenfranchised adults, then it is additionally unsurprising that McEwan, in exploring his cultural context, often includes children and adolescents. And, as he observes,

> My point of departure was to look for de-socialised, distorted versions of my own existence. Many of those early stories were like dreams about my own situation: they carried only a little biographical content, but they bore the same structural relationship to my own existence that a dream might. Often I understood this only long after a particular story was written [Ménégaldo and Fortin 67].

Perspective (being "long after") lets McEwan see how his cultural context inflects his early stories (like *The Cement Garden*), but it may be too early yet for McEwan himself to see that even his later novels (like *Atonement*) are affected. If his own formative experiences emerge symbolically in his writing "like dreams about [his] own situation," one can indeed see, as I argue above, that isolation in his novels refracts geographic dislocation; loss is symptomatic of a third culture, military brat context, and (patriotic) disenfranchisement indicates a military upbringing.

Secrecy, Guilt and Sex

In third culture literature one often sees dislocation, loss, disenfranchisement and secretive guilt (see my discussion of Alison, Drew, Greenway and O'Neill in chapter one). In other words, third culture novels present features of postcolonial writing (international contexts and repeated relocations with accompanying, sometimes devastating, loss), but add new features, chief among which are characters' detachment from the politics of both host countries and passport nation, and their distinctive guilt about expatriate privilege. The latter lends itself to plots in which characters perceive themselves as secretly to blame for brutal disasters that lead to the deaths of others. International experiences are rendered as fabulous but disordered snapshots that, with their bright vividness, conceal disorientation and darker feelings of culpability. Privilege, "exquisite loss" (to use Drew's vocabulary) and guilt all come hand-in-hand. In the military brat subset of third culture literature, these four key categories emerge with slight variations (see my discussion of Bird, MacDonald and Moser). These are dislocation (which still reflects mobility, but can also imply the mobility experienced by moving frequently from base to base within a single nation) loss, patriotic disenfranchisement (implying the oxymoron of detachment in the context of a national armed force) and sexual perversity (which in Moser includes sexually active youths, and in Bird and MacDonald includes pedophilia). In treating McEwan's work, I utilize the subheadings of the fourth characteristic of both third culture literature generally ("secrecy and guilt") *and* military brat writing ("sexual perversity") because in *Atonement* one sees sexual perversity (in the form of Paul Marshall's rape of adolescent Lola), but it is overshadowed by tattle-tale and liar Briony's secretive guilt (as in third culture literature generally); in *The Cement Garden* one sees sexual perversity *without* guilt (as is more common in military brat writing).

In *The Cement Garden*, lack of affiliation outside the family means no obligation to external codes of moral conduct. The children create their own "laws" of behavior. Between Jack and Julie, the sexual act is guiltless and guileless (though McEwan's unsparing account, lacking what Zadie Smith calls a "judging consciousness," is acutely discomfiting to read). Told from Jack's perspective: "I rolled onto my back and Julie, still laughing, sat astride me, took hold of my penis and pulled it into her" (151). Eventually the two "giggle and [forget] what we were about" (152). The children are lighthearted. McEwan contrasts Jack and Julie's moral ease with the disgust of Julie's boyfriend Derek on finding the siblings copulating: "'It's sick,' he said loudly, 'he's your *brother*'" (150). Derek is part of a moral world external to that of the parentless, isolated children. Julie cautions him, "Talk quietly Derek ... or you'll wake Tom up," revealing that not only is she unrepentantly betraying him by copulating with her oldest brother, but her youngest brother is there to bear witness as well (150). Derek is further revulsed: "'Sick!' [He] repeated, and the bedroom door slammed shut" (150). Julie "locked the door and leaned against it," literally shutting out the outside world's assessment (150).

The interaction between Jack and Julie can be read as an extreme expression of third culture detachment from the moral norms or obligations connected to specific nations. However, it is also an expression of the challenge to social hierarchy often seen in military brat writing. If military contexts are characterized by strict rules and hierarchies to which dependent children must unquestioningly adhere, Jack and Julie signify a consummate (and consummated) challenge to both rules and social order. The sexual interaction can happen because order has fallen apart: there are no "real" parents here, no one is "really" in charge, but the two youths playact the roles of mother and father in bed together. They assume a most adult agency in choosing to have sex with each other, and yet it is in play. Like Phil and El (*Skinny Dipping*), or Fumiko or Bernie (*The Yokota Officers Club*), Jack and Julie are laughing as they go about their business. But theirs is a carnival day of incest, not a permanent or far-reaching dismantling of social and moral order, for as they finish the police arrive to definitively end their foray into pretend adulthood.

Though not biologically related, *Atonement*'s Robbie and Cecilia are also *de facto* siblings. Robbie Turner is the "only son of a humble cleaning lady"; he "had been subsidised by Briony's father through school and university, had wanted to be a landscape gardener and now wanted to take up medicine" (38). "Subsidised" by the Tallis family, and growing up among them, he is an adopted son to the household. The lovemaking between Robbie and Cecilia requires them to overcome an incestuous closeness: "That they were old friends who had shared a childhood was now a barrier" (134). Coitus is an act of defamiliarization: "At last they were strangers, their pasts forgotten" (136). Their lovemaking reads as a quelling of their own fears that they have transgressed a significant boundary:

> The son of Grace and Ernest Turner, the daughter of Emily and Jack Tallis, the childhood friends, the university acquaintances, in a state of expansive, tranquil joy, confronted the momentous change they had achieved. The closeness of a familiar face was not ludicrous, it was wondrous.

As in *The Cement Garden*, the lovemaking between "siblings" is ultimately presented as positive and guiltlessly immoral, although Robbie and Cecilia have to work at overcoming their feelings of being too closely related to be lovers. Their lovemaking translates a military brat challenge to military hierarchy into class terms—Cecilia (moneyed) loves Robbie (the son of her cleaning lady). As in *The Cement Garden*, in *Atonement* the challenge to mandated order happens within the very close confines of family life.

Briony in *Atonement* is like Derek from *The Cement Garden* in that she sees the lovemaking and judges what she has seen. Unlike Derek (a complete outsider), Briony is part of the family. This explains some of the vehemence of her reaction. As many children might when catching elders "in the act," she thinks she has seen something violent: "her immediate understanding was that she had interrupted an attack, a hand-to-hand fight" (123). But Briony has a story in her mind already, based on her interception of Robbie's crudely lustful letter to Cecilia. She imagines herself as "her sister's protector" (123). What she sees reaffirms her position as an isolated child in a closed, peculiar world (like a child in a military context might be). Briony therefore challenges order and empowers herself in the only way made available to her: she wrongfully accuses Robbie of raping Lola. Deprived of the sexual agency that might make her feel more adult and powerful, Briony adopts authorial agency: "Her words summoned awful powers" (169).

Briony spends the rest of the novel (and her life) rewriting Robbie and Cecilia's relationship and secretively, guiltily, making amends for her lie. But the fact remains that the lie which disempowered Robbie and

Cecilia gave Briony agency — the ultimate agency, in fact, as she creates the narrative that describes all of their lives. As she muses, later in life,

> The problem these fifty-nine years has been this: how can a novelist achieve atonement when, with her absolute power of deciding outcomes, she is also God? There is no one, no entity or higher form she can appeal to, or be reconciled with, or that can forgive her [371].

If the Tallis family on its estate is like a military base in its inhabitants' experience of isolation, loss, disenfranchisement and sexual perversity, Briony is like a military brat in her efforts to resist the rigid, eccentric, adult laws of a closed community, by means of adopting adult agency (in this case, not by engaging in a sexual act, but rather by describing the rape of someone else and, by making herself an author, assuming power).

The emphasis on family life, and on sexual interactions within the family, suggests the significance of Oedipal issues in McEwan's novels. The recurrence of children engaged in sexual activity in the work of Moser, Bird and MacDonald suggests that what McEwan's work can teach us is the broader significance of Oedipal issues in the writings of former military brats.

Oedipus Militem

> In the Theban tragedy of Oedipus, King Laius banishes his infant son Oedipus because of a prophecy that the son will kill the father. During a chance encounter, Oedipus kills his father without knowing Laius' identity, then marries his victim's wife Jocasta, without knowing she is his mother. Oedipus's discovery of his guilt of parricide and incest causes him to blind himself and flee....
>
> According to the explanation offered by [Freud's] theory of the Oedipus complex, the sexual development of boys and girls differs, although both begin by desiring the mother, their first love-object, who is seen as all-powerful and capable of fulfilling the desires of the child. Eventually the boy child begins to see the father as sexual rival for the mother, but, being small and relatively helpless, he fears castration by the father as punishment for his unacceptable desires and represses them, later to transfer them onto other women when he reaches puberty [Green and LeBihan 154].

Consider the military context: the father (sometimes excessively dictatorial and militant with his family) is often away; the mother is left in charge (but the isolation and responsibility are sometimes overwhelming); the children relocate frequently, so that their closest — indeed, only — sustained and continuous relationships are with each other and their mother. It is a combination of factors that, if one holds with Oedipal theories, seems ripe for exaggerated Oedipal responses, which indeed (if one examines the incest and precocious sexuality of the children in the literature in this chapter) manifest in striking ways.

A significant feature of military life is control: the organization controls serving individuals and their dependants, who are in turn expected to control themselves by obeying rules more stringent than those in the civilian world. Controlling their emotions is one of the ways in which servicemen and -women and their dependants sacrifice themselves in order to serve their country. In his introduction to psychoanalysis, Terry Eagleton writes, "We are prepared to put up with repression as long as we see something in it for us; if too much is demanded of us, however, we are likely to fall sick. This form of sickness is known as neurosis" (152). For military parents, serving their country is "what's in it for them." For military children, however, a lot, and often too much, is demanded. One can speculate that this results in neuroses, specifically in terms of disruptions to Oedipal identity formation within the family.

Frances and Gale write that the military child is "used to having his needs met within the family, which makes individuation and Oedipal issues more complicated" (in Wertsch 189). Familial isolation and the absence of the father figure can have a heightened effect on military sons. As Wertsch puts it, "Oedipal struggles are not meant to be won," but yet, by virtue of the military father's frequent absences, a son *can* perceive himself as having won, if not his mother's bed, then at least his father's role as man of the house: "The father's abdication puts [the son] in the psychologically dangerous position of *winning* the Oedipal struggle — not by 'killing' the father and 'sleeping with' the mother, but by taking over the place in his mother's life the father should by rights occupy" (190). Wertsch imagines a displacement of the Oedipal struggle into familial *roles* (the son takes the missing father's place as husband).

McEwan presents the Oedipal struggle (the son kills the father and then sleeps with the mother) quite literally in *The Cement Garden*. He gives us Jack, whose masturbation coincides with his father's death, suggesting that symbolically the son *has* killed the father (23); Julie, who assumes the leadership (if not exactly nurturing) role of mother after both parents have died (61); and Jack and Julie engaging in sex, the son thereby assuming the role of the father in "sleeping with" his mother. Oedipal issues also emerge in *Atonement*: Jack Tallis is frequently absent. When Emily retreats to her room because of migraines, Cecilia takes her role as head of the household. Robbie, in seducing Cecilia, copulates with both sibling and mother figure. But Briony also strives for the role of mother in the family. Robbie had been, at one time, Briony's childhood crush: Briony throws herself into a weir to get him to rescue her, and then, once rescued, confesses to him, "I love you" (232). Coitus between Robbie and Cecilia, while momentarily empowering to them, is profoundly disempowering to onlooking Briony, as it reaffirms that she is *not* mother figure to Robbie as father/lover.

As McEwan writes it in *The Cement Garden* and *Atonement*, expressing the atmosphere rather than actual conditions of military contexts, military brat–type isolation and disenfranchisement, including detachment from moral norms, lead to what is literally incestuous closeness between siblings. The incest in these novels is guilt-free, as the taboos of the nation do not apply to the closed community the family creates in and of itself. If one follows Lacan's elaboration of Freudian psychoanalytic theory, the incest McEwan presents is additionally fascinating. Eagleton explains Lacan: "The father signifies what Lacan calls the Law, which is in the first place the social taboo on incest" (164). In a military context, the father enforces the Law, and all laws, with heightened authoritarianism, inflexibility and aggression (think back to Pat Conroy, and to Duvall's Oscar-winning violence in the film of *The Great Santini*). The military father, when home, is the Law to an extreme extent. *But* the military father is often away, which means the Law may simply not be enforced. Thus the Oedipal contest can be won when the father is away (the son takes his father's place) *and* taboos regarding things like incest are also disregarded when the father and his Law are absent.

The fact that incest intersects with Oedipus in both McEwan novels is striking: in both the lovers are brother-sister *and* son-mother simultaneously. This suggests that there is more than meets the eye about the pleasure that the lovers in these novels experience. The daughters (Julie and Cecilia) are already role-playing as mothers. The pleasure comes, at least in part, from the sexual act that lets them play at power, and gives the sons/brothers (Jack and Robbie) power too as they become father figures. For both Julie and Cecilia, the assumption of a mother-lover role is a carnivalesque moment; for neither is it a permanent change. Julie giggles as she dismounts, becoming a girl again. Cecilia composes herself for dinner. The sexual act disrupts order fleetingly, and then the (albeit odd and dysfunctional) status quo returns. In some respects this makes the sexual acts even more distressing to read. They should, with utmost pathetic fallacy, rupture the worlds in which they take place, and yet they do not. There are no thunderbolts, the sky does not fall, and facile chit-chat resumes.

Reading *Skinny Dipping* through the lens of Oedipus, the Law, and McEwan, Phil's sexual act, though not incestuous, becomes a challenge to his father's authority, to military authority and to family order. By becoming sexually active at age thirteen, he challenges his father's role: the father should be the adult, sexually active male in the family, not the son. By engaging in sexual activity with El, Phil symbolically emasculates his father. In *The Yokota Officers Club*, Bernie's dancing is neither actually sexual nor incestuous. But if, according to Freud, the girl initially recognizes her genitalia as "lacking" and seeks to compensate (Green and LeBihar 155), then Bernie's dancing like Lovely Assistant (the Okinawan woman giving the python a blow job) does just that: she mimes the actions that would give her the snake/phallus. This, too, displaces the father's Law and authority, as well as masculinist military Law. In *The Way the Crow Flies*, Marjorie and Grace rape Claire with a corn cob: they claim a phallus and use it. Though not incest, this is extremely aberrant behavior and it also displaces the Law of father/military organization.

In each of these texts by former military brats, children's sexual activity challenges the order of the family (Law) and the order of the military. But when Oedipus kills Laius in the myth, Laius stays dead: the father (and his Law) do not come back. Oedipus subsequently punishes himself by blinding himself. These fictional texts, however, show Oedipus as ultimately unsuccessful in killing the father, and also as punished by him: the children cannot retain the adult positions they claim for themselves and military Law is re-imposed. It is as if Oedipus merely concussed his father— but imagine the consequences. Laius, were he to wake, would surely punish his son most severely for both his sexual transgressions and the attempted murder. Likewise, in the fiction writing of former military brats, the return of the Law (father/military) does not herald a return to normalcy but rather the crushing reenlistment of the children under a new, even more severe version of their father's order; they now adhere to an even stricter new Law. That children's sexual activity *incompletely* wins the Oedipal contest is devastating, for they have tried and lost, falling back to a more repressed and damaging position than the one from which they started.

The Doors' Jim Morrison was a military brat, as Wertsch notes; his father was a U.S. naval officer. "The End" provides a quintessentially Oedipal lyric: "'Father?' 'Yes, son.' 'I want to kill you. Mother ... I want to Fuck You!'" (Wertsch 192). Apparently Morrison once performed this song with his mother in the audience, and sang it directly to her, drawing out the final syllables to grotesque effect. The vehemence of Morrison's challenge, like the vividness of perversion in the fiction texts in this chapter, emphasizes that a military brat cultural context is not a blandly international or intranational one: if these writings are artistic responses, they are responses to a cultural context whose egregious difficulty for dependant children is generally not acknowledged, but from which extremes of violent resistance emerge, as well as troubling intimations that resistance is indeed futile.

CHAPTER THREE

When Your Parents Work for God: The Fiction Writing of Former Missionary Kids

Nobel Prize winner Pearl S. Buck's novel *The Good Earth* (1931) is canonized as a "classic" literary text: the copy I have in front of me is in fact a 2009 "Simon & Schuster *Enriched Classic*" (their emphasis), which boasts on its back jacket that it provides "enduring literature illuminated by practical scholarship." The text has earned "enduring" recognition, even if it has been "ignored by literary critics of almost every decade since its publication" (412). It occupies the paradoxical position of being well known as a title and seldom read, especially by contemporary readers. That Buck was the daughter of American missionaries in China (making her a "missionary kid") is widely known. *The Good Earth*, then, is a piece of writing that rests its reputational laurels on the fact that it is by a former missionary kid: Buck's experience in China legitimates her knowledge and discussion of a Chinese peasant family's rise to landowner status. In the novel, Buck makes no mention of missionaries or Americans, but rather writes from a Chinese perspective. Nonetheless, her text is imbued with the ultimate third culture fantasy: belonging to a place. Wang Lung experiences good fortune when he is working "the good earth": "He belonged to the land and he could not live with any fullness until he felt the land under his feet" (129). When the wealthy Hwang family meets their economic downfall, Wang Lung surmises, "It comes of their leaving the land" (165). Wang Lung's *house* is even part of the land: "the kitchen was made of earthen bricks as the house was, great squares of earth dug from their own fields" (2). The land sustains, the house is made from the land (it also sustains) and the inhabitants of the house are rooted in both the edifice and the land itself. This is the fantasy Buck extends over her famous novel's 385 pages.

Fame is a feature that most third culture literature *does not* enjoy. Indeed, part of the goal of writing this book is to provide a vocabulary for literature that too often fails to be recognized because of the ambiguous national identifications of its authors. Not so with the literature of former missionary kids (a subgroup of third culture literature). Here one sees a proliferation of commercial success: Frank Schaeffer's *Portofino* and its film adaptation starring John Lithgow, for instance, or the more than forty books and films of paperback thriller author Ted Dekker (only one of which I will treat here), or romance writer Catherine Palmer (again, I'll treat only one of her thirty-plus texts here). The big commercial successes of Dekker, William Paul Young (whose only major publication, *The Shack*, was, according to Nielsen, the top-selling fiction and audio book in America in 2008), and Palmer come in mass-market paperback formats.

Mass-market paperbacks tend to be classified according to genre: thriller, romance, mystery, and so forth. Conversely, *trade* paperbacks tend to classify as either "fiction" or "nonfiction" and then consider authors in terms of where they are from. Mass-market paperbacks are, in some respects, "disposable" plot-driven reads printed on cheap paper. Pricier trade paperbacks get reviewed in the *London Review of Books*; they are, as the *New York Times*' Elsa Dixler writes, "the novels that reading groups choose and college professors teach." Importantly, in regard to the commercial success of former missionary kids in the mass-market paperback market, trade paperbacks might promote an "Australian fiction writer" but mass-market paperbacks might promote a "thriller writer" instead. Thus former missionary kids can perhaps more easily reach prominence in mass-market paperback fiction formats that do not demand their national identification, and so their internationalized upbringings do not complicate the marketing of their books. That there is an abundance of former missionary kids who have become best-selling mass-market paperback authors inclines one to speculate that the extremities of missionary kid experience provide an especially rich background for mass-market genres. In this chapter I will first treat *trade* paperback fiction by former missionary kids: Catherine Palmer's one non-romance offering, *The Happy Room*, Paula Nangle's linked short story collection *The Leper Compound* and Richard Lewis' *The Flame Tree*. I will then examine two mass-market paperback bestsellers: William Paul Young's *The Shack* and Ted Dekker's *BoneMan's Daughters*.

It is striking that, of all the subgenres under the umbrella of "third culture literature," fiction produced by former missionary kids displays lurid violence, fear and illness, but *not* sexual abuse, despite sexual abuse or impropriety appearing extensively in the works described in chapters one and two. American and European churches are frequently in the news for abuses of minors, and it appears that in missionary contexts, and especially in mission boarding schools, abuses are equally, if not more, prevalent. The October 2010 "Final Report of the Independent Review Panel of the Presbyterian Church (USA)" runs to 546 pages despite the fact that it only covers alleged abuses in American Presbyterian missions overseas between 1970 and 2010 (Evinger, Whitfield, and Wiley). Missionary Kids Safety Net (*www.mksafetynet.net*) provides links to analogous investigations of and reports about the missions of the Christian and Missionary Alliance, United Methodist Church and the New Tribes Mission. In 2008 that same organization asserted that "missionary kids from 21 other Christian denominations [i.e., other than the Christian and Missionary Alliance] and mission-sending organizations have reported child abuse occurring at countless missionary boarding schools" (*All God's Children* closing comments). The documentary *All God's Children* (2008) (an official selection in the 2008 Sarasota Film Festival) chronicles the experiences of children sent to one West African mission boarding school (Mamou, in Guinea), only to be abused there by mission teachers. It is a glaring and consistent omission that, in the fiction texts I study in this chapter, children suffer other abuses at boarding schools or places that are symbolically equivalent to boarding school, but those abuses are everything *but* sexual.

In the books I treat below, children are abandoned, frightened, malnourished, isolated from family, abducted, circumcised against their will (years beyond infancy and without anesthetic), tortured by serial killers, and killed. But they are not sexually abused. Children are, in this third chapter, as in chapters one and two, significant and predominant characters in the literature of former missionary kids. Third culture is a result of being outside one's passport home (first culture), an outsider in a foreign place (second culture), and part of a community of expatriates (third culture) *while a child*. In military contexts and life "on base," there is a tightly enclosed community of fellow dependant expatriate transients with which military brats come to identify. By contrast, in missionary contexts families are generally isolated from other mission families and also from other expatriates. For children, their peers are thus the local children, and there is much more interaction with the host culture than in the case of military children, or even children of diplomats or business people (who tend to reside in larger towns and cities with expatriate communities and schools). There are missionaries who homeschool or allow their elementary-school-aged children to attend local schools, but most middle- or high-school-aged children are sent to boarding schools. On the one hand, those (typically younger) children who do not go to mission boarding schools suffer from isolation, difficult living conditions and, frequently, the hostility of their parents' potential converts; fictional renderings depict these conditions as abuses. On the other hand, there are the mission schools, which, for the children sent to them (typically older, though sometimes as young as age six), mean complete immersion in a world of expatriate children, and complete isolation from their parents.

In order to fully dedicate themselves to their calling, missionaries are often *required* to send their school-aged children to regional boarding schools that are frequently hundreds of miles away. For the Christian and Missionary Alliance, for instance, there was one school in Guinea that served *all* of West Africa until the mid–1960s, after which another school was opened in the Ivory Coast. If you had children over the age of six and did mission work for the C&MA in Nigeria, Togo or Ghana, your children would be required to make the trek to one of these distant regional boarding schools. Once there, they would not see you again for months, possibly even for the entire school year.

That the sending away of children is demanded of many missionary parents is a source of tremendous conflict for missionary children. Parents are asked to prove their faith by *sacrificing* their children and children are required to accept that they have been sacrificed. The subtitle of *All God's Children* is "*The Ultimate Sacrifice.*" Within minutes of the documentary's start, Beverly Shellrude Thompson explains that the central metaphor of Christianity is the father sacrificing his son. As Richard Darr adds, "Missionaries emulate God in sending their sons and daughters to boarding school.... It makes them into heroes" (*All God's Children*). The church looms as the organizational force behind mission life, demanding that missionary kids ricochet between two extremes: isolation from the expatriate world while accompanying their parents on mission, or complete isolation from their parents and the host community with which they may have formed bonds. The church mandates that they be tertiary to their parents' objectives: they are given away, symbolic sacrifices to God.

In *Theories of Adolescence*, Rolf E. Muuss asks:

> What are the crucial processes that make [frequent] transition smooth or problematic? In the case of the frequently relocated Army officer, the overall well-being of the family microsystem seems to play a major role in determining whether such an ecological [cf. Bronfenbrenner's four ecological systems[1]] transition is smooth, difficult or traumatic [334].

Certainly in *The Yokota Officers Club* or *Atonement* (chapter two), or even *Natives and Exotics* or *White Ghost Girls* (chapter one), authors explore what happens to adolescents undergoing transitions when the family microsystem is dysfunctional as a result of parental disengagement and/or absence: children are required to comport themselves as adults and respond inappropriately by adopting adult sexuality. For missionary kids, even more than in the army family Muuss alludes to, the family microsystem is significant and unusual, as it includes God: all members of the family "are God's children," including the parents. And the parents' mission work is indivisible from the family. Parents and children all work explicitly for God, and children are conscripted into mission work to please both their parents and, more onerously, God himself.

In his 1986 *It's OK to Be an MK*, a text that analyzes data from surveys sent to missionaries and their children, William C. Viser observes that "MKs [missionary kids] are closely identified with the work of their parents" and are typically expected to be involved in furthering their parents' mission even from a young age (85, 86ff). He continues:

> When I sent out the survey worldwide to my missionary colleagues asking them if they involved their children in their work, 83 percent responded yes, 15 percent no, and 2 percent were unsure.
>
> Many mentioned over and over again that their children were involved as "door openers." Through their interest in them as light-skinned, blond-haired children, their parents were able to witness. It reminds me so much of Isaiah 11:6, "A little child shall lead them" [89].

While all third culture kids, including military brats, are aware of themselves as outsiders, the parents of missionary kids "over and over again" *exploit* their children's visible differences from their host culture: children are used as God bait by their parents. This seems, to return to Muuss, to raise the potential for dysfunction in the family microsystem quite dramatically. Missionary children are made extremely aware that they are so far outside the culture of their host country that they are curiosities. They are useful because their Western appearance intrigues potential converts; they are aware that they must perform their whiteness in just the right way, in order to help, not harm, God himself.[2] Devout missionary parents quite literally require their children to perform, to be the "door openers" for faith. Children are exploited for "the greater good" by their own parents (a dysfunction, or at least distortion, of family dynamics) and then, often, are sent to school: having done their work, they are sent far away, abruptly removed from the attentions of parents, mission and perhaps even God himself. This is a difficult transition for children, made more complicated by God's interposition in the family and by familial distortions/dysfunctions in the service of God. It is hard to reconcile "the greater good" with the exploitation of children or with parents setting their own children aside in order to prioritize God.

In the literature of former missionary kids, one often sees characters imagining the world as it might be, rather than as it is. In particular, the fictions tend to imagine a "greater good" in which parents want to love their children, or want to be forgiven for failures to protect them. To return to houses, one sees the extent to which Buck's house (a sanctuary made from the earth itself) is a fantasy of the protection and safety children should feel while "at home" with their parents. More frequently, the houses in literature by former missionary kids offer a pretence of security but suffer significant flaws, making the inhabitants unusually, even excessively, vulnerable: the parent-as-house fails to protect the child inhabitants. Paranoid imaginings centering on home (the actual edifice) as susceptible to attack and unable to protect the individual, or root them in a location, abound in the literature of former missionary kids. Another way the house fails as a home is that the child is required to leave it: children are sent from their already insufficiently protective home to a boarding school, or a facsimile of one, in which the adults not only fail to protect their charges but also actively victimize them. Houses represent what should be (but is not) parental protection; boarding schools represent what happens when children's parents have abandoned them in God's name. In documentary accounts of mission boarding schools (as in *All God's Children*), children are often sexually abused by teachers or boarding house staff; in fiction, the issue of sexual abuse is overwhelmed and replaced by that of parental abandonment and its complex religious logistics. In the fiction of former missionary kids, children ask such questions as the following: Have I been abandoned by my parents, or by God? Is this God's will, or my parents'? How can I be happy in fulfilling God's will if it causes me so much grief? Who is responsible for my well-being: my parents or God? Why am I not being taken care of?

In chapter one I present four key characteristics in third culture literature: dislocation, loss, disenfranchisement and secretive guilt. In chapter two, which focuses on the literature of former military brats, I nuance these four characteristics so they become dislocation (acknowledging that multiple moves in the military are not always international, but produce a third culture experience nonetheless), loss, disenfranchisement (despite one's family being deployed in defense of one's passport nation), and, instead of guilt, hierarchy-challenging sexual perversity. In this chapter, with its focus on the literature of former missionary kids, one sees the categories nuanced again: In common with both preceding chapters, one sees dislocation, loss and disenfranchisement. But where in third culture literature generally one sees secretive guilt (chapter one), and in the literature of former military brats one sees sexual perversity (chapter two), in the literature of former missionary kids one sees a strikingly different fourth characteristic: children who are sick or damaged (seemingly embodying, and suffering from, the sacrifice that their parents make by going on mission).

In this chapter I will use a structure similar to that of chapters one and two: first establishing and analyzing a (sub)genre of third culture literature (in this case, the literature of former missionary kids) and then examining a significant, high-profile anomaly that actually fits the genre quite well (in chapter one, this was O'Neill's *Netherland*; in chapter two, McEwan's *The Cement Garden* and *Atonement*). Thus, in this chapter, I deal first with Catherine Palmer's *The Happy Room*, Richard Lewis' *The Flame Tree* and Paula Nangle's *The Leper Compound* in order to characterize and analyze the literature of former missionary kids. I then consider two high-profile (apparent) anomalies to show how they fit the genre — in this case mass-market best-sellers by Ted Dekker (*BoneMan's Daughters*) and William Paul Young (*The Shack*).

Palmer's novel *The Happy Room* tells of the experiences of three former missionary siblings raised in Kenya, now adults repatriated (with varying degrees of success) to the United States of, roughly, the 1990s. Of the two daughters, Julia (married with children of her own, and pregnant) initially seems fairly well adjusted. It is only in confrontation with her now relatively elderly parents (who have retired from mission work but are still extremely active in church work) that Julia's unresolved issues with her childhood, and her experiences in a missionary boarding school in Kenya, surface. The brother, Peter, who at heart wants to be a Maasai warrior, experiences a plethora of problems in his adult life, including difficulty sustaining a relationship with the mother of his young son. The youngest daughter, Debbie, suffers from anorexia, is hospitalized for it (a period during which Peter and Julia recognize that her ailment has some connection with the dislocations of their upbringing and their vulnerability both at home and at school) and dies. This occasions oddly restorative conflict between siblings Julia and Peter and their parents.

Paula Nangle's collection of linked short stories, *The Leper Compound*, takes as its topic a white family in Rhodesia (the deceased mother of the family was there in the first place because she was a missionary). Nangle's own missionary kid upbringing infuses her reflections on white Rhodesians with the sense of dislocation, loss and disenfranchisement typical of third culture literature, as well as with other characteristic hallmarks of the literature of former missionary kids in which the children are sacrificed to the parents' objectives. One follows the life of Colleen from her unguarded home on a coffee plantation with her father and sister in an increasingly anti-white area to a boarding school in the city. Colleen gets sick with malaria; her sister suffers from schizophrenia. When Rhodesia becomes

Zimbabwe in 1979–1980, Colleen leaves Rhodesia for South Africa, and there she becomes the adult sacrificing a sick infant by suffocating it with a pillow ("there had been a sacrifice") (158).

Richard Lewis' *The Flame Tree* chronicles the experiences of Isaac, the American son of missionary doctors who work at a hospital annexed to a mission boarding school on the Indonesian island of Java. Lewis mentions that *The Flame Tree* was written for an adult audience ("Richard Lewis," Bookbrowse); however, because of its child protagonist, it has been marketed as juvenile literature (as is the case with Yann Martel's *The Life of Pi*). This publication quirk indicates, again, how awkwardly uncategorizeable third culture texts currently are. It is easier to market a novel as *juvenile* literature than to figure out how to market its complexly international plot and author in an adult market that typically demands to know where its authors are "from." Isaac lives through the rise of Islamic militants connected with Osama bin Laden, the Indonesian reaction to the 9/11 attacks, and rising anti–American sentiment: he experiences outsider status on the grounds of both his passport nationality and his faith. His parents are Christian missionaries but for a time he is unwillingly incarcerated in a madrasah. His experiences are also paralleled with those of his Muslim, Indonesian peer, the almost too-revealingly named Ismail (suggesting the biblical pairing of Ishmael and Isaac, as well as Abraham's near sacrifice of Isaac, his son, to God).

Then there are the two paperback best-sellers, both with roughly contemporary settings (early 2000s). First, William Paul Young's *The Shack*, which describes a father's response to the abduction of his young daughter by "the ladybug killer." Four years after the abduction, Mack, the father, receives what seems to be a note from God, inviting him back to the (titular) shack in which his daughter's dead body was recovered. Mack goes, and proceeds to have an encounter with God, Jesus, and the Holy Spirit in which theological conundrums are explained and Mack is expunged of his guilt. Through his daughter Missy's death, Mack eventually understands his faith: in some respects she is sacrificed in order for him to be "saved." God takes over as father, redeeming Mack. The shack itself, like the houses in Nangle, Lewis and Palmer, seems indicative of parental inadequacy, but in Young, when Mack encounters God, it is remade as a dream-haven in which God (the ultimate father, or, as the novel would have it, "Papa") resides.

Finally, Ted Dekker's *BoneMan's Daughters*, a text I originally picked from among the plethora of Dekker offerings on the basis of the fact that, as DeWayne Hamby points out, *BoneMan's Daughters* and *The Shack* have uncannily similar covers (both depicting a decrepit farmhouse/barn). *Bone-*

Man's Daughters was a fortuitous discovery, for in this text the former missionary kid idiom of a child sacrificed to the parent's goals is investigated in military terms: Ryan's abandonment of his daughter Bethany in order to serve in Iraq. What follows allows Dekker to explore the ramifications of failing to adequately parent a child (and the extent to which a child can feel lost/abandoned) as well as a father's belated effort to prove his love for his daughter by rescuing her, at great bone-breaking and dramatic cost to his own health and safety, from the BoneMan. Dekker's novel presents a fantasy, like that in *The Shack*, of the father being able to absolve himself of guilt.

All of these novels feature parents with preoccupations (God, farming, patriotism); all feature a child or children abandoned or sacrificed by his/her parents so that the parents can fulfill an obligation perceived as more important. All are influenced by the missionary cultural context of their authors. Palmer, Nangle, Lewis, Young and Dekker were all raised overseas by missionary parents. To establish the similarity of their culture (expatriate, mobile, missionary), it is necessary to spend some time with the biography of each author.

Of her life, Palmer notes, "I grew up as the daughter of missionaries. When I was three years old, we served in East Pakistan (now Bangladesh). When I was seven, we began serving in Kenya. I moved to the United States for college" ("Catherine Palmer Answers"). In other words, Palmer spent four years of her childhood in what is now Bangladesh and the remaining eleven in Kenya. Palmer spent a total of *fifteen* years outside her American "home" during her developmental years. In another interview, Palmer states, "Of all the settings in my romance novels, I'm most in love with Africa. That's where I grew up, and my heart will always belong to Kenya" ("Catherine Palmer," *Focus on Fiction*). Perhaps most intriguing is the extent to which other former missionary kids (MKs, or adult missionary kids, AMKs) claim Palmer's authenticity on the basis of *The Happy Room*. As Dan Elyea writes in a review of *The Happy Room*, "Catherine Palmer is *one of us*. Only an AMK from Africa could have written this book. It shows the touch of one who has 'been there and done that'" (emphasis added). Elyea is clear that Palmer's novel is not an outsider's imagining of what it would be like to be raised by missionaries, but rather an insider perspective. Similarly, Donia "fivefishsticks" reviews *The Happy Room* for Amazon.com:

> Having graduated from the same missionary boarding school [the Rift Valley Academy] as Palmer, but over a decade later (I think), our experiences were quite different. Although we still ate from metal trays in the 1980's, there were neither metal fragments or worms in our cafeteria

meals [*sic*]. This barely fictional account vividly describes the wonder and beauty some of us found as children in Africa, while candidly portraying the inner conflict felt by many missionaries and their children as a balance is sought between "God's work" and what is best for the family ["*The Happy Room*, Review"].

Again, the emphasis is on substantiation: *The Happy Room*, both Elyea and "fivefishsticks" assert, does not represent a far-fetched fantasy but rather something that resonates clearly with other adult missionary kids as a plausible, almost documentary-like, expression of the experience of being a child raised by missionaries in Africa.

The Leper Compound's book jacket tells its readers that "Paula Nangle was raised by missionaries in the U.S. and Southern Africa and now lives in Benton Harbor, Michigan where she works as a psychiatric nurse." This is the standard blurb for Nangle's biography; it is the most typical tagline in reviews (for Amazon.com and the like) trying to pin down her national identity. Nangle's internationalism is domesticated (she "now lives in Benton Harbor"), which reduces the significance of her Southern African upbringing to accreditation: by virtue of some vague association with Rhodesia/Zimbabwe, Nangle is qualified to write about it. But this is an upbringing whose importance, Nangle herself intimates, suggests that "living in the United States after Africa also requires, even demands, a certain renouncement of all things once familiar" ("Nangle Press Kit"). Nangle, at least in the eyes of publishers and reviewers, is an American with some travel experience. But Nangle's regretful acknowledgment of her "renouncement of all things once familiar" suggests a far more influential loss. In *The Leper Compound*'s linked stories, Nangle explores her experience of Zimbabwe's move to independence, considering "what could have happened differently and under what circumstances" ("Nangle Press Kit"). What is ostensibly renounced here is her personal "culture" (the experience of growing up as a missionary kid), so that settled, white Rhodesian farming culture can be examined in some detail. Fascinatingly, what emerges in spite of Nangle's careful omission of biographical material are literary elements common to texts produced by others who share her culture (in other words, texts produced by former missionary kids): dislocation, loss, boarding school, children sacrificed to their parents' goals, and sick children literally suffering from their parents' choices.

Of Lewis, Simon & Schuster writes, "Richard Lewis is the son of American missionary parents. Although he attended university in the United States, he was born, raised, and lives in Bali, Indonesia" ("Richard Lewis, Official Publisher Page"). Elsewhere, Lewis conveniently self-identifies as both a former missionary kid and a third culture kid, as do

Young and Dekker. Lewis says, "My parents worked in Bali, a Hindu island among a predominantly Muslim country, but I went to boarding school in Java. I'm what psychologists call a 'third culture kid'" ("Richard Lewis, An Interview"). Lewis still lives in Indonesia, continuing to be an expatriate and outsider, but evidently more at home there than he might feel if he repatriated to America, which is, according to his nationality, home.

Young, like Lewis, self-identifies as "a missionary kid, a third culture kid" ("Paul Young Part 1"). On his website "Windrumors," Young writes:

> I thought the way I grew up was "normal" but I think most would probably agree that my history and journey have been a bit unusual. I was the eldest of four, born May 11th, 1955, in Grande Prairie, Alberta, Canada, but the majority of my first decade was lived with my missionary parents in the highlands of Netherlands New Guinea (West Papua), among the Dani, a technologically stone age tribal people. These became my family and as the first white child and outsider who ever spoke their language, I was granted unusual access into their culture and community. Although at times a fierce warring people, steeped in the worship of spirits and even occasionally practicing ritualistic cannibalism, they also provided a deep sense of identity that remains an indelible element of my character and person.
>
> By the time I was flown away to boarding school at age 6, I was in most respects a white Dani. In the middle of a school year, my family unexpectedly returned to the West. My father worked as a Pastor for a number of small churches in Western Canada and by the time I graduated, I had already attended thirteen different schools ["Paul Young's Short Bio"].

One sees in his experiences echoes of Viser's description of the child used to open doors in an alien and remote community, as well as of *All God's Children* and the very young child first immersed in a host culture and then sent away to a mission boarding school, not to mention the experience of many third culture kids for whom the number of schools attended before finally graduating is often in the double digits. *The Shack*'s jacket tells us that Young "suffered great loss as a child and young adult." These losses, as with many third culture authors, have to do with what is left behind in innumerable cultural transits. As Young writes, "These facts don't tell you about the pain of trying to adjust to different cultures" ("Paul Young's Short Bio"). But they are also indicative of "life losses that were almost too staggering to bear"—specifically, the sexual abuses Young suffered as a child in both New Guinea (from age four on) and mission boarding schools in Canada ("Paul Young's Short Bio"; "Paul Young Part 1"). In addition, Young states in an interview that

> we had a six-month period where my 18-year-old brother was killed, my wife's father died suddenly and my 5-year-old niece was killed the day after her birthday. So we have that pain. I received a letter from a reader that asked if the character Missy in the book represented something innocent in me that was murdered as a child. And she got it dead on. My stuff goes back to my childhood on the missionary field. My disconnectedness from my own family, sexual abuse in the culture, abuse that happened at boarding school — that's where the center of my pain comes from ["Living *The Shack*"].

The biographical material is cringe-worthy and very reminiscent of work done in documenting the abuses suffered by missionary kids; the fiction Young writes does not diverge nearly as far as one might like from the emotional devastations of his own background.

Dekker, like Lewis and Young, was raised in Indonesia, though he is more fantastical in his description of the experience (his website and press materials are full of references to "head-hunting tribes") and more sparing with concrete information (the tribes are unnamed, as are their languages). For instance, from Dekker's official website

> Dekker was born to missionaries who lived among the headhunter tribes of Indonesia. Because his parents' work often included extended periods of time away from their children, Dekker describes his early life in a culture to which he was a stranger as both fascinating and lonely. It is this unique upbringing that forced him to rely on his own imagination to create a world in which he belonged ["About Ted"].

Intriguing here is the causal presumption: Dekker was and continues to be creative because he had to be in order to create for himself a world in which he belonged. A similar argument could be made about most, if not all, of the authors treated in this book: the rhetoric of nationality and belonging omits their experiences in a way that the worlds of their own imagining do not.

Another source describes Dekker's life as follows, again emphasizing his loneliness and, typical of the authors I treat in this chapter in particular, attributing it to missionary boarding school:

> Ted Dekker was born in Indonesia, to Christian missionaries, John and Helen Dekker. According to Dekker, his early years were lonely ones, having been sent to boarding school, along with his siblings. In his biography, Dekker claims that his happiest times were those spent climbing trees and racing through the jungle with his brother Danny while on vacation from school. After completing high school in Papua New Guinea, he moved to the United States to attend college ["Ted Dekker," Mahalo.com].

There are no allegations of sexual abuse, which makes Dekker's life story markedly different from Young's, despite the fact that the two were close enough in location and age (Young was born in 1955, Dekker in 1964) that they could have attended the same schools, possibly in close succession and maybe even with a bit of overlap.[3]

Dislocation (Palmer, Nangle, Lewis)

In the fiction written by former missionary kids, one sees expressions of dislocation, most typically in the disjunction between the passport home, the home children make on the mission field, and the isolated limbo of boarding school.

In Palmer's *The Happy Room*, Julie, oldest daughter in a family of American missionaries, remembers being "seven years old and sailing on a ship to Africa with her missionary parents" (4). Debbie, "the baby of the family[,] had always been adored. Her long blonde curls and the dimples in her cheeks had stunned villagers in the remote part of Kenya where the Mossmans had lived and worked as missionaries for many years" (10). Peter, the middle child, grew up carrying "a spear around, just like one of the natives" (18). None of the three adapt well to repatriation: the dislocation of their childhoods influences their ability to feel like part of the America they return to. Peter likes the route his Postal Service job has assigned him in New Mexico because it covers "the Hispanic sections ... where people spoke in a different language and children ran around half naked. It felt slightly foreign there, slightly like home" (19). Julie harbors "memories of a long-ago, faraway home they could never return to" (meaning Kenya) (85). Julie and Peter reflect on their younger sister's hospitalization for anorexia and Peter muses, "I wish we could take her back to Africa. She'd get well there" (39). It is also Peter who most trenchantly expresses a sentiment the three siblings implicitly share on their return to the United States: "I hated America, and I hated all those stupid people who didn't know how to speak any language but English and didn't even have a clue where Kenya was on the map" (127). They are dislocated out of belonging to their passport home, and blondly out of place in the Kenya they'd like to imagine as home.

The Mossman children are dislocated from their parents too, as Peter remarks to Julia:

> Family? Julia, when was the last time the Mossmans were a family? Come to think of it, were we ever a family? I mean, during our whole childhood, Mom and Dad were doing their God thing, and the three of us were off at boarding school. Even on holidays, it was clear we played

second fiddle to pastors' meetings, Bible commentaries, sermon preparation — [33].

Going to boarding school is like being exiled from the family, with rare holidays/reprieves and even rarer parental visits. Debbie contracts malaria at school, and her parents come to visit. She thinks, "I can't believe they made that long trip up here to KCA [Kenya Christian Academy] to see me. I feel so special and wonderful inside, like it's Christmas" (137). Debbie's euphoria, however, is shortlived: "Before I barely have a chance to soak it all in, my parents hug and kiss me ... and then everyone walks out the door. They're gone! They've left me behind!" (138). Her happiness is quickly replaced by a sense of abandonment. She feels "like the loneliest person in the world" (138). Peter feels similarly isolated by school, as symbolized by the picture he draws of the family together on vacation (posed idyllically on the beach at sunrise) that then winds up hidden at the bottom of his school trunk (173). Likewise, Julia, ostensibly the happiest of the three at school, has this experience when her parents drop her and her siblings off:

> As I walk out of the dorm with its grey concrete blocks and barred windows, I start feeling pretty bad.... I don't want to cry. I'm not going to cry.... Mom and Dad give me big hugs and kisses. They say they'll be praying for me. They promise they'll write lots of letters. Then they climb into their Land Rover and shut their doors and drive away.
>
> Debbie and I stand there watching until we can't see the car anymore. We stand until we're sure they are completely, totally gone. We stand until we know, beyond a shadow of a doubt, that they're not coming back. Not today. Not for three months [196].

The dislocation of being overseas is compounded, then, by this additional displacement: the children are in a foreign country *and* are left at school, hundreds of miles away from their parents and the host community in which they have started to eke out a place for themselves.

Although Nangle writes of settled white Rhodesians in *The Leper Compound*, her young protagonist Colleen experiences her surroundings very much as missionary kid would. Nangle fills her stories with details of both Colleen's conscious world (as the daughter of a white Rhodesian coffee farmer) and Colleen's dreams. In these dreams, Nangle inserts the experience of a missionary kid (particularly dislocation) into a narrative otherwise not explicitly about missionary children: "She might be in a typical dream, the way she jumbled up South Africa and Zimbabwe and places on the BBC *World News*, and the shore became some jagged peninsula in the North Sea, with Baobab trees, and the landmarks contradicted each other until she was nowhere" (177). In another dream, the Land Rover in which Colleen is riding crashes and "they are all sliding, all of them, over the edge, tumbling on top of one another, African, European, the American, sick, dying, vigorous" (17). Places, and even nationalities, collide. In dreams, Nangle has Colleen express the magnitude of disorientation produced by the kinds of dislocation third culture kids, and missionary kids, experience.

The boarding school passages in *The Leper Compound* are one of the features that most strongly hints that these stories are literature by a former missionary kid, despite the author's focus on white Rhodesians, not missionaries or their children. At boarding school, Colleen's nightmares express her anxiety and isolation: "It seemed all she did was have nightmares more real than her everyday life" and the dreams become like "hallucinations," which are, to Colleen, "a way to cope with being a type of orphan" (23, 26). Life away at school is thus equated with being "a type of orphan"; dreams and hallucinations are envisaged as appropriate responses. The school appears in the first line of the first story ("Penny spotted the anopheles mosquito one mid-morning break at Hatfield Girls' High School") (7). The sanitorium Colleen's schizophrenic sister Sarah lives in is "Rest Haven," which, in a coincidence that becomes important if considering how missionary kid influences creep into this story collection, was "started by a missionary" (43). Similarly, at Colleen's school, "the boarding master and boarding mistress were evangelicals from Wisconsin who'd come to Rhodesia after UDI [the Unilateral Declaration of Independence]" (23). Colleen and Sarah are sent away when their mother dies (at which time Colleen is only seven) (8). The school compounds an identity crisis for Colleen: "How could one ever define oneself, announce with any sureness, 'I am this,' or 'I'm that,' if one knew so little?" (28). Colleen knows so little because of her dislocations, of which boarding school is the apotheosis.

In Lewis' *The Flame Tree*, protagonist Isaac lives with his parents (American missionary doctors) at the hospital annexed to a mission boarding school. He attends that school during the day:

> Behind him was.... The American Academy of Wonobo, Java, a boarding school of the Union of American Baptists.... Isaac did not board in the dorm there. He lived with his parents in a house on the residential side of the tangerine trees and hibiscus hedge that divided the large mission compound. Graham and Mary Williams were doctors at the Union of American Baptists Immanuel Hospital [1].

When the novel begins, Isaac has just returned "home" to Indonesia from vacation in Connecticut (2). The problem that plagues him is a quintessentially third culture one: he is "neither American nor Javanese" (266), a fact that makes his school peers, newer to Indonesia than he, criticize him even though they are fast becoming third culture kids themselves ("You're not a real American. You shouldn't be in this school") (119). The Indonesians he lives among are likewise perplexed when Isaac, dancing one day at a rally, impresses them with a triumphant show of skill.[4] The stage announcer sees Isaac's whiteness as Americanness ("the only good American is a dead American," he says as Isaac comes on stage) (28), and then the Indonesian *dangdut* music starts and Isaac dances: "*dangdut bulé! dangdut bulé!*" roars the now appreciative crowd ("dangdut white boy! dangdut white boy!") (29).

Isaac's dislocation involves America, Indonesia and the amorphous area his identity occupies somewhere between the two. He doesn't live at the Baptist boarding school, but the novel nonetheless includes a dislocating, identity-confounding, boarding school experience: Isaac is kidnapped and held against his will at an Indonesian madrasah (a school for teaching Islamic theology). The kidnapping is only possible because Isaac's parents fail to evacuate Indonesia when asked to by the American government. Isaac's experience is a dislocation that emphasizes the rift between him and his parents, occasioned by their decision to stay. Captive in the madrasah, he hears that his parents are alive and "wait[s] for a flood of happiness at the news. All that came was a trickle of relief that he did not have to worry about his parents" (169). Isaac's displacement has driven him so far from his family that he no longer responds as a child, a son. At the madrasah (functioning in this novel as an exaggerated version of a mission boarding school, and similarly guided by the teaching of religious precepts), Isaac is circumcised against his will, with no anesthesia (212–215). Both he and his faith are attacked, for the circumcision comes with an attempt to convert Isaac to Islam. Lewis has this "boarding school" emphasize how lost and vulnerable the child is, alone to defend himself in impossible circumstances. When Isaac is finally reunited with his mother, the media is there: "The cameras zoomed in on Mary scrambling over the sawhorse and sweeping her son into her arms for her embrace. They showed the world her tears and Isaac's dry eyes" (231). Isaac is not American, not Javanese, and, after separation from his parents, not part of the family anymore either.

In all three texts, one sees geographical dislocation and displacement, as well as the dislocation of children out of the family and into a boarding school setting. The exiling of children from the family is common in the literature of former missionary kids but not common to third culture literature as a whole. In addition to losing place and home, missionary children sent to boarding school also lose family.

Loss (Palmer, Nangle, Lewis)

In previous chapters, I've argued that loss is a prevalent theme in third culture literature; so, too, in this subset, the literature of former missionary kids. In third culture literature, losses are generally accompanied by an acknowledgment of the great privileges associated with third culture lives. Growing up overseas gives third culture kids exposure to different cultures, places and languages. People who have not grown up mobile, or exposed to so much, tend to envy the wealth of experience and consequent cultural flexibility enjoyed by third culture kids. For the children of diplomats or business people overseas, privileges are generally also material ones (expatriates tend to enjoy a much higher standard of living than locals). This may be somewhat true of military brats as well, depending on the location of the bases on which they have lived. For instance, Canadian residents on a military base in Germany may not have a higher standard of living than local Germans, but Canadian residents on a military base in Kosovo might. Third culture kids, and third culture literature, suggest how unexpected it may be, especially to non–third culture individuals, to discover that such a literal and figurative wealth of experience is accompanied by tremendous grief and multitudinous loss.

In the case of literature by former missionary kids, the question of privilege is complex: missionaries are committed to abjuring material wealth, which means their children often endure quite harsh conditions, and the boarding school experience is sometimes also a tremendous hardship. As Palmer's Peter quips in *The Happy Room*, "It was the main message of our childhood. Be good and sweet and perfect all the time.... And whatever you do, don't look like you have any money" (280). Looks *can* be deceiving, but missionaries generally are not wealthy, or are at least impoverished by their isolation and unfamiliarity with surviving in the conditions that their host countries provide. Though they may not necessarily be starving to death, living in conditions in which "first world" staples are hard to obtain generates a certain kind of hardship. As Mrs. Mossman observes in *The Happy Room*, "These days I can hardly pull a meal together to feed my family. Do you realize I haven't had any flour in three months? And safari ants invaded the storeroom again, a whole stream of them" (19). At boarding school Julia realizes, after meals that are either all starch or vegetables "infested with worms or tiny black bugs," "We're malnourished! I bet some of us are bordering on kwashiorkor [protein deficiency]" (101).

In *The Flame Tree*, Isaac is reminded of his privilege by a teacher who taunts him, saying, "You're like a little rajah [lord], aren't you? Wandering around Wonobo as if you ruled it" (35). Here, and also in *The Leper Com-

pound, privilege comes with a loss of *security*. Isaac is aware that the privilege marked by his Americanness and whiteness makes him a target. He realizes this in his experience at a rally his friend Ismail has brought him to: "Isaac's skin prickled. The Tuan Guru [political speaker], seated upon a plush velvet armchair, once again swung his gaze to Isaac. Isaac wanted out, he wanted to become invisible, he wanted Scotty to beam him up. *This is not good. I should not have come here*" (31). Isaac cannot become invisible because of his whiteness and the privilege it connotes. This privilege puts him at a somatically marked disadvantage.

Likewise, in Nangle's stories, Colleen discovers the dangers of her family's privileged life on a coffee estate with servants and a generous house (complete with parquet floors and mosquito netting) (9). Colleen's dog Kimmy has "the menacing look of European guard dogs at gates in the cities" (12). This setup is very characteristic of white Southern Africa, and especially Rhodesia. Colleen, like Isaac, is a target:

> By this time, Colleen had turned sixteen. She'd begun to understand parts of the speeches, especially the liturgical-sounding chants.
> The people of Zimbabwe are many
> The settlers are few.
> She started to wish she was not white, or at least not a farmer's daughter [90].

Lewis and Nangle both pair privilege with loss of security. The feeling that one is visible because of one's racial privilege is not, of course, a trait unique to missionary kids or the literature they may grow up to produce. However, these characters' awareness and tacit legitimation of the threats to which they are exposed are distinctive of a third culture perspective in that they imply a heightened cultural sensitivity. Conspicuously characteristic of former missionary kids' literature is the additional connection of vulnerability with boarding school.

Lewis and Nangle both, like Palmer, come back to the boarding school experience as one that expresses most fully the loss and deprivation of missionary kids. While Palmer's Julia thinks she and her classmates may be malnourished, Lewis' Isaac bathes at the madrasah with "harsh lye soap," in a room in which "algae grew in corners of the unevenly tiled floor" (171). He dries himself with a towel so thin that he's still damp when he puts his clothes back on and it looks as if he's wet himself: "You have a toilet in there and still you manage to piss in your pants," snipes his keeper, Mas Bengkok (172). Like Palmer, Lewis writes of a circumstance that is not life-threatening, but *is* hardship for a child used to material comfort. Isaac is uncomfortable; his physical discomfort is exacerbated by the mockery of Mas Bengkok, the man who, like a boarding house master, is tasked with looking after him. In *The Leper Compound,* Colleen grieves her isolation from her sister ("Colleen sometimes felt she and Sarah might as well not be related. There was no need" [42]). Colleen, like Isaac, is also humiliated in a bathroom by her boarding house mistress. First, Colleen is chastised for hiding and studying in the bathroom at night when she tries to avoid the colony of termites living under her bed (24). Then she gets her first period and is accosted loudly in front of her classmates by Mrs. Fairbridge: "Has a family member talked to you about menstrual periods or pregnancy?" (25). As in Lewis' novel, there is nothing life-threatening in these incidents in *The Leper Compound,* but there is hardship (termites) and, more devastatingly, humiliation.

In both cases the bathroom is the location for a child's humiliation by an adult: the power dynamics are significant. The adult makes the isolated, vulnerable child feel abject. The children's identities are threatened by a moment in which they seem to have lost control of their bodies, and because an authority figure has callously drawn attention to that apparent disruption of self-control, there occurs a symbolic rupturing of the ability to control who the self is, or identity altogether. Julia Kristeva writes, "Abjection is above all ambiguity. Because, while releasing a hold, it does not radically cut off the subject from what threatens it — on the contrary, abjection acknowledges it to be in perpetual danger" (9). Trapped in the bathroom by a menacing adult, Isaac and Colleen are abjected. Their identities are threatened by the sudden emergence of things they cannot control about themselves. Their inability to circumscribe (or even understand) their own identities is especially traumatic because it is observed and commented upon by an unsympathetic audience — the adult authority figure. The bathroom incidents emphasize Isaac's internal debate of "*Who am I? What am I?*" (Lewis 83) and Colleen's frustration when she is reminded that even though she can speak the native language, she is not and can never be African. As Colleen's friend Vaida points out, Colleen's adages are "spoken as though you are one of us," but "as though" is a long way from "are" (Nangle 92).

Nangle's Colleen loses her mother to malaria (8), her sister to schizophrenia (33) and her first lover to political strife (101). Lewis' Isaac loses his friend Ismail to religious conflict between Christianity and Islam (69), and perhaps even loses his faith; he has lost a connection to America from being away too long and a connection to Indonesia from being too American. Palmer's Debbie has, like so many third culture kids, lost the accoutrements that add up to "home," as she notes when leaving America for Kenya: "I remember our house where I have lived all my life, for four whole years. We won't ever go back to that, or our green plastic swimming pool, or our doggy" (50). Julia adds, describing their frequent moves and losses as children,

> Say good-bye to your grandparents and aunts and uncles and friends. Say good-bye to your teachers and classmates. Say good-bye to your house and your pets and your city and your country and your continent! And now — say good-bye to your parents — and be sure not to care about any of it. Do it over and over again. Be big and accept all this, because it is God's will for your life [297].

For Julia, as for the third culture kids described in chapters one and two, every move is tantamount to losing everything and everyone. There are too many good-byes, and too many unacknowledged griefs, but in the midst of such a fortunate life, especially when one is acting according to God's will, one isn't *supposed* to be devastated by loss. Julia is supposed to "accept" a list of losses that is clearly immense.

The shared third culture Pollock and Van Reken carefully delineate in *Third Culture Kids* includes the "irretrievable losses of [a third culture] childhood" that can make third culture kids feel isolated. They write that certain "normal" childhood memories are lost to the more exotic, but also less stable, experiences of a third culture upbringing (171). In other words, for example, the third culture kid whose parents' home is in the Western world, but who gets raised in various parts of Asia, may get to see lantern festivals and Thaipusam, but miss things like school picture day or *Sesame Street*. Pollock and Van Reken's shared third culture also includes the fact that geographical transitions make childhood memories especially intangible for third culture kids: "People who live as adults in the same country where they grew up can usually go back and revisit their old house, school, playground, and church. In spite of inevitable changes, they can still reminisce 'on site,' but a highly mobile TCK often lacks this opportunity" (172).

In *The Happy Room*, Peter defines the specifically *missionary kid* loss he and his siblings experience:

> Their childhood was not without its high points. They had met interesting people, seen cultures of every imaginable variety, had some amazing adventures. Not for anything in the world would Peter have traded the joy of running through the bush with his Maasai friends. The day he had killed the lion had been the greatest day of his life.
> But something had been wrong during their childhood too. Something sharp and painful, like a thorn from an African acacia tree — a barb that had buried itself inside his chest and would never come out.
> The thorn was abandonment by his parents, he realized. And then one loss after another had driven that thorn into the flesh of the Mossman children. He knew it was true, even if Julia wouldn't admit it. He

wondered if any of them knew what it meant to be loved. Truly loved [63–64].

Peter expresses the privilege and loss typical of a third culture experience in terms that, as the fiction bears out, are those of an adult missionary kid. Here the privileges are what one would expect, but the loss is, above all else, the loss of the parents, producing what is perceived by the children as their *abandonment* by their parents. As an adult, Julia whispers to herself, "*Your parents abandoned you. They hurt and neglected you when you needed them most.... Your mother and father put their church work above their family. They always did. They always will*" (315).

In Lewis' *The Flame Tree*, the American sent to help Isaac's parents evacuate is appalled when they plan to send the boy off on his own: "'You don't want to be with your son when he gets on that helicopter?' Sheldon asked, with surprise. 'It's going to be a stressful time for him. What comes first? Your child or your career?'" (127). Clearly the answer is their career, or, more specifically, the "calling" of doing God's work. Isaac boards the helicopter alone, in the midst of a riot successful enough that it forces the aircraft to crash. Isaac survives the crash, only to be abducted by the Muslim militants who take him to the madrasah in which he is held as a student/captive. Implicitly, none of this would have happened to Isaac if his parents hadn't prioritized their work for God over their love for him: like Peter, Julia and Debbie, he is abandoned. In this case, it is as if Lewis has written a story of abandonment in which a cosmic revenge is embedded: the Baptist missionary doctors are punished for their abandonment of their son when they are forced to see the extent to which they *and their God* nearly lost him altogether.

In Nangle's *The Leper Compound*, dreams are, once again, the wellspring of missionary kid experience. In one story Colleen becomes the parent sacrificing a child, thereby abandoning it. Colleen's infant son Gavin shares a hospital room with another infant, Ramona, "a cocaine baby" whose incessant screaming disrupts the room in which Colleen nurses her own son back to life night after night (150). But Ramona dies:

> The room was empty, cluttered with used syringes and tourniquets. Ramona was lying underneath a sheet. Colleen balanced Gavin on her hip and lifted the sheet from Ramona's face ... she remembered the dream. "Was it a dream?" she asked. She remembered a soft pillow. "I did it. I killed her" [157].

And later:

> Someone permitted Colleen to push Gavin in a stroller around the halls. She was haunted, nothing mattered, not this healing baby perched

> forward, looking ahead, side to side, kicking its feet. There had been a sacrifice: she had knowledge of it. She was dangerous. Over and over again came the thought. Dreams and reality layered on top of each other, and behind each other, mixtures and reminders of wrongdoing and banality and the covert [158].

Nangle presents the parental side of the story of sacrifice/abandonment as envisaged by Lewis and Palmer: Colleen (parent) "sacrifices" a child for the greater good, written here in a secular scenario that sounds biblical: a girl dies so that a boy may live.

It's not far from there to the biblical story of Isaac and Ishmael: both of whom are Abraham's sons. Ishmael is the oldest, born to the servant Hagar after Abraham and Sarah experienced biblical-era infertility and decided that if they were going to have a son, they'd need another woman to bear it. Not so long after Sarah's servant Hagar bore Ishmael, Sarah herself finally became pregnant with Isaac. When Isaac was established as the rightful heir, Hagar and Ishmael were sent away to roam the wilderness and finally settled in the desert: abandoned, sacrificed. Ishmael, like Ramona, is the child sacrificed by his parent. Isaac, like Gavin, is the heir who prospers. Nangle's story thus also provides a tidy connection to Lewis' story of Isaac and his Muslim friend Ismail in *The Flame Tree*, a novel that more explicitly plays with the Genesis story in its rendering of a Christian Isaac and a Muslim Ismail.

Loss, in literature by former missionary kids, comes especially in the form of parents "letting their children go." Though the literature of former missionary kids includes the other types of loss typical to third culture literature (the losses of place, people, pets and other markers of home, and losses expressed drastically in terms of death), parents abandoning their children is the key, most returned to, most emphasized loss. In other words, what distinguishes loss in the literature of former missionary kids is the abandonment of children by their parents — parents sacrificing their children to serve God.

Disenfranchisement (Palmer, Nangle, Lewis)

In the literature of former missionary kids, as in other types of third culture literature, characters feel out of place, or as if they have no right to claim any place as their own. In Palmer's *The Happy Room*, the siblings are "heading for forty" but none feel as though they belong in the North America in which they now live: "[N]one seemed to have found a comfortable skin to fit into.... Why were they still struggling to figure out who they were? Why didn't they fit?" (32). Peter's strident assertions that they are "natives" of Kenya, that they "are Africans," only convinces a naked, deranged (and possibly also drunk) Kenyan roaming the streets of Nairobi. But even this incapacitated man, though somewhat willing to go along with Peter's claim, points out the obvious: "But you are white!" (76). The children do not belong to Kenya (and cannot claim it), but they feel out of place in North America too.

In *The Leper Compound*, Colleen refers to Nyadzi, her father's coffee plantation, as home (8), but then Nangle provides an excruciating vignette involving a chicken the dog Kimmy has killed, showing Colleen's longing, and inability, to belong:

> "I could pluck it for you," Colleen offered, though she had only seen Mapipi scattering quills to the wind, brushing off his cutting board in readiness. She wanted to stay longer in the swept yard with its poinsettias and lemon trees and the green wall of maize.
>
> Miss Maenga picked up the chicken by its legs and carried it dripping to the step. "Let's both do it," she said.
>
> They sat, tugging at feathers, the bird between them steadied by their hands. Sometimes Colleen did not pull hard enough at the feather's shaft and bits of down remained on her side of the chicken. She suggested tweezers. Miss Maenga returned from the kitchen with a match. She held a flame to the tufts. There was a smell of burnt hair, the smell of boarding school on a civvies day [14].

In a regrettably colonial incident, Colleen's dog has killed Miss Maenga's chicken: the colonist has imposed egregiously upon the indigene. Colleen wants to apologize and, in the same layered moment, wants to belong. She offers to help. Accepting the implied apology, Miss Maenga lets the girl "help," extending the token possibility that they are doing this together even though it is clear Colleen cannot actually help much at all. Colleen wants to be a part of the setting, with its poinsettias and maize. Her effort to belong to the African village actually culminates in a reminder of the smell of burnt hair—like boarding school on a "civvies," or non-uniform, day, when hairstyling is permitted—and thus also of her isolation and expatriatism.

Lewis' Isaac refers to Indonesia as "home" in *The Flame Tree*, even though he's aware that he is a "little hybrid ... neither American nor Javanese" (2). As it was for Colleen, a symbolic moment in Isaac's unbelonging comes in his effort to sustain a friendship. Ismail is Isaac's friend until religious conflicts in Wonobo drive them apart. Ismail takes part in a raid on Isaac's family's church: "'I want your shoes,' Ismail said again, pointing down at Isaac's new Reeboks. He stared at Isaac with eyes so alien and hostile that it was as though the Ismail whom Isaac had known, with whom he had flown kites and stalked the cane fields and hunted for treasure, was someone else" (82). For all the time the two have spent together, and during which Isaac has behaved as an Indonesian boy, the incident is reminder of Isaac's outsider status (symbolized by his Reeboks) and *his* foreignness, for though it seems Ismail has become "someone else," it is Isaac who is reminded that he is the outsider and forced to embody Americanness and Christianity.

As in third culture literature generally, including military brat writing, in the literature of former missionary kids the feeling of disenfranchisement comes in tandem with a counterintuitive irresponsibility or obliviousness to local politics. One would think, with their enhanced cultural sensitivities, that third culture kids would be especially politically aware. What third culture literature hints at, however, is detachment, which, while it enables adaptability, also results in some problematic areas of nonchalant ignorance. Lewis' Isaac is perhaps the most politically aware of the protagonists I treat in this section, but even he gets caught up in a political rally, one he should have had the sense to stay away from, and is scolded: "This is why your State Department advises Americans in Indonesia to stay away from crowds" (34). He is also too easily reassured about the political situation when his mother says, "We don't have to worry at all because God will take care of us" (39).

Colleen is more staggeringly, and dangerously, oblivious to the resistance movements going on around her, and the connections with rebels across the border in Mozambique. When her friend, Tambudzai, writes to tell her that Hersekwe, her former lover, "*is gone*," Colleen realizes there is more to this information than she can decipher: "'What does it mean?' She obsessed about it. She paced in the empty courtyard. She stared blankly at her textbooks" (94). Thinking back over her time with Hersekwe, she realizes how much "she did not know" (101). One day she taunts a white soldier, "not afraid because he won't hurt her, she is white" (96), but this episode contributes to an attack on her own village, the one she so much wants to be part of. She pleads with a surviving African friend, "Say I didn't do this, please." The response: "Vaida was silent" (105).

In *The Happy Room*, Palmer absolves the children of responsibility but suggests that their parents are inappropriately disengaged from local politics. Though the Mau-Mau rebellion is over, Mau-Maus still hide out around Nairobi and victimize whites. The Mossman parents leave all three of their children in a Land Rover parked on a Nairobi street during a shopping visit to town. While their parents run errands, the children are accosted by the irate, deranged, drunk man mentioned earlier. He is, apparently, also a Mau-Mau. Thanks to Peter and his swift talking, they are not injured, and merely have their shoes stolen. On returning to their car, the Mossman parents are insufficiently rattled by the incident that has terrified their children: "They are very concerned and ask us lots of questions, but we can't seem to make them realize how terrible it was" (80). The children are aware they could have been killed or abducted; their parents, seemingly, are not.

Although privilege seems to be paired with insecurity in the literature of former missionary kids, insecurity, and indeed fear, are also connected with disenfranchisement. The missionary families are vulnerable because they do not belong. In the literature of former missionary kids, insecure *homes* in particular are frequently symbolic of their inhabitants' feelings of vulnerability. In *The Happy Room*, Mrs. Mossman hears that "a missionary family not too far from here was attacked one night," and knows that "families in [their] mission have been shot, drugged, held up, mugged and all sorts of things" (224). She insists that they "have metal bars installed in the windows and a sturdy metal roof. This means if there's ever a fire inside [they're] doomed. But it also means no one is likely to break in while [they're] at home" (222). Peter has a fit when he doesn't get a rifle for Christmas. He is concerned for the family's safety, and feels as if it has come to him to protect them all because his parents are not doing enough. He says of the Maasai spear he manages to procure from his friends:

> I wanted to protect our family ... I knew about the attacks, the robberies, the muggings. You and Mom tried not to say much, but we could hear right through those thin walls. We knew everything — all the bloody details. And I knew our house wasn't secure. Someone broke into it every time we went on vacation [232].

His father responds, "I never realized you were so worried about our safety" (233). But Peter and his siblings *were* worried, and felt the house that was meant to shelter them was but inadequate "thin walls." Home itself is far too insubstantial and the children perceive themselves to be in immediate, mortal danger because the things that should protect them (houses, parents) only do so "thinly," which is not enough to actually keep them safe.

In *The Flame Tree*, Isaac sees a secret gate in the perimeter wall of the hospital/school compound: "someone had cunningly detached a four-foot-square section of wall and then rebricked it within a thin frame ... a small gate, but nonetheless one that would allow even a large man to leave the compound. Or enter" (4). The compound seems like a fortress, but it has a strategically hidden weak point through which Isaac can exit, and, more menacing, through which someone (perhaps the unknown person who made the gate in the first place) could enter. The gate is a symbolic rupture of a boundary that ostensibly keeps the community "safe." Isaac shows the secret gate to a classmate, as a way of buying some social cachet, and is surprised when his peer muses, "I wonder if we should tell someone about this.... What if some Muslim fanatic leads his army through here?" (47). As the Islamicist groups gain power and threaten the mission more forcibly, Isaac finally realizes "how ominous the whole idea of a secret gate in the wall really was" (74). Here, as in *The Happy Room*, the walls that are meant to protect do not: they have flaws and inadequacies that make their inhabitants extremely aware that they are *not* "at home," they are not part of the community — indeed, that they are even *disliked* by the host community and subject to violent expulsion, or even extermination, because they are foreign.

In *The Leper Compound*, a neighbor calls when he hears a strange noise at the farm: "Gwen and I were worried" (39). They are worried because, as Rhodesia moves toward independence, it is entirely possible that the farm of white settlers will come under attack. Colleen comes home from boarding school on the train one holiday "alone in her six-bunk compartment," because "no one wanted to take the night train anymore": it is not safe (57). She is returning to a village in which there has been "an occurrence," as her father cryptically puts it: "Over a period of three days, thirty-four students [at the village school] had absconded, crossing the border to guerrilla training camps in Mozambique. The mission school had been closed by the RDF. Some teachers and students were arrested" (57). The farm, like all white-owned farms, is vulnerable. Colleen's father draws her attention to their own equivalent of a secret gate: Mapipi, their farm help, drums messages in code. As her father says, "Listen sometimes when the army is around. He's warning the chappies up in the hills" (73). "The army" would be defending Rhodesia, and the "chappies in the hills" fighting for a new Zimbabwe. Mapipi is part of the threat against the farm, and lives inside its fences. "Home" is vulnerable from within. Colleen and her family are not safe even within the borders of what they claim as their own land.

In subsequent years they lose the farm, and Colleen's father resides on another increasingly embattled plot of land until his death, land on which, even while he is alive, squatters encroach: "Inside her father's gate, the headlights flashed on what must have been the squatter's camp, the corrugated metal sheets" (179). Inside the house, "she saw the ten speeds parked inside her father's study — brought in from the carport, probably before the looting of the outbuildings ... they were padlocked" (183). Nangle describes a house whose land is already encroached upon and that is so vulnerable to attack that even though the bicycles have been brought inside, they are still padlocked to stymie thieves: the presumption is that thieves *will* come to loot the house. The threat here, as in Lewis and Palmer, is not an abstract dread, but a concrete, definite possibility. The inhabitants of these houses are not at home; they will be attacked; they are far from safe.

Sick Children (Palmer, Nangle, Lewis)

In chapters one and two I discuss third culture literatures in which children are forced, too young, into adult roles. In military brat literature in particular, the result is an excessive, precocious, and perverse sexuality — child characters claim agency in the most adult way they can muster. In the literature of former missionary kids, overt, excessive sexuality (or, indeed, any sexual activity at all) is conspicuously absent. What one sees instead is children who are sick. Child characters perceive themselves as abandoned; the authors write them as *sacrificed* to their parents' calling. In *The Happy Room*, *The Leper Compound* and *The Flame Tree*, children also contract malaria, a tropical disease they are unlikely to have been exposed to were it not for their parents' vocational choices. In each text, the malaria emphasizes the extent to which the children suffer while their parents, seemingly oblivious, continue with their mission.

In Palmer's novel, Debbie, the youngest, gets malaria at boarding school. Her parents come to visit, but leave before she is better. She convalesces for too short a time and then is sent back to her dorm: "My legs feel like spaghetti ... something deep inside me wishes I had never gotten up and crawled to the infirmary [in the first place]. I think it would be better right now to be a pile of bones bleaching in the sun" (138). The problem for Debbie is that her parents came *and then left*, an experience that devalues her so absolutely that she would rather not have lived through it. It is her malaria, and her parents' abandonment while she is sick, that brings on the anorexia that eventually kills Debbie: "I look at myself in the mirror ... I look like a ghost. I feel like one, too. I think about that for a long time, and I decide that the best thing ... the very best thing in the world ... would be to fade away. Disappear [*sic*]" (139). Debbie, by not eating, eventually does make herself disappear. She takes her parents' prioritization of their mission work as indicative that she has been sacrificed, set aside, and rendered so invisible that she may as well not be there.

In Nangle's first story in *The Leper Compound*, Colleen is "hot with guilt," for she is at boarding school, well briefed on the prevalence of the anopheles mosquito, and yet has not been taking her quinine: "Colleen told the boarding mistress and gave her the aluminum packet.... The woman held it before Colleen's face, its intact green pills in horizontal rows, something to read from left to right and understand completely" (7). What is understood is this: Colleen will inevitably get sick. She will get malaria, and a fever, just as her mother did. Colleen's mother died of fever, and her father needs to work the coffee plantation, which is why Colleen has been sent to school in the first place. The mother's death is an abandonment. Like Debbie, Colleen wishes she could meet that abandonment with her own death. "Getting over malaria, while [my] father waited," notes Colleen, "felt like a developmental milestone, required, demanded" (15). She must get better — her father requires it. Her sickness is making him wait. Her sickness, even at its worst, is less important than his waiting, less urgent. Intriguingly, Nangle's collection is not about a missionary context, and yet Colleen and her (self-)sacrifice, her decision to catch malaria, and the fact of her malaria when she does catch it, mark a distinct similarity with Palmer and Lewis: in the work of all three, children contract this tropical disease and languish because of the sacrifice their parents have made — the children themselves. Nangle has given Colleen experiences that may resonate with her own culture as a former missionary kid even while she is writing about white settlers.

In *The Flame Tree*, Lewis' Isaac plays by the river even though he has been warned not to because of the malarial mosquitos there (14–15). He gets bitten, and the disease incubates, finally emerging as a fever after his parents have put him on the evacuation helicopter, alone, and the rioting crowds have managed to get the craft to crash: "Nausea struck. He doubled over and heaved, bringing up slimy bile. His teeth chattered against a sudden chill. A powerful headache gnawed the inside of his head and chewed on the back of his eyeballs" (150). The disease has most effect when Isaac is alone: it is connected with his parents' choice to send him off by himself symbolizing the sacrifice of Isaac's well-being to their mission. The boy collapses and begs, "*Dear Lord, please help me.* But the ramparts of heaven were shut, and Jesus did not come to His child" (151). His parents have sent him away, and even God does not intercede on his behalf. For Isaac, as for Debbie and even Colleen, malaria indicates that *no one*—divine or mortal — is watching over him.

In each of these texts, the children get sick because their parents are paying attention to something other than their children, a "higher" priority. Debbie is at boarding school, as is Colleen. Isaac is roaming. All three children experience illness as emphasizing their aloneness, and particularly a growing rift between them and their parents. They make their own choices; they suffer their own consequences. No one is protecting them. Thus the literature of former missionary kids suggests how absolutely children are sacrificed when their *parents* are God's children. Colleen's agency (her choice not to take the pills), like Debbie's (her choice not to eat) and Isaac's (his choice to play by the river), suggests that Nangle, Palmer and Lewis also embed an element of punishment in these texts. Childishly angst-ridden perhaps, the malarial youths enact a "cast me aside and I will become ill to punish you and to make you pay attention" trope. The fictions allow these authors to dramatize scenarios that would make any missionary parent feel guilty for neglecting their children by favoring God. *The Happy Room*, *The Flame Tree*, and *The Leper Compound* ultimately emphasize the price children pay for their parents' commitment to God: abandonment, illness and even death. The missionary kid, according to Palmer, Lewis and Nangle, perceives him-/herself as negligible in the estimation of the parents and perhaps even God himself. Young and Dekker's mass-market paperbacks reflect similar assumptions.

William Paul Young's *The Shack* and Ted Dekker's *BoneMan's Daughters*

Young writes a frame narrative in which he himself gives voice to the story of "Mack," whose young daughter Missy is abducted by a serial killer and murdered: "What you are about to read is something that Mack and I have struggled with for many months to put into words. It's a little, well ... no, it is a *lot* on the fantastic side [*sic*]" (12). Mack gets a note from God telling him to come to the shack where Missy was killed. He goes, and meets God (in the form of an African American woman named Elouisa who is happier if Mack calls her "Papa," his usual name for God), Jesus (a Jewish carpenter) and the Holy Spirit (Sarayu, an Asian woman who is extraordinarily gifted with plants). As Timothy Beal remarks, "Who knew that a perichoretic model of the Trinity based on an exchange of love could become such a big hit?" ("Theology for Everyone"). Dekker writes a thriller with a personal frame too. Just as Young insists on being the interlocutor for Mack's story, so Dekker insists on presenting a didactic personal postscript. "Now, I would like to think that I am a good father," he quips, as himself, before presenting an anecdote about one of his daughters and then advising, "For your part, go to your daughter, your father, your son, your mother. Hold them close and cherish them forever" (407, 410). Both Young and Dekker present themselves as the frame for the stories they write, which means that both novels are explicitly framed by the sensibility, culture and wish-fulfilling desires of their authors; both authors, as noted previously, self-identify as former missionary kids.

BoneMan's Daughters features Commander Ryan Evans (a military intelligence agent) deployed in Iraq until a traumatic incident in which he is taken hostage and psychologically tortured (his captors force him to watch as children have their bones broken one by one until they die). After his escape, he is discharged from service to recuperate. On returning home, his daughter Bethany is abducted by a serial killer whose technique, like that of Ryan's Iraqi captors, involves breaking bones until the victim dies. Ryan sets out to rescue her and prove his worth as father. The military context makes it sound as if this novel could, conceivably, have fit in chapter two with the writings of former military brats, but Dekker's emphasis on abandoned, sacrificed, and physically (but not sexually) damaged children makes it clear that *BoneMan's Daughters* fits extraordinarily well here, in the chapter about works by former missionary kids: Dekker's culture as a former missionary kid clearly exerts a powerful influence on his text.

In terms of the main analytical *categories* I have been using to establish "third culture literature"—dislocation, loss, disenfranchisement, and a fourth variable (sick children, in the literature of former missionary kids)—these mass-market paperbacks seem to fit only slightly. In *The Shack*, there is no international dislocation, barring the occasional reference to the world at large (as in Mack falling asleep in front of the TV news and hearing "a piece on a high school senior in Zimbabwe, who had been beaten for speaking out against his government") (23). It is *perhaps* revealing that Mack falls asleep to international news—a theological novel *not* written by an adult missionary kid would possibly not include this detail, and it might not have God enjoy listening to "Eurasian funk and blues" (90). In *BoneMan's Daughters*, American military presence in Iraq provides an international component, but one that is a backdrop rather than the focus for the plot. Loss permeates both texts: Mack, crushingly, loses his daughter Missy when she is murdered; Ryan loses his wife Celine—first to his own inattentiveness and then to the BoneMan—and he subsequently loses his daughter Bethany in the same way. However, places are not lost here, nor are the appurtenances of home. The word "lost" hints at lost faith—it does so even in Palmer's *The Happy Room*. Palmer's Debbie says repeatedly that she feels "lost" (86, 87, 159, 288), as does Young's Mack. Mack says to Papa (God), "I feel totally lost" and "I feel so lost" (97, 114). Papa responds, "I know Mack. But it's not true. I am with you and I'm not lost. I'm sorry it feels that way, but hear me clearly. You are not lost" (114). The possibility of geographical disorientation is overshadowed by spiritual disorientation and the potential for disbelief, or lost faith. Disenfranchisement is taken for granted: Mack pursues a spiritual quest on his own and is, in that sense, disenfranchised; Ryan is similarly disenfranchised in that he pursues his daughter as a solitary renegade without police or military sanction. And, finally, children are not merely sick here; they are dead (Missy) or broken (Bethany). Malaria — an obvious symbol of the effect of parents going on mission to a tropical, treacherous place — does not appear in Young or Dekker.

It is clear, then, that *The Shack* and *BoneMan's Daughters* reach far away from the kinds of contexts Palmer, Nangle and Lewis explore: going through the motions of looking for dislocation, loss, and disenfranchisement in these mass-market paperback texts is of limited use. And yet key tropes unique to the writings of former missionary kids appear in these novels in vivid, emphatic detail: the abandonment or sacrifice of a child by a parent (even by "God" as parent/father); the idea of house/home itself as vulnerable and symbolic of lack of parental protection, contrasted with a "boarding school" experience of being away from the family; and, of course, damaged children. In Young and Dekker's texts, the apparatuses of third culture contexts are omitted and, in their stead, the distilled extremes of missionary kid experiences are expressed.

The Shack and *BoneMan's Daughters* both consider what it would feel like to be the parent who abandons or fails the child as well as how the abandoned child might feel. In terms of his inability to meet his own parental responsibilities, Young's Mack is especially haunted by imagining "Missy screaming for her father and no one answering" (53). She is the babe lost in the wilderness, and he the parent who leaves her there. While waiting for news and imagining that his daughter might still be alive, Mack abdicates his paternal responsibility, and hands it to God instead: "Dear God, please, please, please take care of Missy. I just can't right now" (60). Missy dies, and Mack's grief is couched in what Young writes as her father's failure: Mack weeps, "Missy, I'm so sorry. I'm sorry I couldn't protect you" (78). Implicitly, God could have protected her, but has chosen not to. Mack-the-father and God-the-father have both left Missy to die. From the perspective of the sacrificed child, Young has Missy ask, before her abduction, whether Jesus felt snubbed when his daddy allowed him to die, to which Mack responds, "Sweetheart, Jesus didn't think his daddy was mean. He thought his daddy was full of love and loved him very much. His daddy didn't *make* him die. Jesus chose to die because he and his daddy love you and me and everyone in the world" (31). Mack's answer, while full of reassurance, is also distressing: If God and Jesus are so full of love, and Jesus' willing sacrifice is at the heart of their relationship, should all children *want* to be sacrificed for the greater good? Young hints that Mack does not believe the answer that he gives his daughter at this juncture — that he suspects God did sacrifice Jesus, just as further along in the novel it seems that God sacrifices Missy and even Mack himself. When Mack speaks to Elouisa/God/Papa, he says that the effect of Missy's death was his own loss of faith. Mack accuses God of abandoning Jesus, and abandoning him too: "You abandoned him just like you abandoned me!" (96). There are thus various kinds of abandonment associated with Missy's death: Mack's abandonment of Missy, God's abandonment of Mack, God's abandonment of Missy and God's abandonment of Jesus. There is no escaping the trope: someone vulnerable is sacrificed by someone who should be parenting them. Significantly, Mack recognizes and acknowledges a pattern of abandonment. Young, as an adult missionary kid, writes a fantasy in which he gets to imagine father as well as child and, most importantly, he gets to imagine a father who understands why his child feels abandoned and is wracked by remorse because of it. Young's Mack even loses his faith in God. Young is able, as one might not be in real life, to have the father admit how he has failed the child and insinuate, albeit only fleetingly, that the father's responsibility to the child *could be* more important than faith in God.

Dekker creates a similarly repentant father—a fantasy of a father a missionary kid might wish to have—in that Ryan eventually recognizes how his actions have affected his daughter Bethany. Ryan thinks of the "sacrifice" he has made in leaving his wife and daughter to join the military (8): "The cost of separation was an acceptable sacrifice for such a noble and worthwhile calling" (9). The military is presented as a "calling," just as mission work would be; the wife and child left behind are, as they might be in a Christian context, "sacrifice[d]." He initially thinks his actions are justifiable, but gradually recognizes his culpability. At first this is only a grudging recognition: "He was guilty of ignoring them, but not because of evil in his heart—his heart had always been good" (124). Ryan accepts blame, but does not at this early stage accept the idea that he is a bad person, or bad father. When Bethany rejects him, Ryan is startled into questioning his own actions, actions he had previously been able to justify: "I didn't know ... I didn't know she felt like this. What could I do? I tried, I tried. I thought I was doing the right thing for my country, for her, for Celine. I was sacrificing everything for what I knew how to do" (138). He thinks he has done the right thing by sacrificing Bethany, until she suggests otherwise. Dekker's abandoned child gets an opportunity to chastise her father into repentance, for it is only after Bethany's rejection that Ryan thinks "abandoning children is as bad as killing them" (156). Only after Ryan is forced to hear Bethany's opinion regarding "his abandonment of them both [Celine and Bethany]" (21) does he see that he may have done a terribly selfish, even bad, thing. And Dekker, in his characterization of Bethany, gets to express a vengefulness that missionary kids (expected to willingly self-sacrifice) usually do not. Bethany notes that she "hated Ryan more than anyone she knew for not adequately occupying the role of her father" (346). He is an inadequate father: *that* is her most forceful allegation. She *hates* him for it.

Dekker adds BoneMan, a man who refers to himself as "Satan" (145). Thus Young's Mack gets to talk to God, while Dekker's Ryan gets to talk to the devil. What the BoneMan wants in torturing and killing Bethany is actually to punish her father. As a serial killer of young women, his goal is "punishing fathers, all fathers, because all fathers were the fathers of lies" (143–44). All fathers are assumed to be unable to love their children as they should and are therefore worthy of punishment. Regarding Bethany and Ryan in particular, BoneMan wants "to crush the father's heart who, having been rejected, would be forced to live out a terrible life with knowledge of his utter failure" (376). The best punishment for Ryan? To have Bethany reject him, and force him to live with the knowledge that he has been rejected because of his inadequacy as a parent. Dekker develops the abandonment trope into an explicit fantasy of punishment. The punishment is notable because it gives the child agency: the daughter will reject the father; she will have the chance to abandon him. Is this not a very particular fantasy, and one that a reader can see arising from a missionary kid context? This fiction allows the child to abandon her parents, particularly her *father* (even as a metonymy for God himself). Most important, the fiction requires that the father know why he has been abandoned by his child.

The wealth of material on abandonment and sacrifice in these two texts is overwhelming. Dekker's language frequently evokes the idea of religious sacrifice, and he often examines what it means to be a father who has abandoned his child. In Young, Mack's remorse lurks behind his actions throughout the novel: his grief is predicated on his failure to protect/parent Missy adequately. Though the other hallmarks of third culture literature (displacement, loss, disenfranchisement) recede into the background or out of these texts altogether, children abandoned by their parents, and even by God himself (a key trope in the literature of former missionary kids), is so prevalent as to be unavoidable in these texts. Dekker and Young teach us that a presiding concern, even *the* presiding concern, in the literature of former missionary kids is exploring the ramifications of what children perceive as parental abandonment.

As I note above, *The Shack* and *BoneMan's Daughters* also have uncannily similar covers, each depicting a dilapidated rural edifice. In both novels the disintegrating building is the setting for key events: Young's Missy is killed in the shack, but it is also the setting for Mack's encounter with God; Dekker's Ryan is asked by the BoneMan to kill someone in that text's shack. Dekker adds a complication in that the BoneMan also owns *another* dilapidated building — an old house — which he uses as a holding pen for his victims, and sometimes also as a place to break their bones and kill them. It is this second house that becomes especially significant. Dilapidation and unpleasantness are requisite: these sites (one in Young, two in Dekker) are emphatically not the "homes" they could have been but rather houses of horror. Symbolically, the vulnerable "home" in the literature of former missionary kids has become a nightmare image of the absolute failure of home. If fathers are inadequate, the "shacks" in these texts forcefully symbolize a familial enclave emptied of the love and safety that home should provide.

In Young, forensic analysts determine that Missy's death happened in "the shack," which is "rundown" though "a century or so earlier [it] had probably been a settler's home" (61–62). The building could have been, and likely once was, a home, but it has decayed. In Dekker, BoneMan uses a bunker "built into the side of a hill" (258). Inside "orange light silently flickered on the concrete walls, illuminating the numerous drawings" of ways to break bones that the BoneMan has left there for Ryan to see (277–78). This is the unhomely location for many murders. But BoneMan houses his victims, including Bethany, at a different location: an old country house. Here, "paint that had once been white peeled away from the house in flaking strips, revealing rotting grey wood beneath. The front door hung at a slight angle on only one hinge, following the whole house's tilt to the right" (391). It is replete with "glassless windows" (399) and a "rusted refrigerator" (400). With these descriptions, as in Young's shack, we have the trappings of home decayed and decomposed into something that seems inherently corrupt.

In both *The Shack* and *BoneMan's Daughters*, the decrepit houses are on the one hand the settings for nightmarish atrocity ("homes" that have absolutely failed) and, unexpectedly, are on the other hand the scenes of transformative realizations. When Mack goes to meet God at the shack, it is miraculously changed because of God's presence there: "the dilapidated shack had been replaced by a sturdy and beautifully constructed log cabin"— it was "a place Mack could only have imagined in his best dreams" (81). The edifice is fascinating as a fantasy: it is a broken home symbolic of inadequate parental protection, and then becomes a dream of what home/parents/faith *should* be. In its second, fantastical incarnation, it is also a kind of boarding school at which Mack becomes a pupil, for it is here that Mack meets the Trinity and is schooled back into his faith. Just as the vulnerable house is re-envisioned as an idyll, so a boarding school education becomes a wonderful thing: Mack profits immensely from his time away from his family. Papa remarks to Mack that "while you have been with us, you have healed much and have learned much," to which Mack responds, chuckling, "I think that's an understatement!" (234). The horrors of being away at school are re-cast here as a dream: "school" teaches Mack and heals him.

In Dekker, whose novel errs on the side of retribution more often, and more strongly, than Young's does, Bethany says of the house where BoneMan is tied up, "I hate this place.... This house is hell to me. It will haunt me" (403). Ryan responds, "Then burn it" (403). After this, "Ryan took his daughter's hand and together they walked away from the burning house" (404). The edifice that symbolized Ryan's failure to create a "home" for his daughter is finally burned down, destroying the symbol of his inadequate fathering. Its incineration marks the new understanding shared by father and daughter: they walk away hand-in-hand.

If there is a boarding school analog in *BoneMan's Daughters*, it is the room in which Ryan is held by his Iraqi captors at the novel's start. That space features the following: "Concrete walls. An old wood door. No windows. A metal table on his right, stacked with papers ... one dim bulb hung overhead, shrouded by a green metal shade. An empty corkboard hung on the wall directly ahead of him" (25). It is a space that looks, thanks to the table with its papers and the corkboard, a bit like a schoolroom. And it is here that Ryan is "taught" by his torturers that he can no longer fight in a war in which there is collateral damage. After his "schooling" at the hands of his captors (perhaps uncomfortably similar in emotional effect to the "schooling" meted out by some abusive mission school teachers), Ryan "couldn't possibly continue life as he had once known it" (87–88).

Last in the tropes Young and Dekker share with other former missionary kid writers is that of the damaged child. In Palmer, Nangle and Lewis, children suffer malaria — an illness that expresses how those children suffer due to their parents' missions, as though mission work is a disease whose symptoms manifest in the innocents dragged into the whole affair. In Young and Dekker, there is no malaria, but instead definitive bodily harm. Missy's body is hidden, but the police find her "torn and bloodsoaked dress" in the shack: Missy's blood was shed — lots of it. Ryan finally gets to Bethany at the BoneMan's rural house and sees "that her left hand was swollen. Three of her fingers were crooked. [BoneMan] had broken three of her fingers" (372). The physical injuries are visible but in both instances these are just the tip of the iceberg. We see Missy's blood and Bethany's swollen hand, and presume that there is additional, invisible damage that may be far worse. Missy's dress is off her body (we wonder if she was sexually abused); Bethany has broken fingers after being in Bone-Man's basement for days (we wonder the same). Unlike, say, McEwan or MacDonald (in chapter two), sexual abuse is not described in the work of Young or Dekker, although the injured children make us suspect it. Though not malarial, these images can also be read as symbols: innocents are dragged into the preoccupations of their fathers/parents, and suffer. In Young and Dekker (as in Palmer, Nangle and Lewis), suffering is writ physical: one can see the harm that is being done to the children by the choices and actions of their parents.

In *The Shack* and *BoneMan's Daughters*, the injuries suffered by children are not, by any means, the end of the story. Both novels indulge in fantasies of redemption: the injuries are not in vain — indeed, something magnificent is gained from them (restored faith in Young; father-daughter reconciliation in Dekker). It is as though these texts explore, as elaborately and imaginatively as they can, the problems of missionary kid experiences from adult points of view, highlighting, through unrealistic plots, what is dysfunctional, but then these novels engage in fantasy again to posit gloriously implausible resolutions to the problems they have explored. What is perhaps most surprising is that mass-market authors Young and Dekker are not alone in presenting fantasies of redemption: surprisingly, and revealingly, the texts of Palmer, Nangle and Lewis do so as well.

Fantasies of Repentance, Justification, and Apology (Young, Dekker, Palmer, Lewis, Nangle)

In the accounts of abuse provided by the U.S. Presbyterian Church in their documentary film *Witness to Truth, Witness to Healing*, participants discuss three common and problematic responses given by congregation members to the testimonies of abuse victims: (1) How could you impugn such and such a person? (2) Yes, it happened, but I have moved on and so should you. (3) Find it in your heart to forgive and forget. This last is, for one abuse victim in the documentary, the most annoying. "It's not scriptural!" she rails, but the question of scripture is a red herring. Forgiving your abuser, for an abuse victim, is beyond the pale, especially if your abuser never acknowledges that s/he committed a crime against you in the first place. In *All God's Children*, Dianne Darr Couts notes that abuse victims are against forgiveness as a solution to the problem of abuse because it doesn't force anything to change. For the victims of abuse at Mamou boarding school, it took ten years for the Christian and Missionary Alliance to grudgingly acknowledge that there *might* be some legitimacy to their many claims. But even when the C&MA admitted abuse had happened, it did not punish the perpetrators. A handful were "reprimanded" within the church, many opted not to "cooperate" with church inquiries, and *no legal charges were brought against any Mamou staff member.*

The case of Mamou *may* be an isolated one but it is also likely that it is representative of what Missionary Kids Safety Net describes as "child abuse at countless missionary boarding schools" (www.mksafetynet.net). Missionary Kids Safety Net implies that the problem of child abuse is endemic to isolated mission settings in which children are far from their families and church school employees far from witnesses. Forgiveness (as a Christian ideal) does not work for abuse victims, especially those in church contexts, because it means the abuser does not have to change his/her behavior and may not even, thanks to church protection, have to acknowledge his/her crimes. Acknowledgment that wrong has been done, accompanied by genuine apology, would be far better, were it possible to obtain such a response from abusers. It is easy to see why fiction coming out of a missionary kid context might fantasize about acknowledgment and apology.

But Palmer, Nangle, Lewis, Young and Dekker write fantasies of apologetic *parents*, not apologetic abusers. And yet even this turn makes sense: *parents* send children to the schools at which the children are abused; *parents* choose to go on the missions that expose children to so much duress. The suffering of missionary children emerges most directly from choices their *parents* make. In *All God's Children*, Howie Beardslee says of his inability to forgive his parents for sending him to the boarding school at which he was abused, "It's not OK. I have to live with it, and they [his parents] have to live with it." His mother Ann retorts that "it was a question of obedience to God." Herein the conundrum: Ann believes she did what she had to do to meet God's demands; Howie believes her responsibility to him, as her child, should have taken precedence. David Darr says this of the choice his parents made: "I was sacrificed, abandoned. It was not necessary." He thinks his parents *could* have chosen not to send him away. Regardless of how they felt about God, they *could* have made other choices.

If the key presiding concern in the literature of former missionary kids is parents abandoning or sacrificing their children in order to follow God, then the presiding fantasy the literature presents is that of parents who recognize what they have done and sincerely beg for their children's forgiveness.

When Dekker's Ryan returns from Iraq, he says to his wife Celine, "I'm so sorry. I beg your forgiveness. It's been my fault, all of it. I'm the one to blame. I've been a fool for leaving. Will you please, please, just take me back?" (121). When he attempts to reconcile with Bethany, it is because "he loved her more than even he could possibly have realized" (122). What a grand idyll! The father who has abandoned the family (and especially the child) recognizes that he is to blame, begs for forgiveness and pleads his love. Would not any child who feels wronged by a parent wish for this? Ryan even proves his love by undergoing nearly impossible feats to rescue his daughter. Ultimately he *earns* her love back by rescuing her from Bone-Man. "I want to be your father," Ryan declaims (399). "You came back for me. You are my father and I'll never leave you," Bethany replies (400), expressing a histrionic but trenchant fantasy: the father who abandoned her has returned to claim her, and now she can finally love him. Interestingly, Ryan rescues Bethany from BoneMan (a.k.a. Satan), a figure who himself uses "father and God interchangeably" (314). If Ryan finally gets to be father/God, then he has rescued Bethany from Satan and returned her to God as well.

Lewis' *The Flame Tree* presents a similar scenario. Isaac's mother recognizes what she has done, and how it might have felt to her son. She formally apologizes and begs for his forgiveness:

> Isaac, I've done you a very great wrong. When I decided to stay here while you got on that helicopter, I thought I was following the Lord's will, putting His calling first. But I wasn't. I was putting my pride first. I put my pride before my love and duty to you. You feel I abandoned you ... and you are right, I did abandon you. I should have been with you the whole time, I should have ... I should have.... I was so very wrong. Please forgive me [254].

Isaac's mother apologizes, pleads, and tries to win her son back (much like Ryan, above). In this more explicit mission context, she also exculpates God, blaming her own pride and misunderstanding of her mission rather than her faith. Isaac experiences a desire to "hurt her cruelly" by rejecting her, for "she *had* abandoned him" (254–55). "But he loved her," he thinks to himself and then says to her, "Of course I forgive you" (255).

In Young's *The Shack*, we get a different fantasy — one in which God explains what has happened to the child to make it clear that the parent did not abandon anyone. Here we get parental repentance, divine justification *and* parent-child reconciliation. Mack is taken by Jesus to a place where he can see Missy in "an anteroom of a greater reality to come," a pre–Heaven holding cell of the most fabulous and wonderful kind (167). Missy can't see him: "She knows you are here, but she cannot see you," says the beautiful Hispanic woman who administers Mack's access to this vision of Missy.

> Mack focused on [Missy], trying to memorize again every detail of her expression and hair and hands. As he did so, Missy's face erupted in a huge smile, dimples standing out. In slow motion, with great exaggeration, he could see her mouth the words, "It's okay, I..." and now she signed the words, "... love you" ...
> Mack watched every move his precious Missy was making. "Has she forgiven me?" he asked [the Hispanic beauty].
> "Forgiven you for what?"
> "I failed her," he whispered.
> "It would be her nature to forgive, if there were anything to forgive, which there is not" [167–68].

This, too, is a missionary kid fantasy: the father feels he has failed, the divine steps in to exonerate him, and child and father are reconciled, becoming able to fully love one another. Missy forgives Mack ("It's okay"), even though there is, apparently, nothing to forgive. Mack admits he has failed, even though apparently he has not. Missy loves Mack, and Mack loves Missy.

Pollock and Van Reken observe, "Some mission people see an admission of painful feelings as weakness or, worse, a lack of faith. TCKs who want to keep their faith often feel they can't acknowledge the pain they have experienced" (173). That may be the case in Young's *The Shack*, but this idea is even more explicit in Palmer's *The Happy Room*. Peter, the most combative of the three adult siblings, argues outside the hospital in which his sister is dying until his father starts speaking Kenyan Maa: "Hearing his father speak in Maa, Peter suddenly saw his father differently and felt a newfound respect for the older man's years of experience and his greater wisdom" (258). This respect comes out of nowhere and seems jarringly out of place in a novel that is otherwise consistently observant of the difficulties missionary life imposed on the children, especially boarding school, and quite consistent in also suggesting the parents ought not to have prioritized God instead of their children. Peter and his father begin reenacting a Maasai ritual. "I worship you," Peter says to his father several steps into the ritual, "I follow your guidance down the path that is my life" (261–62). Then,

> Peter opened his eyes and saw that his father was weeping. There was still one more thing Peter needed to do. Still crouching on the sidewalk next to his father, he tugged a clump of green grass from the lawn. In the Maasai gesture of asking for forgiveness, he held out the grass to his father.
> "Oh, Peter," Dad said, taking the grass and clutching it tightly. "You don't need my forgiveness."
> "I've not only wronged God," Peter said. "I've wronged you" [262].

This reads as a retreat from what is, in other parts of the novel, a strong critique of the effect of mission work on children. In this novel that largely condemns missionary parents, we detour into a dream of how it is *supposed* to be. Fathers are supposed to be figures their children respect. Sons are supposed to be pious. Palmer backs away from what she elsewhere implies (that missionaries tend to compromise their own children's well-being) to present instead a moment of fealty and orthodoxy. The son once again loves his father and also God, with unquestioning respect.

In Nangle's short story "The Cry Room" in *The Leper Compound*, abandonment and fantastical reconciliation happen simultaneously. Colleen's son Gavin is hospitalized for a heart defect. He needs surgery. He is "skeletal. His neck was a long stem and his bobbing chin pointed" (145). Ramona, the baby with whom he shares a room, is beautiful, "with eyes of a doll — blue, glazed play jewelry," but cries incessantly "all night. Whimpered. Cried and cried and cried" (150, 149). During surgery, Gavin's heart is "stopped still" but he survives: "Gavin had come back. His body was suspended tightly, tied across the bed like drying meat, a pelt, the skin a swollen ice" (152, 153). Ramona inherits her mother's addiction to cocaine, but might survive. Gavin has a major defect, and should perhaps not survive. Colleen rocks them both, her son and then Ramona, "back and forth with the crying that never stopped" (156). Gavin heals and Ramona dies, likely suffocated by Colleen herself. Colleen watches the nurses try to help the already-dead Ramona, holding "her live baby" Gavin (156). Colleen has abandoned Ramona, perhaps even killing her: the child needs too much mothering, or, as she snaps to her husband, "I'm not the world's mother" (150). Ramona is "Colleen's waterlogged lullaby doll" (156). And yet she "sacrifice[s]" Ramona: Ramona dies so that Gavin may live (158). The sacrifice of Ramona is devastating, but Colleen gets to hold Gavin — she gets to be with him. The fantasy here is of parental inadequacy (Colleen decides not to parent Ramona) *and* parental triumph (because Colleen breastfeeds and nurtures Gavin, he is able to thrive). Nangle presents failure (Ramona — dead baby) and fantastical wish-fulfillment (Gavin — baby who recovers from heart defect) simultaneously.

In all five of the novels I have used as examples in this chapter, one sees children abandoned or sacrificed, and amazing, fantastical resolutions in which parents and children get to understand and love one another (and maybe also God). With remarkable consistency, these texts by former missionary kids show the grief of children who have been sacrificed. Troublingly consistent is the appearance in all five texts of far-fetched, fictional fantasies that justify, redeem and explain the abandonment of children. What the literature of former missionary kids tends to intimate is that when *parents* are God's children, children themselves are compromised. Because the sacrifice of missionary kids by their parents is "God's will" and therefore, to the faithful, beyond critique, the literature of former missionary kids plays a significant role in allowing, through the medium of fiction, analyses that may not always present God, faith or missionaries in the most positive light. Concomitantly, God, faith and missionaries may not be able or willing to provide the acknowledgment and apology that missionary kids who feel abandoned or sacrificed crave. The fiction is significant here as well, providing recognition of wrongs done, apologies, and reconciliations.

Conclusion

Barbara Kingsolver's *The Poisonwood Bible* as Third Culture Literature

The U.S. Department of State has a webpage for issues arising when American third culture kids repatriate. Apparently intended for K–12 educators, it begins:

> **Who is the most recent immigrant to your school?** You may be surprised to find that the answer may not be Roberto who immigrated from El Salvador nor Kamini from India, but rather Bobby or Katie who were born to United States (U.S.) citizens and recently moved back to the U.S. from Poland, Santo Domingo, or another foreign country. Every year, there are an estimated 300,000 U.S. students living overseas of whom 100,000 transit back to the U.S. and enter U.S. schools (Gerner, Perry, Moselle, & Archbold, 1992). Because these students, who are known as Third Culture Kids (TCKs), are American citizens and often were born in the U.S., educators are not always aware of who they are, what they might need, and what special gifts they have to offer [Kidd and Lankenau].

The U.S. Department of State acknowledges, in short, that about 100,000 American third culture kids repatriate to the United States *every year*, and makes it clear that because "Bobby or Katie" look American and have American passports/parents, people may not recognize that their experiences are different from those of their peers. These children are what Pollock and Van Reken refer to as "hidden immigrants": they look like their peers, but they think differently (246).

Feroza Jussawalla begins a 2003 article on Barbara Kingsolver's *The Poisonwood Bible* by asking, "Can an American writer really be considered a 'postcolonial' writer? Can a 'White American' writer be considered postcolonial when in fact most theoretical positions associate American Literature with imperialism?" (6). Jussawalla criticizes Kingsolver for being white and American (privileged) and yet, apparently, taking on such a postcolonial topic as decolonization. She makes no mention of the year Kingsolver spent in the Congo as a child (and indeed, there's no reason that she should, for a year as an expatriate child does not a *postcolonial* author make). Kingsolver is no "Roberto" or "Kamini": she does not bear visible marks of alterity, or even linguistic traces of otherness. Her experience is akin to that of "Katie" or "Bobby." In America, Kingsolver looks and sounds American; the experiences she had as a child in the Congo, regardless of how profound they may have been, are hidden. Because of her experiences in the Congo as a child, Kingsolver has a third culture perspective, but it is invisible.

The Poisonwood Bible is largely set in the Congo, and critiques, on the one hand, the American interventions that toppled the Congo's independence in 1960 and facilitated the slaughter of recently elected Patrice Lumumba, and, on the other, the grievously zealous American Baptism that the character Nathan Price inflicts on a small Congolese village. The five female narrators (four daughters and their mother, Orleanna Price) are American. Kingsolver writes from the empowered, not disempowered, side of the colonial equation, and about characters who similarly enjoy American privilege. But the juxtaposition of the U.S. Department of State's webpage and Jussawalla's questions makes it, at least to me, almost painfully obvious that Kingsolver ought to be treated as a "hidden immigrant" and a third culture kid. *The Poisonwood Bible* can be usefully analyzed if one adopts the idea of third culture. Without third culture as a conceptual category and analytical framework, *The Poisonwood Bible* raises myriad questions for which there are no answers.

Kathleen Gilbert defines third culture kids as "persons who accompanied their parents to live all or part of their childhood outside the country for which they hold a passport" (93). Her study is tellingly titled "Loss and Grief Between and Among Cultures: The Experience of Third Culture Kids," and was published in the journal *Illness, Crisis and Loss*. Though Pollock asserts that a third culture upbringing is neither "pathology" nor "disease," not "something from which to recover" (in Pollock and Van Reken xxii), for children in their developmental years it clearly has a profound, often devastating, impact in its combination of privilege with guilt, rootlessness, powerlessness, fear and, perhaps most of all, loss. Third culture literature reflects the profound disconnection between all that is wonderful about being raised overseas or in multiple locations and all that is terrible (and especially grievous for being generally unacknowledged) about it. In this chapter, I argue that Kingsolver's *The Poisonwood Bible* exhibits the characteristics of third culture literature and that Ruth May Price's death — the presiding event in the text — is a consummately third culture expression of loss (which third culture literature suggests is itself the presiding effect of a third culture upbringing).

The Poisonwood Bible tells the story of the Price family. They leave Georgia to be Baptist missionaries in the Congo, despite the fact that their church advises Nathan Price against it (163–64). Nathan is accompanied by his wife Orleanna and four daughters, Rachel, Leah and Adah (twins), and Ruth May. Though his self-importance transports the family into the jungle, Nathan's is not one of the five voices that tell the story. Instead, his female family members reflect upon the failures of his mission, his vegetable garden and his sanity while staking out distinct identities for themselves, shaping themselves into independence in the Congo, just as the Congo shapes itself into independence from Belgium (it is revealing that for neither the women nor the country does "independence" come easily or completely). The Prices embark on a short "twelve-month mission," but each of the five narrators is profoundly changed (13).

Kingsolver uses the four child characters in particular to suggest four different outcomes in terms of identity development, investigating what might happen to a youth's American identity in light of a significant stint overseas. Ruth May dies, suggesting that the American self in Africa is impossible. Leah becomes as African as she can, eventually marrying an African, bearing African children and straining to "work [her] skin to darkness under the equatorial sun" (526). She thus attempts to replace her American self with an African one. Adah does not die, despite being lame and left without help during an ant invasion. After this traumatic event, she in fact starts to heal herself: the Congo teaches her about her own strength, which she applies in the United States. Rachel moves to the French Congo and runs a hotel: the American self learns to relish what it is to be an expatriate, an overseas American in Africa permanently. Kingsolver can separate out four strains in these characters, strains that might, for a single third culture kid, actually be woven together, with the potential for losing one's first culture self, trying (but failing) to fully assimilate, finding new personal strengths, and locating an expatriate community all being combined.

The Price daughters are dramatically influenced by their year abroad as third culture, missionary kids. I find this significant in terms of Kingsolver's own Congo sojourn, which she frames as too brief to have had much impact on her. Describing her life in the appendices of a 2005 edition of *The Poisonwood Bible*, she emphasizes her upbringing "in the middle of an alfalfa field" in eastern Kentucky (P.S. 2) before going on to sheepishly acknowledge living "briefly" in the Congo "as a child" (P.S. 7).

Kingsolver almost sounds as though she is apologizing for having the audacity to write her "D.A.B." (Damned Africa Book), given how "briefly" she experienced the Congo and how young she was (P.S. 5–14).

Pollock and Van Reken, however, emphasize that the duration of an experience is not predictive of its role in shaping a third culture kid:

> Time by itself doesn't determine how deep an impact the third culture experience has on the development of a particular child. Other variables such as the child's age, personality, and participation in the local culture will have an important effect. For example, living overseas between the ages of one and four will affect a child differently than if that same experience occurs between the ages of eleven and fourteen [27].

Kingsolver was eight in 1963 when her family spent a year (the same amount of time the Price family originally intends to stay) (13) in a Congolese village where her father (a physician) provided medical care. Eight is an age of which most adults retain clear memories. Significant experiences at that age *can* profoundly shape an adult. And yet Kingsolver seems ambivalent about how to process her experience. It provides "memories of playing with village children and exploring the jungle [that are] acutely sensory and indelible" on the one hand. But, on the other, these childish experiences are, she claims, not pertinent to a reading of the novel: "The thematic material of *The Poisonwood* [sic] is serious, adult stuff. I wrote the book not because of a brief adventure I had in place of second grade, but because as an adult I am interested in cultural imperialism and postcolonial history" (Kingsolver, "FAQ"). Supposedly separate, then, are the "adventure" she experienced as a child and the novel, which is painstakingly researched and derived from adult interests.

Kingsolver sounds unnecessarily defensive about her biographical connection to the material in her novel. It is as if she is anticipating critics who might accuse her of producing a juvenile, imperialist reflection on the complexities of postcolonial politics, or, perhaps worse, of claiming some kind of Africanness for herself. Possibly Kingsolver might find negotiating her position vis-à-vis her carefully astute adult fiction and her childhood Congo year easier if she could draw on the idea of third culture. In an interview with Ellen Kanner, Kingsolver says of returning from the Congo, "I came home with an acutely heightened sense of race, of ethnicity. I got to live in a place where people thought I was noticeable and probably hideous because of the color of my skin. These weren't easy lessons ... but they were priceless" (Kanner). Indeed, Kanner concludes that Kingsolver "has not forgotten what the Congo taught her. It made her the person, the writer, she is." The idea of "third culture" would perhaps allow Kingsolver to acknowledge the influence the Congo had on the shaping of her identity, for would she be interested in "cultural imperialism and post-colonial history" had she not lived there? Would she have written a novel in which such an experience (a year abroad in an African country) profoundly, and variously, affects four different child characters? Acknowledging herself as a third culture kid, Kingsolver might feel able to position herself as an American changed by her encounter with another culture without fearing that doing so is to claim that twelve months of experience at age eight granted her either Africanness or the *adult* knowledge of politics and history she later so carefully acquired by dint of research.

Critical foundering in response to Kingsolver's "Damned Africa Book" suggests that it raises questions which are difficult to answer without the vocabulary of third culture literary analysis. *New York Times* reviewer Verlyn Klinkenborg asserts that *The Poisonwood Bible* "turns on several axes," hinting that the five narrative voices mean one cannot discern a *single* point around which the novel's content is oriented. In her article on the representation of missionary work in *The Poisonwood Bible*, Elaine R. Ognibene comments briefly and concretely on Kingsolver's *oeuvre*: "In all her fiction, Kingsolver grapples with clashing cultural values, social justice issues, ecological awareness, and the intersection of private and public concerns" (34). But Ognibene is unable to be as clear about what exactly Kingsolver grapples with in this novel: "*The Poisonwood Bible*, however, is more complex; its images resonate across levels of meaning, allusions are multiple, and the stories of its narrators carry deep spiritual meaning. As re-told narratives cross and refract, shedding different shades of light on the same truth, ethical questions multiply" (34). Klinkenborg and Ognibene are alike in finding that the novel's narrative-in-five-voices is hard to sum up as coherent and unified. There are, according to the two critics, numerous axes, questions and allusions; these axes, questions and allusions remain, for Klinkenborg and Ognibene, undefined, even undefineable. The problem is that neither critic is asking what it is to be a third culture kid (as four of the novel's five narrative voices are — Rachel, Leah, Adah and Ruth May), and they have no vocabulary for discussing third culture literature (which the novel exemplifies). Reading *The Poisonwood Bible* as third culture literature reveals concerns that *do* provide unity and coherence across the different narrative perspectives.

An author's culture is influential in terms of themes and tropes that appear in their fiction writing. Kingsolver's case is interesting: As a child she went to the Congo so her father could practice medicine there. She was, though she may not yet be aware of the term herself, a third culture kid. But her father was not part of a missionary or military organization and presumably could act relatively autonomously. Her experience as a third culture kid was consequently different in significant ways from the typical experiences of missionary children. Kingsolver did not have to attend a mission boarding school, for instance, and the novel's insights about third culture life imply a freedom from the direct responsibilities to God that a missionary kid would have felt subject to. Though third culture, certain elements that tend to typify the writings of former missionary kids are missing in *The Poisonwood Bible*, which makes perfect sense: what we have here is a novel about missionary kids by an adult third culture kid who was not herself a missionary kid. Kingsolver has a capacious enough imagination to evoke a great deal of what the Price girls might have experienced, so what one gets in the novel are the characteristics of third culture literature generally, with some elements of what one sees in the writings of former missionary kids, as well as some significant departures.

Dislocation

The Poisonwood Bible, quite obviously, presents dislocation, the first of the four characteristics indicative of third culture literature. The Prices leave the United States to take up residence in the Congo. They move, leaving their home behind, to a destination with which they are markedly unfamiliar. In the new place, the family itself becomes an isolated enclave of foreignness.

Leah describes how the Prices try to bring America with them into the jungle despite the airline's restrictive luggage allowance:

> We struck out for Africa carrying all our excess baggage on our bodies, under our clothes. Also, we had *clothes* under our clothes. My sisters and I left home wearing six pairs of underdrawers, two-half slips and camisoles; several dresses one on top of the other, with pedal-pushers underneath; and outside of everything an all-weather coat. (The encyclopedia advised us to count on rain). The other goods, tools, cake-mix boxes and so forth were tucked out of sight in our pockets and under our waist-bands, surrounding us in a clanking armor [15].

Clearly the family would not get through security at an American airport these days, but what Kingsolver highlights here is that the appurtenances of American life are comical and literally weigh the family down, causing discomfort rather than helping them. The description prepares a reader for how utterly out of place the Prices are once they arrive in Africa. The hammer smuggled with them (one of the above-mentioned tools) "turned out to be a waste of a good two or three pounds, because there appear to be no nails in the mud-and-thatch town of Kilanga" (32). The stove in their Kilanga abode "looks less like a stove than a machine hammered together out of parts of another machine" (65). As a consequence, Rachel's birthday comes and goes with no use of the cake mix carried in their pockets on the journey. "Normal cake production proved out of the question" because "normal" is no longer anything like American (65). "If I'd of had the foggiest idea," says Orleanna, "just the foggiest idea. We brought all the wrong things" (65). The family is as dislocated as the Kentucky Wonder Beans that Nathan tries to plant in his failed vegetable garden: the vines grow, developing unusually large leaves, but they have no insects to pollinate them. Nathan eventually realizes there is a problem and says to Leah, "Look at this [insect]. How would it know what to do with a Kentucky Wonder Bean?" (80). He might just as easily have said, "Look at this villager. How is s/he to know what to do with people like us?" or even, "Look at us, we are as out of place here as these beans, so completely out of place that we will die out before we belong."

The Prices do slowly recognize exactly how out of place they are, Nathan most slowly of all (or, arguably, never). Orleanna, for example, "cannot stop being embarrassed" when she remembers her own obliviousness the day Leah tried to step across a row of produce at the market (89): "straddling a woman's market-day wealth ... Leah there with her genitals — bare, for all anyone knew — suspended over a woman's oranges" (89). Leah has been rude; Orleanna has let her blight the market-woman's wares. Neither intended to cause offense, but they do, and then feel rightly but severely chastised: "A foreign mother and her child assuming themselves in charge, suddenly slapped down to nothing by what they all saw us to be" (89). They are "foreign" missionaries, arrogant for having assumed "themselves in charge" and exaggeratedly aware of how humblingly dislocated they are when they see themselves through the eyes of Congolese villagers. Orleanna says, "Until that moment I'd thought I could have it both ways: to be one of them and also my husband's wife" (89). The incident makes it clear that she and her children are irrevocably outsiders.

Moreover, they become outsiders everywhere else as well because of their Congolese experiences. Repatriation to America (for Orleanna and Adah) and relocation to the French Congo (for Rachel) do not make for a return to feeling at home, any more than remaining in the Congo does for Leah, for Africa "happened" to the family, and it is impossible to change that, or for them to go back to the way they were before. Orleanna says to the deceased Ruth May, "Try to imagine what never happened: our family without Africa," but the time in Africa cannot be un-spent (385). "My little beast, my eyes, my favorite stolen egg. Listen. To live is to be marked. To live is to change," says Orleanna (385). Their year in the

Congo is what changes the Price women, and those changes cannot be undone. There is a dislocation of identity for all of them that no circumstance can turn back into a complacent feeling of belonging.

Orleanna wonders if the family is more disconnected than they know: "Are we lost right now without knowing it?" she asks (90). The fact that she asks the question at all implies that they are. Leah feels out of place next to her playmate Pascal because she has no Congolese skills ("My own hands lumbered like pale flippers on a walrus out of its element") and yet she also deeply resents her Americanness ("I felt a stirring of anger against my father for making me a white preacher's child from Georgia") (115). Leah is dislocated from both places, and experiencing her feeling of not belonging to the Congo alongside her sense of no longer belonging to Georgia results in her inner turmoil: "My embarrassment ran scarlet and deep" (115). The novel's plot essentially revolves around how disconnected the Prices are from the Congo, and how the Congo experience disconnects them from their American past.

Loss

In Kingsolver's novel, loss overshadows by far the privileges her characters enjoy. Loss is, as in every other literary example in this book, highlighted, taking a reader past the "you're so lucky you got to live in X country!" response to what characters experience and well into "I had no idea it would entail so much grief" instead. *The Poisonwood Bible*, set as it is on the cusp of Lumumba's election (and assassination) in the Congo, alludes clearly to the question of white privilege in Africa. Conrad's *Heart of Darkness* and the legacy of King Leopold II are perhaps foremost among Kingsolver's allusions. Jussawalla takes refuge in the possibility that *The Poisonwood Bible* is "postcolonial in intent," just as Conrad's *Heart of Darkness* might also be "postcolonial in intent" (6, 7). Does "postcolonial in intent" mean the author seeks to point out colonial inequities, and perhaps even suggest how to redress them? Kingsolver (though not otherwise very much like Conrad at all) *is* like Conrad in that she writes about the Congo from a position of privilege and creates characters who are privileged. Her characters become aware of how privileged they are, which is a means of pointing out inequities. However, tragic losses in Kingsolver's novel (notably Ruth May's death) are not retributive. They are not punishments for colonialist intrusions. Instead, they express the deep feelings of loss that arise from a third culture experience: loss of people, places and pets that connote home, and of the secure sense of identity that goes with feeling one has a home.

In terms of privilege, the Prices live in a house that is "different from all the other houses in Kilanga," with "a wide front room and two bedrooms in the back, one of which resembles a hospital scene from Florence Nightingale's time, as it is chock-full of cots under triangles of mosquito net for the family surplus of girls" (60). "Unlike the other villagers' houses, our windows are square panes of glass and our foundation and floor are cement," remarks Adah (60). Their house is "different" and "unlike" others because of its size, glass windows, cement floor, and mosquito netting. It is a rich house, regardless of how deprived the Price family may feel in it. *Fufu* (a paste made of pounded manioc) is the village staple, and yet the Prices expect fruit, meat and vegetables: they require what by village standards would be "three Thanksgiving dinners a day" (93). What largesse, what excess. A boy named Nelson is enlisted to help them, and, in marked contrast to the girls (who arrive wearing their entire wardrobe), he has "no more than an intact seat to his brown shorts [and] a red T-shirt he wears every day of his life" (143). In their early weeks in the Congo, the girls have time to play, and it turns out that this is a luxury too. Leah realizes this on spending time with a boy named Pascal:

> It struck me what a wide world of difference there was between our sort of games — "Mother, May I?," "Hide and Seek" — and his: "Find Food," "Recognize Firewood," "Build a House." And here he was a boy no older than eight or nine. He had a younger sister who carried the family's baby everywhere she went and hacked weeds in the manioc field. I could see that this whole business of Childhood was nothing guaranteed [114].

The girls lose their childhoods in their encounter with the Congo, first in terms of how they occupy their time, for Orleanna succumbs to bedridden depression, leaving Leah to tend malarial Ruth May, and Rachel to take over the cooking (despite her ineptitude). They may not be hacking weeds in the manioc fields, but they are no longer playing Hide and Seek either: "Our childhood has passed over into history overnight," Adah observes, "The transition was unnoticed by anyone but ourselves" (218). They lose their childhood in a second way as well, for they also lose an *American* childhood. There are no brownies to eat after school; indeed, there is no school, but rather homeschooling in the "Ding Dong Schoolhouse with Mother" (160). There are also no bicycles to ride or television shows to watch, no swimming lessons, no birthday parties. They lose the childhood they had expected for themselves. (Orleanna's "Ding Dong Schoolhouse" also marks one of the differences between *The Poisonwood Bible* and fiction texts by former missionary kids: the girls do not go to boarding school.)

Systematically, the Prices lose most of their material privileges when Nathan's salary stops coming after he refuses to return to the United States. To the villagers who continue to try and sell things to the Prices, the family "spelled out our position as best we could: *fyata*, no money! ... Yet our neighbors in Kilanga seemed to think: Could this really be, a white person *fyata*?" (206). Colonial history set the precedent that white people *always* had more money than Africans. When the Prices first arrive, despite being impoverished missionaries, they still have more money than the Congolese around them. It is a significant change—in fact, almost inconceivable—when that is no longer true. Leah observes that "Mama Mwanza from next door was the only one who felt sorry for us. She made her way over on the palms of her hands to give us some oranges.... Really you know things are bad when a woman without any legs and who recently lost two of her own kids feels sorry for *you*" (206–7). One critical response to this change of circumstance is to see it as postcolonial in its reversal of the material-racial norms of colonialism: "It is clear that Kingsolver's perception of missionaries makes them, unlike their colonial predecessors, marginal figures in the new society" (Varela-Zapata 108). The missionaries, in this reading, are postcolonially marginalized. However, a third culture reading lets one examine the Price family's circumstances as indicative of the erosion of their identities. Material wealth is one thing that flags them as outsiders: here they lose their foreign material wealth and become, not insiders, but rather outsiders whom Africa has marked. The Congo has changed the Price family and is remolding them. They are not African but they are not simply American anymore either. They are becoming third culture and are doing so especially because of what they lose.

If pets are one of the appurtenances of home in the Western world, then the parrot Methuselah's death is symbolically significant. Inherited from the family's missionary predecessor, the bird is technically part of their household, but he is exiled from the house by Nathan because of his foul language and lurks in the foliage until killed by a civet cat. His remains are found by Adah: "clusters of long wing feathers still attached to gristle and skin" in the grass (185). His death is the death of home. The family and its abode do not offer sanctuary, but rather send members of the household out to be savaged by the world beyond. His death echoes both the "death" of Adah (who is presumed to have been killed by a lion, but in fact has not been) (140) and the actual death of Ruth May. Methuselah, as his biblical name suggests, should live forever, but the Prices will not, do not and cannot protect him, just as they will not, do not and cannot protect themselves.

Predators also invade the family house, revealing it as inadequate in terms of providing a safe haven. The Price house, like the houses in books by former missionary kids (*The Happy Room*, *The Leper Compound* and even *The Shack* and *BoneMan's Daughters*), is vulnerable, signifying how vulnerable the family members themselves are. Ants (*nsongonya*) swarm the village one night, and, in a consummately third culture moment, the Prices have to run, leaving everything behind. Like the pet hamster forgotten in the garage or the songbird abandoned when military families are quickly "reduce[d] in force" (see Bosco's comments in *The Yokota Officers Club*), what the Prices leave behind is quite literally dead to them: the chickens in the Price family coop cannot escape on the night of the ants and are eaten alive, "their bones laid clean and white" (311). The girls return to the house and the chicken skeletons, with their symbolic bones (white, like the girls are, but also laid in the dust as if telling a fortune by African witchcraft), indicate a new development: the Price girls feel that all constructions of "home," African or American, have been called into question. The idea of "home" itself is newly insecure, and they themselves are conspicuously laid bare, "clean and white," as they try to restructure their identities.

Leah says "You can't just point to the one most terrible thing and wonder why it happened. This has been a whole terrible time, from the beginning of the drought that left so many without food, and then the night of the ants, to now the worst tragedy of all" (327). Loss agglomerates over the months and culminates in Ruth May dying from a snake bite. After the green mamba kills Ruth May, Rachel thinks about how they will tell their parents what has happened: "Now we were going to put one foot in front of the other, walk to the back door, go in the house, stand beside our parents' bed, wake up Mother, say to her the words *Ruth May*, say the word *dead*" (366). It is unbearable. What is most profound about Ruth May's death, though, is that it indicates how absolutely Africa has changed the family.

Kingsolver makes the death of the youngest daughter emblematic of the loss of a secure national self-identity: it is a third culture tragedy. As Rachel expresses it,

> Until that moment I'd always believed I could still go home and pretend the Congo never happened. The misery, the hunt, the ants, the embarrassments of all we saw and endured — those were just stories I would tell someday with a laugh and a toss of my hair, when Africa was faraway and make-believe like the people in history books. The tragedies that happened to Africans were not mine. We were different, not just because we were white and had our vaccinations, but because we were simply a much, much luckier kind of person. I would get back to Bethlehem, Georgia, and be exactly the same Rachel as before. I'd grow up to be a carefree American wife, with nice things and a sensible way of

> life and three grown sisters to share my ideals and talk to on the phone from time to time. This is what I believed. I'd never planned on being someone different. Never imagined I would be a girl they'd duck their eyes from and whisper about as tragic, for having suffered such a loss [367].

There is so much in Rachel's words that expresses third culture loss specifically: "I'd always believed I could still go home and pretend the Congo never happened," but she cannot: she cannot really go "home" again (and, indeed, chooses not to try by staying on the African continent for the rest of her life). The Congo *did* happen, and it did change her, irrevocably. Africa is not make-believe or remote anymore — it has deeply personal significance. African tragedies *are* hers, as she no longer feels like a "much, much luckier kind of person." She is not the same Rachel as before. Influenced by her Congo experiences, she cannot "grow up to be a carefree American wife." What Rachel loses, what all the Price daughters lose with Ruth May's death, is the ability to separate their African experience from their identity. They lose their purely American identity; they are forced to admit that the Congo has shaped them so strongly that a previous *self* has died. Ruth May literally dies, but the "old" versions of Leah, Adah and Rachel die too. This way of expressing loss is third cultural in that, instead of focusing on the tragedy of Ruth May's passing, Kingsolver has her characters focus on how the death of the youngest girl in Africa signifies the great change Africa has wrought upon them all.

If Kingsolver has taken third culture experience and divided its different ramifications among the perspectives of the four girls, then Orleanna, the mother and fifth narrator, provides something a bit different in terms of thinking through the significance of Ruth May's death. On this topic, Orleanna's ideas differ markedly from those of her third culture daughters. In Kingsolver's treatment of Ruth May's death through Orleanna's eyes, we get a synthesis of Africa and America, with the two becoming veritable "blood-sisters." Orleanna muses that the death of her youngest suggests that "the two rivers," her blood and the Congo, "have run together" (385). Ruth May's death and the experience of living in the Congo are continually intertwined, so Orleanna's grief is equally associated with both. "I just go on keening for my own losses," thinks Orleanna, "trying to wear the marks of the boot on my back as gracefully as the Congo wears hers" (385). These descriptions suggest that Orleanna and the Congo are alike — both are mothers to tragic loss. They also suggest it is *possible* for the river of Orleanna's blood and that of the Congo to run together. They suggest, in short, that through Ruth May's death and burial in African soil, Orleanna has a connection to place, which third culture literature generally portrays as being close to, if not absolutely, impossible for a third culture individual. The disjunction is fruitful in that it reminds us that the experience of an adult (already possessed of a clear national and cultural identity) who moves to an unfamiliar place is profoundly different from that of a child (who is still struggling to establish who they are and what their place is in the world). Orleanna can imagine a melding because she has a clear sense of who she was before Africa. There is a "river" that represents her before Africa and it is separate from the one so famously associated with the Congo. Paradoxically, surviving daughters Rachel, Adah and Leah cannot "meld" because they have no clear sense of a preexisting "river of their own blood." Because the girls do not have a stable American self in the first place, they cannot blend that part of their identity with the Congo, and instead develop an identity that indicates "their sense of relationship" with both cultures, "while not having full ownership in [either]" (Pollock). They grow to feel awkwardly peripheral everywhere. It is the Congo, as well as the death of their sister, that requires Rachel, Leah and Adah to find "their own three ways to live with [the family's] experience" (385). Each chooses a third culture response that tries to make sense of feeling like an outsider: Rachel by embracing expatriate life at her hotel, Leah by trying (forever unsuccessfully) to make herself African, and Adah by retreating to a life with more time spent among viruses than humans, a life turning isolation into a humanitarian achievement.

Deceased Ruth May gets the novel's last chapter, speaking of herself as "the forest's conscience" (537). She does not describe herself as abandoned or sacrificed, although abandonment and sacrifice are crucial themes in the writings of former missionary kids. In Palmer's *The Happy Room* or Lewis' *The Flame Tree*, parents pursue their religious agendas and children are damaged by them. Children are forced to go to boarding schools (generally described as terrifying places) so that their parents can focus on God's work. Children are expected to feel good about being cast aside, as it is all for the greater good of God. This vocabulary of sacrifice is almost entirely omitted from *The Poisonwood Bible*. Nathan does instruct Leah that "great sacrifice, [produces] great rewards!" but it is in the context of planting his garden, not that of her sacrificing herself so that God's work may be done (37). Orleanna develops the idea that Nathan is trying to own his daughters, just as he tries to own the land he plants in the Congo: she describes him as "Nathan, who can simply see no way to have a daughter but to own her like a plot of land. To work her, plow her under, rain down a dreadful poison upon her" (191). Kingsolver imagines the father keeping his children close (and thereby destroying them). This is very different from Palmer, Lewis, Young or Dekker, all of whom emphasize the father abandoning the child in some way. The parent, in many cases, works as God's child/servant, leaving the actual children unparented. Kingsolver's girls suffer their father's lunacies, but not his abandonment. Leah, arguing with Mrs. Underdown, suggests that "her father [knew] what was best in the sight of the Lord, and that we were privileged to serve" (182), but none of the daughters *do* actually serve as missionaries, and Leah's comment is clearly meant to silence religious Mrs. Underdown: it is a parry, not an unburdening of Leah's soul. Orleanna does try to explain to Nathan that "he's putting his own children in jeopardy" (176) by refusing to leave the Congo when asked, but "jeopardy" is still a far cry from the father quite intentionally offering his child as a sacrifice, as the Bible's Abraham does with Isaac.

We've seen the fantasies of repentance and apology that proliferate in the writings of former missionary kids. Fascinatingly, though one doesn't see much of the theme of abandonment/sacrifice, *The Poisonwood Bible* does conclude with the deceased Ruth May forgiving her mother:

> I forgive you, Mother.... The teeth at your bones are your own, the hunger is yours, forgiveness is yours. The sins of the fathers belong to you and to the forest and even to the ones in iron bracelets, and here you stand, remembering their songs. Listen. Slide the weight from your shoulders and move forward. You are afraid you might forget, but you never will. You will forgive and remember [543].

The thing is, Ruth May is forgiving her mother for *everything* from colonialism to slavery — everything, that is, that has to do with the Western world wronging Africa. Ruth May suggests Orleanna will forgive herself too — but she will remember the wrongs of "the fathers" (colonists, slavers) even while she moves forward from them. It is an oddly generalized conclusion in that it encompasses the whole colonial past and all of Africa, not just the death of a much-loved child in the Congo. Its generality is significant, for it suggests a nationally disenfranchised apology, a broad apology for all wrongs that have ever been wrought by those with power on those without.

Disenfranchisement

A third culture upbringing means that one tends to feel somewhat disconnected from all places, including one's passport "home" and the location in which one resides. Third culture is rooted especially in a shared, uneasy feeling of perpetual dislocation, rather than in a physical location. The corollary to perpetual dislocation is feeling that one has no *right* to any place. Despite privilege and good fortune, one can stake no claim to a nation as one's own. No place is really one's own to exert an influence over. Local politics (or, indeed, any politics) are the domain of those who belong (and can vote), and a third culture kid never fully belongs (and often, as an expatriate, cannot vote). In third culture literature, one sees the implications of feeling disconnected, and feeling that one has no rights, expressed in characters' obliviousness to the politics of the places in which they reside: the literature tends to present characters who are clueless about what is going on around them.

Kingsolver makes much of how ignorant her characters are about the Congo's history and politics. Nathan is most oblivious of all. Only Nathan thinks the family has a *right* to try and shape the Congo; the rest of his family is instead shaped by it. Indeed, as Jesús Varela-Zapata has it, "Mr. Price is an uncompromising man who makes no attempt to understand or become acquainted with African culture. He believes in an unqualified superiority of whites, their civilisation [*sic*] and, above all, the particular set of beliefs of his conservative Baptist denomination" (109). Like the fathers in Ann-Marie MacDonald's *The Way the Crow Flies* or Sarah Bird's *The Yokota Officers Club*, Nathan *should* know more about the Congo, for it is his responsibility to be aware of what he is exposing his family to. But Nathan's knowledge is occluded by his righteous convictions. "The Belgians and American business brought civilization to the Congo!" he yells, without acknowledging the evidence offered by his immediate, depleted surroundings, "American aid will be the Congo's salvation" (121). When Nathan refuses to leave the Congo, Mr. Underdown delicately suggests, "Nathan, perhaps you don't understand how serious this is. In all likelihood, the embassy will evacuate from Léopoldville," to which Nathan, asking no questions and admitting no new information to his rigid notions, responds, "I believe I understand perfectly well" (169). It may be that *belief* is the only thing he understands.

Rachel's vacuous imagination spins around Anatole's "autography" (autobiography) and his time in the diamond mines, concluding that because she has seen Marilyn Monroe performing "Diamonds Are a Girl's Best Friend" in the cinema, she knows "a thing or two about diamonds": "Just picturing [Monroe] in her satin gown and a Congolese diamond digger in the same universe gave me the weebie jeebies," thinks Rachel, before she adds, willfully protecting herself from insight, "So I didn't think about it anymore" (127). Leah and Adah spy on Eben Axelroot, trying — and largely failing — to figure out what his "shrieking" radio is communicating to him with such urgency (146). Later, Rachel, of all people, becomes party to some of his dealings in diamonds but misunderstands even when told directly. She describes the end of her conversation with him about the Katanga province's secession from the Congo: "'I am just happy to know somebody has succeeded in something.' ... 'You have no idea,' [Axelroot] said again. I was getting a little tired of hearing I had no idea" (292). Leah presses Anatole for information about the revolutionary *Jeune Mou Pro*. "Things are not so simple as you think," Anatole chastises, and he is not "especially kind" when he does so (308).

As an adult browsing a decades-old newspaper in which pictures of Mobutu and Lumumba appear, Leah reflects back on how little she knew despite her proximity to significant political events:

> I can picture the Georgia housewives shuddering at the communist challenge, quickly turning the page on that black devil Lumumba with the pointed chin. But I was hardly any less in the dark, and I was in Bulungu, the very village where Lumumba had been captured. My sister [Rachel] married a man who may have assisted in his death-sentence transport to Shaba, though even Rachel will never know that for sure. We have in this story the ignorant, but no real innocents [447].

Ignorance characterizes most of the Price family's interactions with the Congo: they do not know what is going on. Adah remarks, "The things we do not know, independently and in unison as a family, would fill two separate baskets, each with a large hole in its bottom" (209). This does not, however, make them innocent. Ignorance, as Kingsolver writes it, allows for complicity. The Prices are complicit with the terrible things that have happened in the Congo, and are perhaps complicit with all the terrible things the West has ever done to Africa.

Kimberly Koza argues:

> By making the Price women the narrators, Kingsolver has limited the novel's perspective to an American point of view; none of the African characters is given a voice. This choice is revealing, suggesting that Kingsolver's purpose is to tell an American story. Her novel is driven by its political goal: a critique of the arrogance and moral blindness of the American role in, what Orleanna terms, "murder[ing] the fledgling Congo" [285].

Koza's claim, however, is slightly inaccurate: African characters *do* speak within the narratives of Kingsolver's five main speakers. We hear, among others, Anatole in conversation with Leah, as well as Mama Tataba, Nelson, and Pascal. Beyond that inaccuracy, Koza's comments suggest that this is a very *enfranchised* novel: for her, it is an American text, critiquing America from the perspective of Americans. However, reading *The Poisonwood Bible* in light of Eileen Drew's *The Ivory Crocodile* or Joseph O'Neill's *Netherland* makes it clear that, certainly in the closing stages of the twentieth century and opening ones of the twenty-first, America-bashing is a "safe" political position for novels/novelists with an international conscience. For third culture authors aware of the world, regardless of where they hail from and how detached they may be from specific *national* politics, critiquing America is a reliable way to make their work sound engaged with international affairs. You cannot really put a foot wrong: America is consistently unpopular on the international stage. If one is to invest in critiquing a nation, America is the one that can be critiqued without fearing that one has misrepresented the case. Kingsolver has lived in America for most of her life, so perhaps she is cognizant of and attentive to its national politics; she takes pains, as mentioned previously, to talk about the research she did in writing this book. Nonetheless, her treatment of American influence in the Congo is conspicuously like Drew's or O'Neill's treatment of it: America is simply bad. "Bongo Bango Bingo," hums Adah, recalling the popular 1947 American song by the Andrews Sisters about American mission work in the Congo: "That is the story they are telling now in America: a tale of cannibals" (174). She overhears Axelroot speaking on his radio to another man and "the name the two men spoke out loud to each other was The President. Not Lumumba. President: Eisenhower, We Like Ike. Eki Ekil Ew. The King of America wants a tall, thin man in the Congo to be dead" (297). Adah's palindrome tells us how to feel about Ike: Eki, Ew. She takes a third culture position that acknowledges general international ill will toward America. Unmitigated America-bashing, surprisingly, implies a third culture detachment from America. It suggests Kingsolver combines an awareness of how America must be seen by the outside world with a sense that she is not really part of what has happened: in other words, it suggests Kingsolver's own third culture disenfranchisement.

Kingsolver writes of the Bellwether Prize, which she established for "fiction that addresses issues of social justice and the impact of culture and politics on human relationships":

> Fiction has a unique capacity to bring difficult issues to a broad readership on a personal level, creating empathy in a reader's heart for the theoretical stranger. Its capacity for invoking moral and social responsibility is enormous. Throughout history, every movement toward a more peaceful and humane world has begun with those who imagined the possibilities. The Bellwether Prize seeks to support the imagination of humane possibilities [Bellwether Prize].

The "possibilities" imagined by *The Poisonwood Bible* and the "moral and social responsibility" that it suggests arise not from the novel's treatment of America's troubling, foul interventions in the Congo, but rather from the relaxing of nationally and/or religiously specific moral codes. Kingsolver uses Adah's perspective to explore the positive potential of the moral indeterminacy that might arise from a third culture position.

Adah becomes a doctor whose daily work is subtended by the knowledge that her mother left her to die on the night of the ants; having only enough strength to help one child, Orleanna helped Ruth May, not her disabled older daughter. But Adah lived, aware from that moment on of how arbitrary is the choice between who lives (generally the white and the privileged) and who dies (so often African children). Adah thinks

> Africa has slipped the floor out from under my righteous house, my Adah moral code. How sure I always felt before, how smug.... Adah the bridled entitled, Adah, authorized to despise one and all. Now she must concede to those who think perhaps I should have been abandoned in the jungle at birth: well, they have a point. What I carried out of Congo on my crooked little back is a ferocious uncertainty about the worth of a life [443].

In that uncertainty lies the possibility of a more peaceful world, Kingsolver suggests. Uncertainty allows interaction, allows one culture to affect another, and allows people to see past themselves. If one of the drawbacks of a third culture upbringing is feeling uncertain about religious and political issues, if it is often considered a "challenge" to experience the "confused loyalties" that can make third culture kids unwilling to "follow unthinkingly the cultural patterns of preceding generations" (Pollock and Van Reken 80, 81, 83), then what Kingsolver does instead is tout such uncertainty as *the* thing that can support "humane possibilities" in the future. Her third culture literature makes Adah's moral uncertainties visionary. By "believing in all things equally," Adah (or, indeed, a third culture perspective) short-circuits conflict (531). Disenfranchisement is the hope of the future, if we take *The Poisonwood Bible* as our model.

Secrecy, Guilt, Malaria

I have posited the existence of four categories for the analysis of third culture literature. Three are consistent across its various substrains (dislocation, loss, disenfranchisement) and the fourth expresses context more specifically. In third culture literature generally, one sees secrecy and guilt, but in the writing of former military brats, sexual precociousness comes to express children challenging military and adult authority. In the writing of former missionary kids, sick (often malarial) children embody the sacrifices children are forced to make for their parents' careers. In Kingsolver's novel we see smatterings of secrecy and guilt, as well as malarial children —

a commingling likely resulting from the fact that the author is third culture but working hard to create a missionary context.

Guilt over Western exploitation of Africa features prominently (as Kingsolver comments elsewhere, "nearly every industrialized country has arrived at its present prosperity by doing awful things" ["FAQ"]). In *The Poisonwood Bible*, American newspapers frame Belgium as "the unsung heroes, [who,] when they come into a village [,] usually interrupt cannibal natives in the middle of human sacrifice" (161). Khrushchev, according to the same article, wants the Congo as "part of his plan for world domination" (161). America is wrong — it imagines the Belgians are *helping* the Congo. Plus, Khrushchev allegedly wants the Congo, and America-the-devious opens the door to the possibility of offering a heroic "rescue" by getting involved themselves. The Western world certainly looks odious. Secrecy is involved in two ways. First, Rachel marries Axelroot, who appears to be covertly involved in Lumumba's assassination; the Prices, then, are guilty by association. Second, Orleanna continues a private dialogue with the spirit of her dead daughter. She processes, in secret, the implications of the Price family's time on African soil, the implications of the experiences that have changed *them* irrevocably. The Congo is being destroyed by the Western world, and yet Ruth May is above all indicative of what the *family* loses.

Sick, especially malarial, children symbolize missionary parents sacrificing their children's well-being while serving on mission. In Kingsolver, Rachel gets malaria because her dosage of chloroquine has been too low (amusingly, she initially mistakes the fever for lust) (148). Ruth May sticks her malaria pills on the wall behind her bed, where her mother finds rows and rows of them after Ruth May has been sick for weeks (272). The image is like Nangle's *The Leper Compound* and Colleen's rows of untaken pills. Both Ruth May and Colleen *choose* to be ill, exerting a perverse agency in the face of the adults who "protect" them with medication when they might have better protected their children by not exposing them to malarial climes in the first place. The image of the malarial child is striking if read as third cultural, not just as specific to the literature of former missionary kids (a latitude Kingsolver's novel lets us take, straddling as it does the line between third culture literature generally and the fiction writing of former missionary kids). Travel overseas is routinely touted as so *good* for children: it exposes them to new cultures and languages; it makes them more sensitive, adaptable people. To have sickness befall these children contradicts those assumptions. Travel overseas may be *bad* for children: it might expose them to new diseases and tragedies; it might disorient them utterly, for the rest of their lives.

In all chapters of this book, third culture literature expresses the extremity of third culture dislocation, loss and disenfranchisement by developing a fourth theme, be it secrecy and guilt, sexual precociousness, or malarial children. In Kingsolver, these elements combine. In expressing dysfunction, third culture literature draws attention to the severity of loss and displacement experienced by third culture individuals: the privilege of being third culture is, in these literary expressions, far outweighed by the losses. Kingsolver returns us again and again to Ruth May's death. In the eyes of a parent or sibling, what is bigger than the loss of a child? She gives us what may be one of life's most extreme griefs. *The Poisonwood Bible* presents a family confronted with an event that utterly changes all of their identities: Ruth May's death in the Congo. More correctly, that is *two* events: Ruth May's death *and* the Congo. That is to say, Ruth May's death expresses all the ways the Price girls cannot belong in the Congo and all the ways they cannot belong in the United States either. In leaving Georgia, the Price girls leave behind American selves (those selves symbolically die); in leaving the Congo, they leave behind Ruth May (who symbolizes all of the parts of the Congo they must leave behind because, as privileged white American girls, they have no legitimate claim there). The Congo influences the Price girls, but they can ask nothing of it in return. Being third culture kids, they are well aware that they have no right to claim to belong. The Price family does not recover from or forget about Ruth May's death, just as a third culture kid neither "recovers from" nor forgets the places and cultures that, however inconsistently, make up their identity.

Kingsolver lightly describes her own "adventure" in Africa, but in writing this novel she reveals the gravity of losing a foundational experience because there seems to be no apt way to acknowledge it. Kingsolver cannot claim to be somehow African on the basis of her twelve-month sojourn at age eight, and yet the inability to reconcile her adult life with that childhood "adventure" overseas represents a loss, perhaps even a loss tantamount to the Price family's loss of Ruth May.

My reading of *The Poisonwood Bible* suggests that it is far from being a postcolonial novel, or even "postcolonial in intent." Reading the novel as third culture literature makes sense of the five narrative voices (which are ways of separating out different facets of third culture experience, especially in the voices of the four girls), and of Ruth May's death (which symbolizes the gravity of what is lost in a third culture experience).

Reading Kingsolver's novel, and the many others I treat in this book, as third culture makes it emphatically clear that these fiction texts can, and *should*, be treated as part of a distinct field of literature. They are not the same as national literatures, and they are neither postcolonial nor "international" in the sense of being from somewhere other than the first world. Third culture is established as *a literature*, as a field, in these categories of analysis, which map an analytical terrain for literatures produced by a culture that has no delimited physical geography. Third culture literature is a cohesive, and substantial field. It needs to be recognized. It can be identified quite easily. It has certain features that an analyst new to the idea of third culture could look for and readily find. It is my sincerest hope that, if you are reading this, you might yourself go off now to test, expand and refine these categories. This book ought to be only the very beginning.

Chapter Notes

Introduction

1. David Cassuto uses Kingsolver's novels to discuss water policy in the American Southwest in his 2001 *Dripping Dry*; Kingsolver's own *The Bean Trees* is often used in discussions of American indigeneity in literature, and her *Animal, Vegetable, Miracle* is a significant referent in studies of the local food movement in the United States.

2. The phrases "third culture kids" (TCKs) and "adult third culture kids" (ATCKs) originated with Ruth Hill Useem and are "neither synonymous with Third World nor with C.P. Snow's Third Culture" (Useem). "TCK" and "ATCK" are used in the social sciences, often by scholars who also participate in an organization called Families in Global Transition (FIGT). Many academics in TCK/ATCK research participate actively in this forum and contribute to the annual convention. Among these scholars are Ruth Van Reken, Ann Baker Cottrell, Anne Copeland, Barbara Schaetti and Janet Bennett. FIGT defines itself and its mission as follows:

> Families in Global Transition creates a forum where members of internationally mobile corporate, military, diplomatic, and missionary families gather with those who assist them: human resource personnel, relocation experts, educators, and counselors. Together we seek to develop practical strategies for dealing effectively with the special dynamics encountered in the cross-cultural lifestyle.
>
> It's our mission to provide an educational forum for the benefit of internationally mobile individuals, their families and those who assist them. Our goals are to increase understanding of the special dynamics encountered in a global lifestyle and to enhance the well being of those who live it ["Welcome to FIGT"].

The focus of FIGT is often practical (generally dealing with what kind of school you might enroll your American-Javanese daughter in when you are living in Turkey, or how best to deal with emergency evacuations and forced "repatriations" to your passport country if you have never actually lived there before), and so it is a useful antidote to a purely conceptual approach to third culture literature.

3. See Paterson and Plamondon; Dewaele and van Oudenhoven; and Bonebright.

4. See Dueñas' "The Postmodern Twist in Yann Martel's *Life of Pi*," as well as Werner's "Migration Towards a Rewarding Goal and Multiculturalism with a Positive Center."

5. Iyer gave the plenary speech at FIGT's 2004 convention.

6. See Robbins' impressively concise and yet comprehensive summary of such critiques in *Cosmopolitics*, "Introduction: Part One."

Chapter One

1. See CNN's post by Peter Hamby from April 29, 2009: "In an interview for the upcoming issue of the *New York Times* magazine, the president said he's grown tired of briefing books and has been spending his evenings with Joseph O'Neill's 2008 novel *Netherland*" (http://politicalticker.blogs.cnn.com/2009/04/29/what-is-president-obama-reading, accessed July 20, 2010).
2. See, for instance, Ellen Kanner's review of *Natives and Exotics* ("The Secret Life of Plants," May/June 2005), linked to Alison's webpage.
3. She calls this phenomenon "global nomad" grief, treating the term as synonymous with third culture.
4. The pathology angle allows one to ponder a connection between what seems to be a puzzlingly large number of contemporary novels about psychiatric problems and third culture literature. Consider an article in *n+1*, a "thrice-yearly print journal of politics, literature, and culture." In September 2009, this journal published "Rise of the Neuronovel." In the article, Marco Roth argues that modern fiction is increasingly, excessively, even weirdly pathologized: mental illnesses abound. How interesting that four of the seven novels listed by Roth (two by Ian McEwan) are by third culture authors (McEwan, a military brat raised in Singapore and Libya; Richard Powers, raised in Thailand from the ages of eleven to sixteen; and John Wray, with dual Austrian and American citizenship, and raised in Austria). Contemporary literary reflections on mental illness are sometimes — and more commonly than one might expect — expressions of third culture dislocation.

Chapter Two

1. The term "brat" is not taken to be derogatory, as Wertsch attests: "Of the eighty military brats interviewed for this book, only five objected to the term — two because they disliked a categorization they felt was imposed on them by the military, one because she did not like the implications of 'brat,' and two because they had always been told to say 'Navy junior' instead. The rest all said they identified with the term *military brat* and used it themselves" (xvii). Donna Musil titled her film *Brats: Our Journey Home*, Ender titled the collection of essays he edits *Military Brats and Other Global Nomads*, and Wertsch's own book is *Military Brats: Legacies of Childhood Inside the Fortress*.
2. More spectacularly than *The Cement Garden* or *Atonement*, "Conversation with a Cupboard Man" (in McEwan's story collection *First Love, Last Rites*) contains an example of a mother who does, in fact, refuse to let her son grow up, treating him as a one-year-old well into his adulthood.
3. That all three books deal with pilots and two are set on Air Force bases may reflect the prevalence of overseas Air Force bases relative to other types of installations, and thus the significant likelihood that inter- and intra-national dislocation and displacement would be a an issue for the children of pilots.
4. MacDonald has been awarded, among other prizes, the Governor General's Award for Drama (*Goodnight Desdemona, Good Morning Juliet*) and the Commonwealth Prize (*Fall on Your Knees*), as well as numerous Dora Awards (*Anything That Moves* and *The Attic, the Pearls and 3 Fine Girls*). McEwan's awards include the Booker Prize (*Amsterdam*), the Whitbread Award (*The Child in Time*), and the Somerset Maugham Award (*First Love, Last Rites*).
5. Another privilege on American bases, notes Kristofferson, is that they tended to be integrated long before the rest of America was. United as "Americans," race could fade into the background in a way that is too often impossible in civilian life.

6. This phrase is used in the title of Eidse and Sichel's collection of memoirs: *Unrooted Childhoods: Memoirs of Growing Up Global.*

7. Peter Childs observes that the 1990s in particular mark a time in which British literature offered many representations of abused children, as in the works of Pat Barker, Martin Amis and Kazuo Ishiguro. McEwan's representations of dysfunctional adult-child relationships are generally distinct from other authors' representations due to the isolation/dislocation that also characterizes them ("Fascinating Violation").

8. See McEwan's description of the portrait hanging over an unusable fireplace: It "showed an aristocratic family ... posed before a vaguely Tuscan landscape. No one knew who these people were, but it was likely Harry Tallis thought they would lend an impression of solidity to his household" (126).

9. Think again of "The Cupboard Man" in *First Love, Last Rites*, in which the speaker's development into adolescence and adulthood is retarded by his mother's insistence on treating him as an infant.

10. McEwan's *The Cement Garden* is often compared to Golding's *Lord of the Flies*. It is interesting to note that Golding's text, like those I consider here, examines a military brat context: it involves children isolated because of a plane crash during an "evacuation" (30), who are eventually discovered by a naval officer (222).

Chapter Three

1. Bronfenbrenner describes an adolescent's environment as an ecological system that can be broken down into "nested structures": the microsystem (e.g., immediate family), the mesosystem (e.g., school, sports teams, band activity), the exosystem (e.g., parents and employers) and the macrosystem (e.g., governmental politics) (Muuss 322).

2. As Catherine Palmer's *The Happy Room* suggests, paradoxically these same children, having absorbed certain aspects of a foreign host culture while on a mission, are often then called upon to demonstrate these aspects when they return to their passport home (in her example, this involves a repatriated American boy asked to do a Kenyan dance for Americans).

3. Facebook posts on pages associated with the Hillcrest International School in Sentani, Papua, Indonesia (formerly the Sentani International School and Sentani Elementary School), allege that both Young and Dekker may be alumni. *The Circle Trilogy's Blog* also claims Dekker attended Sentani Elementary.

4. This is much like Bernie's exuberant dancing in *The Yokota Officers Club*, especially considering that in each case a kind of identity is being performed somewhat inauthentically. Bernie performs a go-go-booted American that she is not; Isaac performs a type of Indonesian that he is not.

Works Cited

"About Jane Alison." www.janealison.com/about.php. Accessed July 25, 2010.
"About Pat Conroy." www.patconroy.com. Accessed July 12, 2011.
"About Ted." Ted Dekker: The Official Author Site. Accessed May 17, 2011.
Albrecht, Donald. *New Hotels for Global Nomads*. London: Merrell, 2002.
Alison, Jane. *Natives and Exotics*. New York: Harcourt, 2005.
All God's Children: The Ultimate Sacrifice. Directed by Scott Solary and Lucy Westfall. 2008.
Appadurai, Arjun. *Modernity at Large: Cultural Dimensions of Globalization*. Public Worlds, Vol. 1. Minneapolis: University of Minnesota Press, 1996.
Appiah, Kwame Anthony. *Cosmopolitanism: Ethics in a World of Strangers*. New York: Norton, 2006.
———. "Cosmopolitan Patriots." In Cheah and Robbins, *Cosmopolitics*, 91–116.
Archibugi, Daniele, ed. *Debating Cosmopolitics*. New York: Verso, 2003.
Bacon, Katie. "The Great Irish-Dutch-American Novel." *Atlantic* (May 2008). Accessed July 10, 2010.
Baudrillard, Jean. *Simulacra and Simulation*. Translated by Sheila Faria Glaser. Ann Arbor: University of Michigan Press, 2006.
Beal, Timothy. "Theology for Everyone." *Chronicle of Higher Education* 56, no. 18 (January 15, 2010): B16–17. Accessed March 15, 2011.
Begley, Adam. "The Art of Fiction CLXXIII: Ian McEwan." In Roberts, *Conversations with Ian McEwan*, 89–107.
"Bellwether Prize for Fiction." www.bellwether.prize.org. Accessed July 25, 2011.
Bennett, Janet. "Plenary." Talk at the Families in Global Transition Convention. Marriott Westchase, Houston, Texas. March 29–31, 2007.
Bhabha, Homi K. *The Location of Culture*. New York: Routledge, 2004.
"Bird, Sarah." American Overseas Schools Archives (online). Accessed July 7, 2011.
Bird, Sarah. *The Yokota Officers Club*. New York: Ballantine, 2002.
Blake, Fanny. "Meet the Author: Fanny Blake Talks to Ann-Marie MacDonald." In MacDonald, *The Way the Crow Flies*, postscript 2–3.
Bonebright, Denise. "Adult Third Culture Kids: HRD Challenges and Opportunities." *Human Resource Development International* 13, no. 3 (July 2010): 351–59. Accessed August 11, 2011.
Brats: Our Journey Home. Directed by Donna Musil. Performed by Kris Kristofferson. Brats Without Borders, 2005.
Brennan, Timothy. *At Home in the World: Cosmopolitanism Now*. Cambridge, MA: Harvard University Press, 1997.

_____. "Cosmopolitans and Celebrities." *Race and Class* 31, no. 1 (July 1989): 1–19. Accessed June 25, 2007.
Buck, Pearl S. *The Good Earth.* New York: Simon & Schuster Enriched Classic, 2009 (orig. 1931).
"Canadian Forces Gender Integration — Recruiting." www.nato.int. Accessed July 14, 2011.
"Catherine Palmer." Focus on Fiction. www.focusonfiction.net/html/catherinepalmer.html. Accessed May 14, 2011.
"Catherine Palmer Answers the Faithful Fifteen." FaithfulReader.com (May 2005). Accessed May 14, 2011.
Cheah, Pheng, and Bruce Robbins, eds. *Cosmopolitics: Thinking and Feeling Beyond the Nation.* Cultural Politics, Vol. 14. Minneapolis: University of Minnesota Press, 1998.
Childs, Peter. "Fascinating Violation: Ian McEwan's Children." In *British Fiction of the 1990s,* edited by Nick Bentley. New York: Routledge, 2005.
_____. *The Fiction of Ian McEwan: A Reader's Guide to Essential Criticism.* New York: Palgrave, 2006.
"*The Circle Trilogy's* Blog." February 25, 2008. Accessed May 18, 2011.
Clifford, James. "Mixed Feelings." In Cheah and Robbins, *Cosmopolitics,* 362–70.
Coetzee, J.M. *Disgrace.* New York: Penguin, 1999.
Conroy, Pat. *The Great Santini.* New York: Dial Press, 2006.
Cottrell, Ann Baker, and Ruth Hill Useem. "TCKs Experience Prolonged Adolescence." TCK World. www.tckworld.com/useem/art3.html.
Dekker, Ted. *BoneMan's Daughters.* New York: Center Street, 2009.
Dewaele, Jean-Marc, and Jan Pieter Oudenhoven. "The Effect of Multilingualism/Multiculturalism on Personality: No Gain Without Pain for Third Culture Kids?" *International Journal of Multilingualism* 6, no. 4 (November 2009): 443–59. Accessed August 5, 2011.
Dixler, Elsa. "Paperback Row." *New York Times* (March 16, 2008). Accessed May 14, 2011.
Dodou, Katherina. "Dismembering a Romance of Englishness: Images of Childhood in Ian McEwan's *The Innocent.*" *Anglistick und Englischunterricht* 73 (2009): 73–86.
Donaldson-Pressman, Stephanie, and Donald Pressman. *The Narcissistic Family: Diagnosis and Treatment.* New York: Jossey-Bass, 1997.
Drew, Eileen. *The Ivory Crocodile.* Minneapolis: Coffee House Press, 1996.
Drummet, Amy Reinkober, Marilyn Coleman, and Susan Cable. "Military Families Under Stress: Implications for Family Life Education." *Family Relations* 52 (2003): 279–87. Accessed May 14, 2011.
Dueñas, Mercedes Diaz. "The Postmodern Twist in Yann Martel's *Life of Pi.*" In *Figures of Belatedness: Postmodernist Fiction in English,* edited by Javier Gascueña Gahete et al. Córdoba, Spain: University of Córdoba Press, 2006.
Eagleton, Terry. *Literary Theory: An Introduction.* Minneapolis: University of Minnesota, 1983.
Eckstein, Lars, Andrea Lutz, Daniela Oss, Marc Shaeffer, Sylvia Tress, and Sabine Vogler. "Literary Missions and Global Ethic." In *Colonies — Missions — Cultures in the English Speaking World,* edited by Gerhard Stilz, 435–56. Tubingen: Stauffenberg, 2001.
Eidse, Faith, and Nina Sichel, eds. *Unrooted Childhoods: Memoirs of Growing Up Global.* Yarmouth, ME: Nicholas Brealey, 2004.
Elyea, Dan. "*The Happy Room,* Reviewed." Simroots. http://simroots.sim.org/bookf-j.htm#happy. Accessed May 14, 2011.

Ender, Morten G. "Beyond Adolescence: The Experiences of Adult Children of Military Parents." In Ender, *Military Brats and Other Global Nomads*, 83–99.
———. *Military Brats and Other Global Nomads: Growing Up in Organizational Families*. Westport, CT: Praeger, 2002.
Evinger, James, Carolyn Whitfield, and Judith Wiley. "Final Report of the Independent Abuse Review Panel, Presbyterian Church (USA)" (October 2010). Accessed February 11, 2011.
"Expatriates Worldwide." www.justlanded.com. Accessed August 29, 2011.
Fail, Helen, Jeff Thompson, and George Walker. "Belonging, Identity and Third Culture Kids: Life Histories of Former International School Students." *Journal of Research in International Education* 3 (2004): 319–38. Accessed August 1, 2010.
Garry, Maryanne, and Kimberly A. Wade. "Actually, a Picture Is Worth Less than 45 Words: Narratives Produce More False Memories than Photographs Do." *Psychonomic Bulletin and Review* 12, no. 2 (2005): 359–366. Accessed August 1, 2010.
Gerson, Joseph. "US Foreign Military Bases and Military Colonialism." American Friends Service Committee (online). Accessed July 28, 2008
Gilbert, Kathleen R. "Loss and Grief Between and Among Cultures: The Experience of Third Culture Kids." *Illness, Crisis and Loss* 16, no. 2 (2008): 93–109.
Golding, William. *Lord of the Flies*. London: Faber & Faber, 1954.
Gordon, Peter. "*White Ghost Girls* by Alice Greenway." *Asian Review of Books* (April 25, 2006). Accessed July 20, 2010.
The Great Santini. Directed by Lewis John Carlino. 1979.
"The Great Santini." Internet Movie Database. www.imdb.com/title/tt0079239/. Accessed July 12, 2011.
Green, Keith, and Jill LeBihan. *Critical Theory and Practice: A Coursebook*. New York: Routledge, 1997.
Greenway, Alice. *White Ghost Girls*. New York: Black Cat, 2006.
Hamby, DeWayne. "'The Shack' by Ted Dekker?" Christian Retailing (online). January 30, 2009. Accessed February 21, 2011.
Hamilton, Ian. "Points of Departure." In Roberts, *Conversations with Ian McEwan*, 3–17.
Hannerz, Ulf. "Cosmopolitans and Locals in World Culture." *Theory, Culture and Society* 7 (1990): 237–51. Accessed June 28, 2007.
"*The Happy Room*, Review." Amazon.com review by Donia "fivefishsticks" (July 6, 2005). Accessed May 14, 2011.
"History of Women in the British Armed Forces." www.mod.uk (2006). Accessed July 14, 2011.
Hylmö, Annika. "Internationally Mobile Children in Children's Fictional Literature: Legitimate Reflection or Reflecting Legitimation?" In Ender, *Military Brats and Other Global Nomads*, 121–44.
"Interview with Sarah Bird." Simon & Schuster, Canada (online). Accessed July 7, 2011.
Iyer, Pico. *The Global Soul: Jet Lag, Shopping Malls and the Search for Home*. New York: Vintage, 2000.
James, David. "'A boy stepped out': Migrancy, Visuality and the Mapping of Masculinities in the Later Fiction of Ian McEwan. " *Textual Practice* 17, no. 1 (2003): 81–100. Accessed November 10, 2010.
Jordan, Kathleen A. Finn. "Identity Formation and the Adult Third Culture Kid." In Ender, *Military Brats and Other Global Nomads*, 211–28.
Joseph, May. *Nomadic Identities: The Performance of Citizenship*. Public Worlds, Vol. 5. Minneapolis: University of Minnesota Press, 1999.
Jussawalla, Feroza. "Reading and Teaching Barbara Kingsolver's *Poisonwood Bible* as Postcolonial." *Revista Estudios Ingleses* 16 (2003): 6–32. Accessed July 22, 2011.

Works Cited

Kanner, Ellen. "*The Poisonwood Bible*: Barbara Kingsolver Turns to Her Past to Understand Her Present." www.bookpage.com (November 1998). Accessed January 10, 2011.

———. "The Secret Life of Plants." Interview with Jane Alison. www.janealison.com/about.php (May/June 2005). Accessed July 14, 2010.

Kaplan, Caren. *Questions of Travel: Postmodern Discourses of Displacement*. Durham, NC: Duke University Press, 1996.

Keenan, Catherine. "Artist's Impression of Love Gone Wrong." *Sydney Morning Herald, Spectrum* (April 17-18, 2004). http://www.janealison.com/about.php. Accessed July 14, 2010.

Kidd, Julie, and Linda Lankenau. "Third Culture Kids: Returning to Their Passport Country." www.state.gov/m/dghr/flo/c22473.htm. Accessed August 18, 2011.

Kingsolver, Barbara. "FAQ." www.kingsolver.com. Accessed July 25, 2011.

———. *The Poisonwood Bible*. New York: HarperPerennial, 2005.

Klinkenborg, Verlyn. "Going Native: The Family of a Baptist Missionary in the Congo of the 1950's Learns Some Hard Lessons about Life." *New York Times on the Web: Books* (October 18, 1998). Accessed July 18, 2011.

Koza, Kimberly A. "The Africa of Two Western Women Writers: Barbara Kingsolver and Margaret Laurence." *Critique: Studies in Contemporary Fiction* 44, no. 3 (Spring 2003): 284-94. Accessed July 22, 2011

Krishnaswamy, Revathi. "Mythologies of Migrancy: Postcolonialism, Postmodernism and the Politics of (Dis)location." *ARIEL: A Review of International Literature* 26, no. 1 (January 1995): 125-46.

Kristeva, Julia. *Powers of Horror: An Essay on Abjection*. New York: Columbia University Press, 1982.

Kröller, Eva-Marie. "Introduction. *Life of Pi*: Reception of a Canadian Novel." *The Cambridge Companion to Canadian Literature*, 1-22. Cambridge: Cambridge University Press, 2004.

Lahiri, Jhumpa. *The Namesake*. New York: Houghton Mifflin, 2003.

Lewis, Richard. *The Flame Tree*. New York: Simon & Schuster, 2004.

"Living *The Shack*: An Interview with William Paul Young." *New Man* (emagazine). June 12, 2008. Accessed May 17, 2011.

Lutz, Catherine. "A US Invasion of Korea." *Boston Globe* (October 8, 2006). Accessed July 28, 2008.

MacDonald, Ann-Marie. *The Way the Crow Flies*. Toronto: Perennial, 2003.

Malcolm, David. *Understanding Ian McEwan*. Columbia: University of South Carolina, 2002.

Malcomson, Scott L. "The Varieties of Cosmopolitan Experience." In Cheah and Robbins, *Cosmopolitics*, 233-45.

Martel, Yann. *Life of Pi*. Toronto: Vintage, 2002.

Martin, Sandra. "Canada Takes the Prize at Squashing Excellence." *The Globe and Mail* (December 3, 2002). Accessed August 1, 2007.

McCaig, Norma M. "Understanding Global Nomads" In Carolyn Smith, ed. *Strangers at Home: Essays on the Effects of Living Overseas and Coming "Home" to a Strange Land*. Bayside, NY: Aletheia Publications, 1996: 99-120.

McEwan, Ian. *Atonement*. Toronto: Vintage, 2001.

———. *The Cement Garden*. New York: Anchor, 2003.

———. *First Love, Last Rites*. New York: Anchor, 2003.

Ménégaldo, Gilles, and Anne-Laure Fortin. "An Interview with Ian McEwan." In Roberts, *Conversations with Ian McEwan*, 67-78.

"Military Brat Registry: Every Brat Has a Story." Militarybrats.com. Accessed July 7, 2011.

Missionary Kids Safety Net. www.mksafetynet.net. Accessed February 11, 2011.
Moser, Gene. *Skinny Dipping and Other Stories: Phil and El Collection One.* Baltimore: AmErica House, 2001.
Muuss, Rolf E. *Theories of Adolescence.* 6th ed. New York: McGraw-Hill, 1996.
Nangle, Paula. *The Leper Compound.* New York: Bellevue, 2008.
"Nangle Press Kit." Literary Ventures Fund. www.literaryventuresfund.org/books/press_kits/Nangle_press_kit.pdf. Accessed May 15, 2011.
Newton, Jay. "Obama's Foreign-Policy Problem." *Time* (December 18, 2007). Accessed July 3, 2010.
Ognibene, Elaine R. "The Missionary Position: Barbara Kingsolver's *The Poisonwood Bible.*" *College Literature* 30, no. 3 (Summer 2003): 19–37. Accessed July 21, 2011.
O'Neill, Joseph. *Netherland.* New York: Pantheon, 2008.
Ong, Aiwa. "Citizenship." In *A Companion to the Anthropology of Politics*, edited by David Nugent and Joan Vincent, 55–68. Oxford: Blackwell, 2004.
Orgun, Gün. "Marginality, Cosmopolitanism and Postcoloniality." *Commonwealth* 23, no. 1 (Autumn 2000): 111–24.
Palmer, Cale. "A Theory of Risk and Resiliency Factors in Military Families." *Military Psychology* 20 (2008): 205–17. Accessed June 28, 2011.
Palmer, Catherine. *The Happy Room.* Wheaton, IL: Tyndale, 2002.
"Pat Conroy Biography." www.awayfromthesouth.com. Accessed July 12, 2011.
Paterson, Bill E., and Laila T. Plamondon. "Third Culture Kids and the Consequences of International Sojourns on Authoritarianism, Acculturative Balance and Positive Affect." *Journal of Research in Personality* 43 (2009): 755–63. Accessed August 11, 2011.
"Paul Young Part 1: Sexually Abused Missionary Kid." YouTube. Uploaded by David Kyle Foster on April 8, 2011. Accessed May 17, 2011.
"Paul Young's Short Bio" Windrumors: The Official Site of Paul Young. Accessed May 17, 2011.
Pollock, David C. "TCK Definition." *Among Worlds* 8, no. 4 (December 2006): masthead.
Pollock, David C., and Ruth E. Van Reken. *Third Culture Kids: The Experience of Growing Up Among Worlds.* Boston: Nicholas Brealey, 2001.
Price, Phoebe Evelyn. "Behaviour of Civilian and Military High School Students in Movie Theaters." In Ender, *Military Brats and Other Global Nomads*, 35–52.
Remnick, David. "Naming What Is There: Ian McEwan in Conversation with David Remnick." In Roberts, *Conversations with Ian McEwan*, 156–75.
"Richard Lewis: An Interview." Bookbrowse.com (2004). Accessed May 15, 2011.
"Richard Lewis, Official Publisher Page." Simon & Schuster (online). Accessed May 15, 2011.
Ricks, Christopher. "Adolescence and After." In Roberts, *Conversations with Ian McEwan*, 19–25.
Robbins, Bruce. "Introduction: Part One." In Cheah and Robbins, *Cosmopolitics*, 1–19.
Roberts, Ryan, ed. *Conversations with Ian McEwan.* Jackson: University Press of Mississippi, 2010.
Rosenberg, Amy. "Into the Enchanted Forest and Up the Faraway Tree: Why Is There a Corner of the Indian Heart That Is Forever Enid Blyton?" *Caravan: A Journal of Politics and Culture* (March 1, 2010). Accessed November 16, 2010.
Roth, Marco. "The Rise of the Neuronovel: A Specter Is Haunting the Contemporary Novel." *n+1* (September 2009). Accessed June 29, 2010.
Rushdie, Salman. *Imaginary Homelands: Essays and Criticism, 1981–1991.* London: Granta, 1981.

Ryan, Kiernan. "Sex, Violence and Complicity: Martin Amis and Ian McEwan." In Rod Mengham ed. and intro. *An Introduction to Contemporary Fiction: International Writing in English Since 1970.* Cambridge, England: Polity, 1999: 203–218.
Sarvas, Mark. "The Joseph O'Neill Interview." *Elegant Variation* (blog) (July 13–17, 2009). Accessed July 14, 2010.
Schaetti, Barbara F. "Attachment Theory: A View Into the Global Nomad Experience." In Ender, *Military Brats and Other Global Nomads*, 103–20.
Scott, Shelley. "Ann-Marie MacDonald." *Literary Encyclopedia.* January 23, 2004. Accessed July 29, 2008.
Sherwell, Philip. "Joseph O'Neill: The Man Who Bowled Over New York." *Telegraph* (August 2, 2008). Accessed July 14, 2010.
Smith, Zadie. "Two Paths for the Novel: *Netherland* by Joseph O'Neill, *Remainder* by Tom McCarthy." *New York Review of Books* (November 20, 2008). Accessed August 3, 2010.
———. *White Teeth.* London: Penguin, 2000.
———. "Zadie Smith Talks with Ian McEwan." In Roberts, *Conversations with Ian McEwan*, 108–33.
Soto-Crespo, Ramón. "Death and Diaspora: Hybridity and Mourning in the Work of Jamaica Kincaid." *Contemporary Literature* 43, no. 2 (Summer 2002): 342–76. Accessed August 3, 2010.
Stanton, Domna C. "Presidential Address 2005: On Rooted Cosmopolitanism." *PMLA* 121, no. 3 (May 2006): 627–40.
"Statistics on Women in the Military." www.womensmemorial.org/PDFs/Statson WIM.pdf (2010). Accessed July 14, 2011.
Stephens, Libby, and Ruth Van Reken. "Third Culture Kids: The Experience of Growing Up Among Worlds." Talk at the Families in Global Transition Convention. Marriott Westchase, Houston, Texas. March 29–31, 2007.
Suleri, Sara. *Meatless Days.* Chicago: University of Chicago Press, 1987.
"Ted Dekker." Mahalo.com. Accessed May 17, 2011
"Ted Dekker Answers the Faithful Fifteen." FaithfulReader.com (September 2004). Accessed May 17, 2011.
"Top Selling Books of 2008." Nielsen.com. Accessed February 21, 2011.
Turpin, Adrian. "A Literary Bomb Ready to Explode." *Sunday Times* (March 19, 2006). Accessed July 14, 2010.
Useem, Ruth Hill. "'Third Culture Kids': Focus of a Major Study — TCK 'Mother' Pens History of the Field." TCK World. http://www.tckworld.com/useem/art1.html. Accessed 30 July, 2007.
Van Reken, Ruth. *Letters Never Sent.* Colorado Springs: Cook Communications Ministries International, 1988.
Varela-Zapata, Jesús. "Staying On After Empire: The Changing Role of Church Missions in Africa from Colonial to Post-Colonial Times." In *Colonies — Missions — Cultures in the English Speaking World*, edited by Gerhard Stilz, 99–110. Tübingen: Stauffenberg-Verl., 2001.
Viser, William C. *It's OK to Be an MK: What It's Like to Be a Missionary Kid.* Nashville, TN: Broadman, 1986.
"Welcome to Families in Global Transition." Families in Global Transition (online). Accessed August 6, 2007.
Werkman, Sidney. "Debate: Resolved: Military Family Life Is Hazardous to the Mental Health of Children." *Journal of the American Academy of Child and Adolescent Psychiatry* 31, no. 5 (September 1992): 984–87.
Werner, Wolf. "Migration Towards a Rewarding Goal and Multiculturalism with a Positive Center: Yann Martel's *Life of Pi* as a Post-Postmodernist Attempt at Elic-

iting (Poetic) Faith." In *Canada in the Sign of Migration and Trans-Culturalism*, edited by Klaus-Dieter Ertler et al. Frankfurt: Peter Lang, 2004.

Wertsch, Mary Edwards. *Military Brats: Legacies of Childhood Inside the Fortress*. St. Louis, MO: Brightwell, 2006.

Witness to Truth, Witness to Healing. Independent Abuse Review Panel, Presbyterian Church. 2006.

Wood, Alan. "Kant's Project for Perpetual Peace." In Cheah and Robbins, *Cosmopolitics*, 59–76.

Young, Robert. *The Idea of English Ethnicity*. Oxford: Oxford University Press, 2008.

Young, William Paul. *The Shack*. Los Angeles: Windblown, 2007.

Index

abandonment 20, 121, 124, 129, 135–137, 142–148, 152–155, 169–170
Albrecht, Donald 49
Alison, Jane: biography 30–31; *Natives and Exotics* 25, 28–30, 34–36, 39–56, 59–61, 80, 91, 119; *The Sisters Antipodes* 31
All God's Children (documentary) 118–119, 126, 151–152
Amis, Kingsley 72
anti-Americanism 44; in Kingsolver 158, 171–173, 175; in O'Neill 51
apology 138, 152–153, 156, 170
Appadurai, Arjun 18
Appiah, Kwame Anthony: "Cosmopolitan Patriots" 21; *Cosmopolitanism* 18
arrogance 21, 172
Atonement (McEwan) 25, 67, 70–71, 96–115, 119

Bacon, Katie 27–28
Banks, Sir Joseph 55
Baudrillard, Jean 85
Beal, Timothy 144
Beardslee, Howie 152
Bellwether Prize 173
belonging 16, 41–42, 65, 116, 127–128, 164
Bennett, Janet 16
Bhabha, Homi K.: *The Location of Culture* 19
Bird, Sarah: biography 7, 71; *The Yokota Officers Club* 25, 64, 67–100, 104–105, 108–110, 115, 119, 171
Blaise, Clark 8
Blyton, Enid 2, 106–107; *The Famous Five* 106; *The Secret Seven* 106
boarding schools 14, 118–121, 126, 152, 169
BoneMan's Daughters (Dekker) 26, 117, 122–126, 144–153

Brats: Our Journey Home (Musil) 68, 76, 79, 180
Brennan, Timothy: "Cosmopolitans and Celebrities" 17–18
Buck, Pearl S.: *The Good Earth* 25, 116, 121

Cable, Susan: "Military Families Under Stress" 67
The Cement Garden (McEwan) 25, 64, 70, 96–115
Christian and Missionary Alliance 118–119, 151–152
Coetzee, J.M.: *Disgrace* 41, 45
Coleman, Marilyn: "Military Families Under Stress" 67
colonialism 1, 21–22, 86, 166
Conrad, Joseph: *Heart of Darkness* 164
Conroy, Pat 8, 63–63, 75, 98, 114; *The Great Santini* (novel) 25, 62–63
cosmopolitan 10, 14, 17; individual 21, 41; literature 8, 17
"Cosmopolitan Patriots" (Appiah) 21
cosmopolitanism 16–19, 21–22; third world 8, 11, 14, 17; vernacular 19
Cosmopolitanism (Appiah) 18
"Cosmopolitans and Celebrities" (Brennan) 17
Cottrell, Ann Baker 21
"The Cry Room" (Nangle) 155

Danner, Blythe 62
Darr, David 152
Darr, Richard 119
Darr Couts, Diane 151
death 13, 20, 109; in Kingsolver 159, 166–168, 176; in McEwan 101–105, 113; in military brat literature 65–66, 70, 81–82, 87, 90, 95; in missionary kid literature 123, 132, 134, 136–137, 141, 143–144, 146–149; in the writing of

189

third culture kids 38–39, 41, 50, 52–53, 55
Dekker, Ted: biography 124, 127–128; *BoneMan's Daughters* 26, 117, 122–126, 144–153
"denizen: for third culture kids" 39–40
detachment 15, 21, 42, 51, 65, 107–110, 114, 139, 173
Dewaele, Jean-Marc 20–21
Dewitt, Helen 8
diasporic 9–10, 14; literature 8, 14–15, 33, 35–36
discontinuity 20, 54–56
disenfranchisement 14, 21, 23–25; in Kingsolver 170–174, 176; in military brat literature 64–65, 73, 83–90, 96, 101, 105–109, 112, 114; in missionary kid literature 121–122, 137–142, 145–146, 148; in the writing of third culture kids 28, 33, 34, 41–44, 48, 50–51
Disgrace (Coetzee) 41, 45
dislocation 3, 11, 13–14, 16–19, 23–25; in Kingsolver 162–164, 170–171, 176; in military brat literature 63–66, 73–79, 96–99, 109, in missionary kid literature 121–122, 125, 128–131, 145–146; in the writing of third culture kids 28, 30–35, 37–38, 41, 48–50, 53, 59
Disneyland 85
displacement 1, 8, 13–16, 23, 63–64, 77, 129, 131, 148, 176
Dixler, Elsa 117
Dodou, Katherine 67, 108
Donaldson-Pressman, Stephanie: *The Narcissistic Family* 76
Drew, Eileen: biography 31–32; *The Ivory Crocodile* 25, 28–30, 34–38, 40, 42, 44–61, 172–173
Drummet, Amy Reinkober: "Military Families Under Stress" 67
Duvall, Robert 62–63, 114

Eagleton, Terry 113–114
Eidse, Faith: *Uprooted Childhoods* 31
Elyea, Dan 124–125
Ender, Morten G. 64; *Military Brats and Other Global Nomads* 15
exile 1, 11, 14, 35, 61, 129, 166
expatriate 2, 7–9, 15, 28, 41, 66, 83, 126, 159, 169; children 3–4, 38, 119 158; community 35, 118–119, 159; privilege 19–20, 45–46, 65, 109, 132; and third culture 7, 9, 118

Fail, Helen 28, 38, 41
fame 117
Families in Global Transition 16, 179*n*2

The Famous Five (Blyton) 106
"Final Report of the Independent Review Panel of the Presbyterian Church (USA)" 118
first culture 9, 28, 31, 66, 118, 159 11
"fivefishsticks," Donia 124–125
The Flame Tree (Lewis) 26, 117, 122–123, 130–133, 136–146, 150–153, 169
Forster, E.M.: *A Passage to India* 22
Frances, Allen 69, 113

Gale, Leonard 69, 113
Garry, Maryanne 57
gender roles 68–69
Gerson, Joseph 86
Gilbert, Kathleen 12, 20, 158; "Loss and Grief Between and Among Cultures: The Experience of Third Culture Kids" 158
global nomad 54, 180*n*3
The Global Soul (Iyer) 12, 14–15
The Good Earth (Buck) 25, 116, 121
Gordon, Peter 32
The Great Santini (film) 62–63, 114
The Great Santini (novel) 25, 62–63
Greenway, Alice: biography 32; *White Ghost Girls* 25, 28–30, 34–56, 59–61, 119
grief 4, 11–13, 20, 22, 38–39, 41, 50, 68, 81, 132, 135, 146–148, 155, 168, 176
guilt 14, 21–25, 28, 158; in Kingsolver 173–177; in military brat literature 64–66, 90, 95, 106, 109–112, 114; in missionary kid literature 121, 123–124, 142, 144, 147; in the writing of third culture kids 33–34, 44–48, 51–53, 60

Hamby, DeWayne 123–124
Hannerz, Ulf 17
The Happy Room (Palmer) 25, 117, 122–125, 128–129, 132–146, 150–155, 169
Heart of Darkness (Conrad) 164
Hiroshima 89
home 2–3; in Alison 46; and dislocation 17–18; in Drew 42; in Kingsolver 163, 164, 166–169, 170; in Martel 12, 14, 24; and McEwan 97, 99–101; military base as 83–86; in military brat literature 63–64, 66, 74–80, 83–86; in missionary kid literature 121, 128, 137–138, 140–141, 145–146, 149–150; nation 7–10, 17, 22, 28, 31, 33, 66, 83; and O'Neill 32–33, 52; for Rushdie 35; sense of 9, 17, 38, 66, and third culture 9, 12, 20, 118; and third culture literature 14–15, 17, 22, 30, 33, 35, 58, 83, 105

Index

homeland 14, 36–37, 58, 105
homelessness 12, 47
house 20, 34, 99, 113, 121, 135; in Alison 36–37; in Bird 77; boarding 19; in Buck 116, 121; in Dekker 146, 149–150; in Greenway 46; in Kingsolver 165–167, 174; in Lewis 130; in MacDonald 74; Martel 12, in McEwan 97–99, 100–101, 103; in Moser 91; in Nangle 133, 134–135, 141, 142; in Palmer 140; in Young 123, 146, 149–150
Hylmö, Annika 19

identity: in Alison 29; Conroy's 75; cosmopolitan 17, 21; and dislocation 31, 33–34; in Drew 37, 42; in Greenway 43, 59; and Kingsolver 159–161, 163–164, 166–169, 176; Martel's 11; in McEwan 105, 108; in military brat literature 65, 73, 76, 113; in missionary kid literature 125, 130–131, 134; national 8, 11, 24, 28, 65, 75, 105, 108, 125, 167; national/cultural 3, 9, 16; in O'Neill 52; plasticity 12, 21, 49; problems with 4; third culture 9, 15–16, 20–22, 27, 28, 39, 42, 66; and Young 126
Illness, Crisis and Loss 158
immigrant 1, 4, 9, 48, 51–53; authors 11, 14; hidden 3, 26, 157–158; literature 29, 61; writing 30, 35–36, 48, 52
international literature 1, 4–5, 8, 177
isolation 15, 112–113, 169; in McEwan 96–97, 107, 109, 112, 114, 181*n*7; in military kid literature 64–65, 67, 68, 95; in missionary kid literature 118–119, 130, 132, 134, 138
It's OK to Be an MK (Viser) 120
The Ivory Crocodile (Drew) 25, 28–30, 34–38, 40, 42, 44–61, 172–173
Iyer, Pico 12, 14; *The Global Soul* 12, 14–15

Jordan, Kathleen A. Finn 20–21, 33, 39, 44
Joseph, May 15; *Nomadic Identities* 15
Jussawalla, Feroza 157–158, 164
"Just Landed" 1–2

Kadena Karnival 85, 93–94
Kanner, Ellen 31, 160
Kaplan, Caren: *Questions of Travel* 18
Keenan, Catherine 31
Kingsolver, Barbara 8, 26, 157–162, 164, 173–174, 179*n*1; biography 26, 158, 159–162, 173–174; *The Poisonwood Bible* 10, 26, 157–177
Klinkenborg, Verlyn 161

Koza, Kimberly 172
Krishnaswamy, Revathi 18
Kristeva, Julia 19, 134
Kristofferson, Kris 76, 79
Kröller, Eva-Marie 11

Lacan, Jacques 114
Lahiri, Jhumpa: *The Namesake* 35
The Leper Compound (Nangle) 26, 117, 122, 125, 129–146, 150–152, 175
Letters Never Sent (Van Reken) 7
Lewis, Richard: biography 7, 124, 125–126; *The Flame Tree* 26, 117, 122–123, 130–133, 136–146, 150–153, 169
Life of Pi (Martel) 7, 10–14, 22, 24–25, 123
Lithgow, John 117
The Location of Culture (Bhabha) 19
loss: in Kingsolver 164–170, 176; in MacDonald 73, 79–83, 99–100; in Martel 11, 13, 24; McEwan 96, 99–105 ; in military brat literature 63–65, 68, 71, 73, 78–83, 95, 109; in missionary kid literature 121, 125, 132–137, 145, 148; in O'Neill 49–50, 53; parental 102–104; as third culture characteristic 3–4, 12, 14, 20, 25, 28, 33, 58 64, 68; in third culture literature 14, 21–23, 33, 35–41
"Loss and Grief Between and Among Cultures: The Experience of Third Culture Kids" (Gilbert) 158
Lutz, Catherine 85–86

MacDonald, Ann-Marie: biography 8, 71–72, 180*n*4; *The Way the Crow Flies* 25, 64, 67–100, 104–105, 108–110, 115, 171
malaria: in Drew 38; in Kingsolver 165, 174–176; in missionary kid literature 24, 122, 129, 134, 142–144, 150; not in Young and Dekker 150–151
Malcolm, David: *Understanding Ian McEwan* 72
Man Booker Prize 4, 10–11
marginality 4, 9, 33
Martel, Emil 11
Martel, Yann 7–8, 10–14, 17, 19, 22, 27; biography 11; *Life of Pi* 7, 10–14, 24–25, 123
Martin, Sandra 11
McEwan, Ian 64, 66–67, 69–73, 79, 95–115, 180*n*4; *Atonement* 25, 67, 70–71, 96–115, 119; biography 8, 71–72, 180*n*4; *The Cement Garden* 25, 64, 70, 96–115
McIntosh, Fiona 8
Meatless Days (Suleri) 36

Military Brats (Wertsch) 75, 180n1
Military Brats and Other Global Nomads (Ender) 15
"Military Families Under Stress" (Drummet, Coleman and Cable) 67
military family syndrome 67–68, 95
Missionary Kids Safety Net 118, 152
Morrison, Jim 115
Moser, Gene: biography 71; *Skinny Dipping* 25, 64, 67–91, 95–100, 105, 108–110, 114
Mukherjee, Bharati 17
Musil, Donna: *Brats: Our Journey Home* 68, 76
Muuss, Rolf E.: *Theories of Adolescence* 119–120

The Namesake (Lahiri) 35
Nangle, Paula: biography 124–125; "The Cry Room" 155; *The Leper Compound* 26, 117, 122, 125, 129–146, 150–152, 175
The Narcissistic Family (Donaldson-Pressman and Pressman) 76
Natives and Exotics (Alison) 25, 28–30, 34–36, 39–56, 59–61, 80, 91, 119
Netherland (O'Neill) 25, 27–30, 48–57, 59, 61, 172
New Tribes Mission 118
Newton, Jay 27
nomad 15, 54
Nomadic Identities (Joseph) 15

Obama, Barack 27
Oedipus 112–115
Ognibene, Elaine 161
O'Keefe, Michael 62
one culture 7
O'Neill, Joseph 8; biography 32–33; *Netherland* 25, 27–30, 48–57, 59, 61, 172
Ong, Aihwa 15
Operation Footlocker 71
Oprah's Book Club 4
Oudenhoven, Jan Pieter 20–21
outsider 2–3; in Drew 42, 58–59; expatriate 28, 31, 49, 66, 83; identity 21 99, 118; in Kingsolver 163, 164, 169; and Lewis 123, 126, 139; in Martel 12; and McEwan 72, 99, 101–102; in missionary kid literature 120; in O'Neill 50, 52; privilege 38, 58, 61

Palmer, Catherine: biography 124–125; *The Happy Room* 25, 117, 122–125, 128–129, 132–146, 150–155, 169
paperback: mass-market 117, 144–146; trade 117

A Passage to India (Forster) 22
patriotic 66, 83, 105–106, 109
patriotism 41, 65, 106, 124
pets 20, 54, 65, 137, 164; in Bird 78–79, 81; in Kingsolver 166–167; in Palmer 135
photographs 55–60
Pierre, DBC 8
The Poisonwood Bible 10, 26, 157–177
Pollock, David: faith 154; grief 39; hidden immigrants 157; identity 9, 21, 42, 51; loss 135, 158; privilege 20, 45; "TCK Definition" 16; *Third Culture Kids*: community 15–16, 41, 51, 169; time 9, 66
postcolonial literature 1, 5, 8, 17, 35, 41, 61, 109, 157–158, 164, 176
postmodernism 14
Pressman, Donald: *The Narcissistic Family* 76
Price, Phoebe Evelyn 68
privilege 2–3, 17, 19, 22, 28, 60–61; in Bird 80; and disenfranchisement 21; expatriate 36, 38; and guilt 109; and insecurity 140; and Kingsolver 158, 164–165, 171, 176; in Lewis 132–133; and loss 14, 63, 65, 68, 132–133, 164–165 176; and military culture 79; in Moser 79; in Nangle 133; in O'Neill 51–52; in Palmer 136; of third culture authors 4–5, 8, 9, 23 44–46
Pullman, Philip 8

Questions of Travel (Kaplan) 18

rape: in Coetzee 45; in Greenway 48; in McDonald 87, 95, 115; in McEwan 71, 96, 99, 104, 110, 112
refugee 11, 35
repentance 147, 153, 170
rootlessness 41, 63, 105, 158
Rosenberg, Amy 106–107
Rushdie, Salman 17, 35–36
Ryan, Kiernan 96–97

sacrifice 24, 65, 122, 155; of children 119, 122, 124, 125 142–148, 155–156; and David Darr 152; in Dekker 124, 145–148; in Kingsolver 169–170, 174; in Lewis 123, 137, 143–144; in Nangle 137, 143–144, 155; in Palmer 142–144; in Young 123, 146–147
Schaeffer, Frank: *Portofino* 117
Schaetti, Barbara F. 20, 39, 53–55
school 1–3, 20, 23, 31, 32, 36, 45, 70, 77, 106; boarding 14, 72, 97, 118–121, 126–133, 138, 140–143, 146, 149–150, 151–152, 154, 162, 169; and detachment 80;

and dislocation 44, 69, 73–74, 90–91, 126; home 118, 165; and military bases 83–84, 86
Scudamore, James 8
second culture 7, 9, 11, 28, 31, 66, 118
secrecy: in Coetzee 45; in Kingsolver 174–177; in McEwan 99; in military brat literature 64–66, 83, 86–87, 88, 90, 109–112; in missionary kid literature 121 140–141; in O'Neill 28, 51–52; in third culture literature 45, 46–48, 59, 109, 121
The Secret Seven (Blyton) 106
security 92, 95, 121, 133, 140–141
sex 20, 25, 40–41; in Alison 47; in McEwan 70–71, 96–97, 102, 107, 109–115; in military brat literature 65–66, 69–70, 73, 79, 90–95; and missionary kid literature, 117–118, 120–121, 142, 151; and Oedipal struggle 112–115
sexual precociousness 23, 25, 66, 73, 174, 176
The Shack (Young) 8, 26, 17, 122–126, 144–154
Shellrude Thompson, Beverly 119
Sherwell, Philip 33
Sichel, Nina: *Uprooted Childhoods* 31
sick children 142–144; as characteristic of third culture literature 20, 25, 121, 145; in Dekker 145, 150–151; in Kingsolver 174–176; in Lewis 143–144; in Nangle 123, 125, 143–143; in Palmer 122, 128, 142; in Young 150–151
The Sisters Antipodes (Alison) 31
Skinny Dipping (Moser) 25, 64, 67–91, 95–100, 105, 108–110, 114
Smith, Zadie 108, 110; *White Teeth* 35, 48, 50
snapshots 55–60
Soto-Crespo, Ramón 36
Stanton, Domna 18, 21
Stephens, Libby 9, 15, 20
Suleri, Sara: *Meatless Days* 36

Third Culture Kids: The Experience of Growing Up Among Worlds (Pollock and Van Reken): community 15–16, 41, 51, 169; faith 154; grief 39; hidden immigrants 157; identity 9, 21, 42, 51; loss 135, 158; privilege 20, 45; time 9, 66

"Third Culture Kids: The Experience of Growing Up Among Worlds" (Stephens and Van Reken) 9, 15, 20
time 30, 53–55, 66
Tolkien, J.R.R. 8
Top of the Pops 3
transience 9, 49, 63, 69, 89
Turpin, Adrian 32

United Methodist Church 118
United States Department of State 157–158
United States Presbyterian Church: *Witness to Truth, Witness to Healing* 151
Uprooted Childhoods (Eidse and Sichel) 31
Useem, Ruth Hill 8–9, 21, 27, 33, 179n2

Vandermeer, Jeff 8
Van Reken, Ruth 7, 154, 160; faith 154; grief 39; hidden immigrants 157; identity 9, 21, 42, 51; *Letters Never Sent* 7; loss 135, 158; privilege 20, 45; *Third Culture Kids*: community 15–16, 41, 51, 169; time 9, 66
Varela-Zapata, Jesús 166, 171
Viser, William C. 126; *It's OK to Be an MK* 120

Wade, Kimberly A. 57
The Way the Crow Flies (MacDonald) 25, 64, 67–100, 104–105, 108–110, 115, 171
Werkman, Sidney 3–4, 23, 68
Wertsch, Mary Edwards 73, 75, 76, 83, 99, 102, 113, 115, 180n1; *Military Brats* 75, 180n1
White Ghost Girls (Greenway) 25, 28–30, 34–35, 37–38, 40–41, 42–45, 47–52, 54–56, 59–61, 119
White Teeth (Smith) 35, 48
Wilson, Angus 72
Witness to Truth, Witness to Healing (U.S. Presbyterian Church) 151

The Yokota Officers Club (Bird) 25, 64, 67–100, 104–105, 108–110, 115, 119, 171
Young, William Paul: biography 8, 124, 126–127; *The Shack* 8, 26, 17, 117, 122–126, 144–154

www.ingramcontent.com/pod-product-compliance
Lightning Source LLC
Chambersburg PA
CBHW032101300426
44116CB00007B/841